D1742256

Political parties in modern Britain
An organizational and functional guide

Political parties in modern Britain An organizational and functional guide

edited and introduced by **John D. Lees** and **Richard Kimber**

University of Keele

Routledge & Kegan Paul
London

First published 1972
by Routledge & Kegan Paul Ltd
Broadway House, 68–74 Carter Lane,
London EC4V 5EL
Printed in Great Britain by
Western Printing Services Ltd., Bristol
© *John D. Lees and Richard Kimber 1972*

ISBN 07100 7133 7

329.942
A781.251

Contents

Preface

Any attempt to provide a wide range of information about political parties in Britain faces a great many obstacles, and inevitably accrues a great many debts. On the latter score we are especially thankful for the co-operation of a range of party officials who gave us information on party activities and permission to reprint official party material without which this guide would have been of limited utility. We are grateful also for the comments and advice received at various stages of our research from Martin Harrison and J. J. Richardson. Small but useful research grants from the University of Keele helped greatly in the gathering of material from which the final selection was made. We would like also to thank formally those who contributed original material, and the authors, editors and publishers who allowed material originally published elsewhere to be reprinted here.

A major research problem in any attempt to study on-going institutions like political parties is that changing events often make some information redundant or irrelevant the moment it is written. We would be less than frank if we did not admit this to be possible in this guide, and the calling of a General Election in June 1970 certainly forced necessary modifications and delayed final production (as well as adding a certain ironic piquancy to the selection of some material contained in Chapter 8!). However, we hope that such deficiencies as doubtless exist do not outweigh the general value of providing the type of introductory comparative guide to British political parties which follows.

University of Keele   John D. Lees
                                                          Richard Kimber

Introduction: **Political parties and the British political system**

Introduction: Political parties and the British political system

Political parties in contemporary Britain are products of the historical, social and political environment in which they exist and compete. They have become more influential and necessary to the extent that party discipline and individual party loyalty help maintain the predominance of the Cabinet in the political system, as well as providing cohesive formal opposition. One consequence of this development is that much study of British political parties has concentrated on those parties dominant in Parliament and on the structural and other factors which help to maintain this dominance. However, while it is becoming common to talk about party government in Britain, it is worth remembering that the origins of organized political parties in British politics are relatively recent, and that not all political parties existing in Britain directly affect government. This guide therefore has the general aim of gathering together evidence about the distinctive features of political parties in Britain *as political parties*, primarily in order to illustrate and compare the range of their organizational and functional attributes.

Development and role of political parties

Two centuries ago there was little evidence of party organization in Britain, and parties existed for some time before they became respectable. Only on achieving respectability, and later an aura of legitimacy, did they begin to increase their potential influence on the governmental process. Political parties were first acknowledged (and praised) by Burke in 1769, and some commentators see the origins of party in the Whig and Tory groups in the late seventeenth century or in the first toleration of organized political opposition within the political process. Others, notably Ostrogorski and Weber, have asserted that the origins of party legitimacy are to be found in the effects of the 1832 and 1867 Reform Acts and the rise of extra-parliamentary mass organizations of the political parties.[1] The growth of a more democratic political process helped further to legitimize, and make necessary, political parties as electoral organizations.

British political parties therefore began within the political institutions and deliberately created their extra-parliamentary organizations to recruit support and maintain a mass electoral base in the face of political and social change.[2] Later parties, most notably the Labour Party, have begun as movements outside Parliament and have sought parliamentary representation in order to further party policy goals. Parties therefore differ in terms of their origins as well as their organization and policies, and political parties exist within the British political system whose major conditioning influences are not those of being responsible for the government of the country or having a reasonable prospect of taking over this responsibility. Yet all political parties seek in some way to influence the workings of the political system and possibly the future decisions of government.

It is possible to analyse British political parties from two different but not distinct viewpoints. They may be seen as voluntary organizations with specific and well-defined structures designed to help attain certain goals, with many of the formal party members being activists in other voluntary organizations also. They may also be seen as organizations which perform legitimate and necessary functions for the effective operation of the political system as a whole which affect, and are affected by, the wider social system within which they operate.

As voluntary organizations, political parties possess distinctive structures which are to some extent independent of party functions. All major parties, and many minor parties in Britain, possess stable, well-defined organizational structures. The pattern of such structures is affected by factors such as relative electoral success, degree of financial support and historical evolution. For example, the structures of the Conservative, Labour and Liberal parties are all heavily affected by the fact that at some time they have been responsible for the government of the country. Some parties develop formal hierarchical organizations employing full-time professional party employees at all levels of organization, while others have a more fluid and less formalized structure.

The nature of the electoral system affects the structure of party organization, leading to the establishment of quasi-independent local organizations whose activities may be co-ordinated by the establishment of constituency, regional and national party organizations which serve to promote unity within a party at and between elections. The specific nature of the relationship between different levels of party organization is also affected by factors of historical development, party traditions and principles, financial and other supports, and electoral success. While political parties in Britain may possess similar organizational structures, the relationships between different levels of organization are often very different. Most parties draw up constitutions which seek to define the responsibilities and duties of individuals holding formal party positions, and the responsibilities of particular party organizations or groups formally affiliated with the party. Most parties hold annual party conferences which are designed to allow for internal party debate about policies, promote internal party unity, and decide major organizational questions. Most parties also have general procedures for the selection of official party candidates to compete in elections, and the selection of national party leaders and officials. However, there are significant differences in the performance of these basic organizational prerequisites.

Functions of political parties

The functions performed by any political party within the political system depend greatly on the nature of their internal organization. As parties become institutionalized and their organizations established in accordance with accepted norms of political organization, so there may develop real differences between the formal structure of internal party authority and the actual pattern of power within parties. Political parties operating within the same political system may therefore not merely exert different influences but provide examples of different patterns of activity which reflect different stages of party development.

Political parties can perform at least four broad functions in any democratic political system. Such functions are affected by factors such as existing political institutions, and the roles which political parties are expected to perform within the political systems. They are affected also by the role which individual parties seek to play in the political system and how far they are prepared to conform to the demands and limitations imposed by accepted political conventions and norms of political behaviour. The four broad functions are as follows:

Office-holding

Political parties operate as voluntary organizations whose prime rationale is to compete for and hold political office at all levels of government. In performing this function they provide orderly competition for political office and also maintain internal procedures whereby individuals are recruited and selected to compete for political office and become political decision-makers.

3

Policy-making

Political parties seek to capture political office by articulating broad principles and specific policies which may obtain support from individuals and groups within the electorate. As a result of this they also aggregate the demands of specific groups in society and reduce an infinite combination of principles, policies and teams of individuals to a few alternatives.

Imperfect channels of communications

Political parties need to provide links between different levels of their organization, between their leaders and other party activists, and between party activists and actual and potential party supporters. As a result of this they may also serve as links between those who govern and the electorate as a whole. This channel of communication and information can be a two-way process, serving to legitimize policy decisions as well as promoting group interests or maintaining political opposition which operates both within and outside the formal institutions of government.

Integrative, nation-building, constituent organs

Some political parties, through formal activities designed to achieve their goals, serve as political educators, maintaining support for the existing political system or channelling demands for radical change into the accepted patterns of competition for political power, thus helping to maintain the stability and integration of the political system, i.e. the Scottish National Party (S.N.P.) channels demands for Scottish self-government through the normal electoral channels of the existing political structure.

Most political parties in Britain appear to perform all of these functions to a greater or lesser degree, though some may be more obvious than others. They are, in part, and often simultaneously, groups of office-seekers and office-holders, bodies of men agreed on certain principles, electoral machines and social groups. A particular party, such as the Liberal Party, may, for example, place more emphasis on political communication and education than office-holding, or, like the Scottish or Welsh Nationalists (Plaid Cymru), be primarily concerned with aggregating specific group demands rather than articulating broad political principles.

Political parties in Britain perform functions directly or manifestly related to their structure and rationale for existence (the nomination and election of candidates for political office, co-ordination of different groups behind a broad party programme for which they seek public support, and support or criticism of existing or proposed public policy) and also latent and less perceptible functions which may help to support the political system as a whole. Not all existing parties perform such latent functions, but the following are among the most significant of these functions:

Recruitment of political leadership

By their desire to select candidates for political office, political parties also provide a major source for the recruitment of governmental decision-makers.

Innovation

Political parties, especially minority parties, present new ideas and policies for consideration, and may recommend fundamental changes in the existing political system which may be achieved without revolutionary change.

Political socialization

Political parties help to promote and maintain political awareness within a society, encouraging members of the public to identify with a particular party and possibly to work within the existing political process to achieve political ends.

This delineation of the functions performed by parties as parties, and as organization operating within the political process, is important in seeking to consider and compare the activities of British political parties. Some activities of certain political parties (the Communist Party of Great Britain or the National Front Party, for example) may fall outside this functional categorization and be excluded from consideration, not because of their lack of significance but because of difficulties in comparison. However, some attempt to compare British political parties of all types in structural and functional terms is useful if only because there is a dearth of attempts to consider and compare British political parties as parties in formal terms, and the selection of material for this guide has been made with this fact firmly in mind.

There are also practical as well as methodological reasons for the use of such an approach. The contemporary British political process is both cohesive and coherent. It involves cabinet control of Parliament through the medium of the majority party in the House of Commons. As Butler and Stokes point out:

5

Politics in Britain, to a remarkable degree, are [sic] based on the competition between cohesive parties which act together in the national legislature and offer unified appeals for the support of the mass electorate. A member almost never goes against the party whips in the division lobbies, and very few candidates diverge from the party line in their election appeals.[3]

At the national level an electoral system of single-member districts, and election to the House of Commons by a simple plurality, strongly favour two-party competition and the dominance of government by the Conservative and Labour parties. This situation is buttressed by the general preference of most British people for stable, effective government and a strong long-term electoral identification with one or other of the two major parties.[4]

A major consequence of this situation is that the Labour and Conservative parties in Britain have become much more than private, voluntary organizations. Though Britain contains great diversities of interests and attitudes, the two major parties have developed into predominantly (even obsessively) 'parliamentary' parties concerned primarily with support for, or harassment of, successive governments. One result of this is that, while the formal organizational features of these parties may differ, within the parties (despite their different origins) relationships between parliamentary party and its mass organization have become essentially the same. As McKenzie has demonstrated, 'the primary function of the mass organisations of the Conservative and Labour parties is to sustain two competing teams of parliamentary leaders between whom the electorate as a whole may periodically choose.'[5]

While, as has been indicated earlier, it is a legitimate function of parties to act as supports, even nurseries, for the cultivation and maintenance of a governing elite, preoccupation with this function may lead to neglect of the need to articulate effectively the demands of diverse interest and opinions. Equally there is the intellectual danger of neglecting consideration of the nature of party organization of other parties which exist with different functions and at different stages of development. The growth and relative electoral success in the short-run of parties appealing to nationalistic sentiments, and the persistence of support for the Liberal Party, are interesting phenomena in themselves, quite apart from evidence of the dangers to the major parties of relying on traditional ties such as class to maintain party support and alleviate disillusion with party performance. This guide is not intended, however, as an examination of current trends in party competition, but is an attempt to provide factual evidence about distinctive structural and functional characteristics of political

parties within the political process in Britain. Our concern is not with political parties simply as instruments of government but as discrete and distinctive phenomena with a wide range of activities operating within a common political framework, thus demonstrating the utility of presenting and comparing evidence about parties at different stages of development, possessing distinctive styles of organization and obtaining different degrees of electoral success. Information is provided about the way in which specific organizational and functional matters are dealt with by parties of many types, along with bibliographic information of available written work to allow for further study.

As a short preliminary guide, this volume presents material which may be difficult for students to obtain on parties both familiar and less familiar. In this respect it may serve as a supplement as well as an introduction to existing studies of party activity in Britain. Part One is intended as a brief comparative analysis of the formal organizational and structural attributes of political parties in Britain. Part Two is concerned with analysis and comparison of the roles and functions performed by political parties and their effects on the political process, emphasizing both the manifest and latent functions of parties and how formal structural forms are affected by the practical realities of party competition at all stages of the political process. Each chapter, except Chapter 1, begins with a general introduction and a select bibliography of sources, followed by a selection of documentary and article material intended to illuminate specific aspects of the matters under discussion.

Notes

1 See H. J. Hanham, 'The First Constituency Party', *Political Studies*, 1961, pp. 188–9.
2 See F. Bealey *et al.*, *Constituency Politics*, London, 1965, pp. 62 and 404–5, also J. Cornford, 'The Adoption of Mass Organisation by the British Conservative Party', in E. Allardt and Y. Littunen (eds), *Cleavages, Ideologies and Party Systems*, Helsinki, 1964.
3 D. Butler and D. Stokes, *Political Change in Britain*, London, 1969, p. 373.
4 Though the intensive study of Butler and Stokes provides fascinating accounts of the short-term nuances of electoral deviations from basic party identification and of the continuing potential for fundamental realignments of party support, much of their evidence supports this basic generalization.
5 R. T. McKenzie, *British Political Parties*, 2nd ed., London, 1963, p. 642.

INTRODUCTION

Further reading

A. Beattie, ed., *English Party Politics 1660–1970*, 2 vols, London, 1970.
S. Beer, *Modern British Politics*, London, 1969.
I. Bulmer-Thomas, *The Growth of the British Party System*, 2 vols, London, 1965.
W. N. Chambers and W. D. Burnham, eds, *The American Party Systems*, New York, 1967 (chapters by T. Lowi, W. D. Burnham and D. Stokes).
M. Duverger, *Political Parties*, London, 1964.
S. J. Eldersveld, *Political Parties. A Behavioral Analysis*, Chicago, 1964.
L. J. MacFarlane, *The British Communist Party*, London, 1966.
R. T. McKenzie, *British Political Parties*, London, 1963.
R. C. Macridis, ed., *Political Parties: Contemporary Trends and Ideas*, New York, 1967.
H. Mansfield Jr, *Statesmanship and Party Government*, Chicago, 1965.
C. G. Mayo and B. L. Crowe, eds, *American Political Parties: A Systematic Perspective*, New York, 1967.
R. Merton, *Social Theory and Social Structure*, New York, 1957.
R. Michels, *Political Parties*, London, 1911.
M. I. Ostrogorski, *Democracy and the Organisation of Political Parties* (2 vols), London, 1901.
G. Thayer, *The British Political Fringe. A Profile*, London, 1965.

Articles

T. W. Casstevens, 'Party Theories and British Politics', *Midwest Journal of Political Science*, 1961, pp. 391–9.
A. King, 'Political Parties in Western Democracies—Some Sceptical Reflections', *Polity*, 1969, pp. 111–41.
C. Leys, 'Models, Theories and the Theory of Political Parties', *Political Studies*, 1959, pp. 127–46.
T. Lowi, 'Towards Functionalism in Political Science. The Case of Innovation in Party Systems', *American Political Science Review*, 1963, pp. 570–83.
J. D. May, 'Democracy, Organisation, Michels', *American Political Science Review*, 1965, pp. 417–29.
R. Rose, 'The Variability of Party Government', *Political Studies*, 1969, pp. 413–45.

8

Part one   The organization of political parties

1   The structure and framework of political parties

Formal and informal structures

One of the consequences of focusing on the concept of 'power' in the political process has been the relative neglect of the role of formal structures in the political system. The quest for the 'power structure' is a quest for an informal structure of the political process, a structure which is often relatively ephemeral or which evolves as the people operating the system change.

This informal structure is, however, usually limited by a set of rules, procedures and functions which are laid down and constitute a formal organization, or structure. Sometimes, of course, informal and formal structures coincide, such as when those formally assigned a specific function actually *do* perform that function: those who are powerful 'on paper' turn out to be powerful in practice. More frequently, however, there is a discrepancy between the formal and informal structures.

Such discrepancies certainly exist within the political parties considered in this study. Each party has a formal set of rules prescribing the relationship between its various officers, committees, conferences and so on. Yet the actual power relationship is often quite different from this. It is the task of the student of politics to explain how and why this is so. Part of this explanation consists in an examination of the formal structure and its role in the political process. Why do parties have constitutions? Why do they provide for the particular types of organizations that they do? Why, for example, do parties have conferences? Are they meant to play the same role in different parties? Do all parties provide for the same kind of central organization? These are a few of the questions which arise in this context.

Of course it should not be thought that constitutions and formal procedures are immutable and remain constant while the informal structures evolve with time. The frequency of amendment of the Swiss Constitution vividly illustrates what can happen to formal rules and procedures.

What concern us, however, are the reasons for constitutional change, and whether parties playing one kind of role in the political system are more prone to show concern for their formal structure than others.

The creation of a formal structure arises from several functional needs:

1. The existence of a formal structure helps to give the party credibility within the system. A clear-cut organization can project a public image more easily.

2. Certain ends, e.g. vote-winning, can better be achieved consistently by means of people operating within a formal, clearly defined, structure.

3. A formal structure plays an important role in determining the pattern of party loyalty. Seen from the point of view of the party, loyalty solely to ideals on the part of party members can at times be dangerous, and possibly threaten the survival of the party. Loyalty given to the formal structure, however, is more lasting. One reason for the survival of the Conservative Party is the part played by what we might term 'institutional' loyalty. Deeds have been done 'for the good of the party' rather than in pursuance of particular ideals, and conflicts have been avoided by appeals to party loyalty. In a sense, the encouragement of such institutional loyalty is a rational strategy for a party; in this way the acquisition and retention of power can be promoted. Conversely, the highly variable performance of the nationalist parties is partly to be seen in terms of a lack of structural loyalty.

4. As parties become larger, communication problems appear, the solution of which requires the creation of permanent communication and organizational channels.

5. Formal structures also provide for some form of balance between leaders and members. Constitutions sometimes offer members opportunities to control leaders, for membership usually carries with it certain rights of participation in the affairs of the party.

6. Formal structures in most organizations, while allocating superior power to key individuals (secretaries, chairmen, etc.), attempt, to a greater or lesser degree, to equalize the power wielded by members generally. Often quite detailed rules are laid down determining members' participation in the affairs of the party.

In any given political party, a *particular* structural feature may have arisen in response to any or all of these needs, or to none of them. It is worth remembering that not every structural feature in society has an obvious functional explanation. Changes in the formal structure can occur for a variety of reasons. It may be that there is concern that some of the basic functions of the party are not being performed adequately, or that those operating the structure find certain restrictions hamper their informal arrangements, or that it is felt desirable to limit the informal structure in some way.

Concern and support for the formal structure is often related to the historical role which a party has played in the political system. Parties whose role has been a relatively minor one, that is, those who have never known substantial representation in Parliament, have usually not needed strong formal structures and hence have been less preoccupied with them. Their central organizations may play a quite different role both in theory and practice from that played by the central organization of the major parties. This is in part due to the fact that the smaller parties simply do not have the resources of finance, publicity, speakers and so on, to provide a central service for their branches, and therefore there is no need for a structure to organize this. Part of the explanation is also to be seen in the tacit acceptance of a different role in the system from that of the major parties. The role of minor parties, such as the nationalists, is often much more akin to that of a pressure group. They place a different emphasis on the function of conferences, central office, party and leadership.

The position of the Liberal Party in this context is an interesting one, being something of a hybrid between the highly structured major party on the one hand, and the loosely structured minor party on the other. Like the nationalists, the Liberals have very limited resources. Central office cannot perform a very positive function within the party and, like the nationalists, Liberal Associations have considerably more autonomy than those of either of the two main parties. However, the party has a structural legacy from the early part of the century when their representation in Parliament was measured in hundreds rather than dozens. Despite the position of the party's central office in terms of real power and resources, the party continued its ambivalent attitude towards its role in the system by maintaining such an office after 1945, even making what proved to be a disastrously expensive decision to move the headquarters to Smith Square alongside the Labour and Conservative headquarters during the revival of party fortunes in the early 1960s, but moving to more modest accommodation in 1969. Improvements in the electoral fortunes of the S.N.P. and Plaid Cymru after 1966 saw both parties strengthen existing central offices and create new offices with permanent organizational staff.

Constitutions

As the main vehicles of structural delineation let us examine some provisions of the constitutions of the parties with which we are concerned.

13

Statement of aims

All the constitutions have a section on the 'aims' or 'principles' of the party. The S.N.P. and Plaid Cymru state their aims simply in a short paragraph: to secure self-government and to safeguard national culture and interests. It is clear both from this and from their pamphlets that the nationalists are almost entirely preoccupied with self-government. This looms so large on their horizon that there is little discussion of what the stance of the party would be if self-government were achieved, or even whether the party would continue. The parties have no constitutional statements which might be said to imply a particular social or economic policy. As Article 3 of the S.N.P. Constitution says: 'The Policy and Direction of the National Party shall be that laid down from time to time in accordance with the Constitution and Rules.'

The Ulster Unionist Party, as one might expect, lays emphasis on defending the position of Northern Ireland, and the Unionist Council sees its role as a largely co-ordinating one. Again there are no policy implications, in the social, economic or any other sphere (save the status of Northern Ireland).

The object of Conservative Associations is to provide an organizational foundation for electoral success, to disseminate information about party policy, and to contribute to the central funds of the party. The National Union, like the Ulster Unionist Council, plays a co-ordinating role. Its functions are encouraging the formation of constituency associations, furtherance of the principles and aims of the party, acting as 'a link' between the party leader and the organizations, maintaining a 'close relationship' with Central Office, and finally, working 'in close co-operation' with the Scottish Conservatives and the Ulster Unionists. As the leader of the party has theoretical control over policy, the objects and functions contain no references to particular policy objectives.

In contrast, both the Liberal and the Labour parties pay considerable attention to their aims in their constitutions. The Liberal Party has a lengthy preamble in which the basic creed is outlined, while of course the aims of the Labour Party are outlined in the notorious Clause IV over which there has been considerable controversy on certain occasions:

Clause IV.—Party Objects

National
(1) To organise and maintain in Parliament and in the country a Political Labour Party.

(2) To co-operate with the General Council of the Trades Union Congress, or other Kindred Organisations, in joint political or other action in harmony with the Party Constitution and Standing Orders.

(3) To give effect as far as may be practicable to the principles from time to time approved by the Party Conference.

(4) To secure for the workers by hand or by brain the full fruits of their industry and the most equitable distribution thereof that may be possible, upon the basis of the common ownership of the means of production, distribution, and exchange, and the best obtainable system of popular administration and control of each industry or service.

(5) Generally to promote the Political, Social and Economic Emancipation of the People, and more particularly of those who depend directly upon their own exertions by hand or by brain for the means of life.

Inter-commonwealth

(6) To co-operate with the Labour and Socialist organisations in the Commonwealth Overseas with a view to promoting the purposes of the Party, and to take common action for the promotion of a higher standard of social and economic life for the working population of the respective countries.

International

(7) To co-operate with the Labour and Socialist organisations in other countries and to support the United Nations Organisation and its various agencies and other international organisations for the promotion of peace, the adjustment and settlement of international disputes by conciliation or judicial arbitration, the establishment and defence of human rights, and the improvement of the social and economic standards and conditions of work of the people of the world.

The Aims and Objects of the Liberal Party

1. The Liberal Party exists to build a Liberal Society in which every citizen shall possess liberty, property, and security, and none shall be enslaved by poverty, ignorance or conformity. Its chief care is for the rights and opportunities of the individual, and in all spheres it sets freedom first.

2. It looks forward to a world in which all peoples live together in peace under an effective and democratically constituted World Authority; in which all people enjoy access to the earth's abundance; in which the various cultures of mankind can develop freely

15

without being warped by nationalist, racial, or religious antagonism; and in which the free movement of ideas, of people, and of goods is guaranteed to the benefit of all. To these ends it sees this country as committed to supporting and strengthening the United Nations, to working steadfastly for the eventual abolition of national armies and armaments, to co-operating with other countries to build a United Europe, and to making a special effort together with other richer nations towards assisting that part of mankind whose essential freedoms are denied by poverty and hunger. It welcomes the establishment of links with other countries in so far as such groupings advance these Liberal aims.

3. At home its goal is a country in which the powers of the state will be used to establish social justice, to wage war against poverty, to spread wealth and power, to ensure that the country's resources are wisely and fully developed for the benefit of the whole community, and to create the positive conditions which will make a full and free life possible for all regardless of colour, creed, race or sex: a country in which, under the protection of law, all citizens shall have the right to think freely, to speak freely, to write freely, and to vote freely: power through a just electoral system to shape the laws which they are called upon to obey; autonomous institutions ensuring genuine self-government; an effective voice in deciding the conditions in which they live and work; liberty to buy, sell, and produce in circumstances which secure for the consumer real freedom of choice; guarantees against the abuse of monopoly, whether private or public; opportunity to work at a fair wage; decent homes in a varied and attractive environment; good education and facilities for the full cultivation of the human personality; an assurance that the community shall enjoy the benefits of publicly created land values; and, as a safeguard of independence, the personal ownership of property by all citizens. These are the conditions of liberty, which it is the function of the state to protect and enlarge.

4. The Liberal Party consists of men and women working together for the achievement of these aims.

Membership

In general, membership is open to those who subscribe to the aims of the party; though the Labour Party, with its tradition of stronger discipline than most parties, puts the point rather more strictly. Members must 'accept the conditions of membership' which are:

Clause III.—Conditions of Membership

(1) Each affiliated organisation must:
(*a*) Accept the Programme, Principles, and Policy of the Party.
(*b*) Agree to conform to the Constitution and Standing Orders of the Party.
(*c*) Submit its Political Rules to the National Executive Committee.

(2) Each Constituency Labour Party, Central Labour Party, and Federation must, in addition to the conditions mentioned in Section 1 of this Clause, adopt the Rules laid down by the Party Conference.

(3) Each Individual Member must
(*a*) Accept and conform to the Constitution, Programme, Principles and Policy of the Party.
(*b*) If eligible, be a member of a Trade Union affiliated to the Trades Union Congress or recognised by the General Council of the Trades Union Congress as a *bona fide* Trade Union.
(*c*) Unless temporarily resident abroad, be a member of a Constituency Labour Party, either (*i*) where he or she resides, or (*ii*) where he or she is registered as a Parliamentary or Local Government elector.

In only two cases are members obliged to sign anything. The S.N.P. asks members to sign a document to the effect that they endorse the party's aims and accept the direction of the party. Oddly, the suggested model rules for Conservative Associations demand that members 'sign an enrolment form' (though this practice is probably not very widespread). All except the Liberal Party (presumably anxious not to deter support) insist on payment of a subscription, though the National Executive Committee is given the power to lay down 'regulations governing the payment of . . . subscriptions'. In practice parties may not operate subscription requirements rigorously, especially the Conservative Party where active party work is valued more than annual subscriptions. Usually, members join the constituency Association or its sub-units, though the S.N.P. allows members to join at headquarters, and allows non-residents to become honorary members.

Only the Labour Party acknowledges an age limit: members must be fifteen years old or more.

Individual membership is not, however, the only form of membership. The Labour Party constitution defines two classes.

Clause II.—Membership

(1) There shall be two classes of members, namely:
  (*a*) Affiliated Members.
  (*b*) Individual Members.
(2) Affiliated Members shall consist of:
  (*a*) Trade Unions affiliated to the Trades Union Congress or recognised by the General Council of the Trades Union Congress as *bona fide* Trade Unions.
  (*b*) Co-operative Societies.
  (*c*) Socialist Societies.
  (*d*) Professional Organisations which, in the opinion of the National Executive Committee, have interests consistent with those of other affiliated organisations.
  (*e*) Constituency Labour Parties and Central Labour Parties in Divided Boroughs.
  (*f*) County or Area Federations of Constituency Labour Parties, hereinafter referred to as Federations.

Other parties do not have affiliated organizations in quite the same way. The U.U. Council comprises representatives of various facets of unionism.

III.—Membership of Council

1. The Council shall be composed of the following members:
  (a) *306 nominated by the affiliated Divisional Associations in accordance with the numbers set forth in the Schedule;
  (b) *234 nominated by the Women's Associations affiliated to the Ulster Women's Unionist Council;
  (c) 122 nominated by the County Grand Lodges of the Loyal Orange Institution of Ireland;
  (d) 20 nominated by the Ulster Unionist Labour Association;
  (e) 20 nominated by the Ulster Women's Unionist Council;
  (f) 12 nominated by the Ulster Reform Club Political Council;
  (g) 12 nominated by the Queen's University Unionist Voters' Association;
  (h) 6 nominated by the Apprentice Boys of Derry;
  (i) 6 nominated by the Willowfield Unionist Club;
  (j) 10 nominated by the Association of Loyal Orange Women of Ireland;

* Where two or more Constituencies for better working unite to form one Association, they shall have representation equal to the total representation of the Constituencies so uniting.

(k)   12 nominated by the Unionist Society;

(l)   **the Northern Irish Peers, the Members representing Ulster Constituencies in the Imperial House of Commons at Westminster, and the Members of the Senate and of the House of Commons of the Parliament of Northern Ireland, who, in the opinion of the Standing Committee hereinafter referred to, are members of the Unionist Party;

(m)   **the wives of such Peers, Senators, and Members of Parliament if they so desire;

(n)   also distinguished persons who may from time to time be co-opted by the Council, but the number of such co-opted members shall not exceed 120 at any one time.

2. The nominated Delegates shall be selected annually by the several Organisations referred to above, and their names and addresses should be sent to the Secretary, Unionist Headquarters, Glengall Street, Belfast, 12, not later than the second Monday in January.

Section 1(a) may include delegates from the Young Unionists.

The Council of the National Union includes representatives of such organizations as the Society of Conservative Lawyers, Swinton College, the Primrose League, the Association of Conservative Clubs, and of course the parties in Scotland and Ulster. The two nationalist parties have no affiliated organizations. The Liberal Constitution 'recognises' certain 'bodies':

3. The following bodies shall be recognised by this Constitution:

(a)   The Association of Liberal Councillors;

(b)   The Association of Liberal Trades Unionists;

(c)   The Liberal Agents Association;

(d)   The Liberal Party Organisation Staff Association;

(e)   The National League of Young Liberals;

(f)   The National Union of Liberal Clubs;

(g)   The Union of Liberal Students;

(h)   The Women's Liberal Federation.

Nothing in this Constitution shall prejudice the independence of these bodies.

Of course parties vary in the extent to which they allow their members to join other organizations. The Conservatives, U.U. and Plaid Cymru have no specified restrictions. The Liberals and the S.N.P. require that members must not belong to other political parties, while

** Ex-officio Members.

the Labour Party publishes a list of proscribed organizations including:

British Soviet Society
British Soviet Friendship Houses Ltd.
Common Wealth
Communist Party of Great Britain
Labour Research Department
Marx House
Militant Labour League
Scottish U.S.S.R. Society
Women's Parliament
Student Labour Federation
International Youth Council in Britain
The World Federation of Democratic Youth
Women's International Democratic Federation
League for Democracy in Greece
British Peace Committee
Welsh Peace Council
Socialist Fellowship
Union Movement
British Youth Festival
International Women's Day Committee
People's Congress for Peace
West Yorkshire Federation of Peace Organisations
World Federation of Trade Unions
The International Union of Students
The International Association of Democratic Lawyers
The International Organisation of Journalists
The World Federation of Scientific Workers
World Peace Council
British-Soviet Friendship Society
British-Polish Friendship Society
British-China Friendship Association
British-Czechoslovak Friendship League
British-Rumanian Friendship Association
The Committee for Friendship with Bulgaria
British Hungarian Friendship Society
Artists for Peace
Musicians' Organisation for Peace
Authors' World Peace Appeal
Teachers for Peace
Scientists for Peace
National Assembly of Women

The Newsletter
Socialist Labour League
Keep Left
Independent Nuclear Disarmament Election Committee

All parties except Plaid Cymru acknowledge the need for some form of disciplinary procedure involving suspension or expulsion for behaviour which is not regarded as compatible with the aims of the party. In the S.N.P. this power is vested in the National Council, with right of appeal to the annual conference. In the Labour Party the N.E.C. has responsibility for disaffiliation and expulsion, and merely reports its actions to the conference. In the other parties expulsion is vested in the enrolling body. The Liberals allow appeals to be made to the Regional Executive, thence to the President, and ultimately to the Assembly. The Council is responsible for disaffiliation of a constituency Association subject to appeal to the Assembly.

Ulster Unionists may appeal to a meeting of their Association, having had the opportunity to rebut any charges made by the executive of the Association. The Conservatives have no appeals procedure as such, though 'any dispute or difference' may be resolved by the area officers, or failing that, the Executive Committee of the National Union, whose decision is final. Presumably, the lack of clear-cut appeals procedure indicates that the party does not envisage the necessity of having to expel many members.

Finally, with the exception of the Conservatives, the various constitutions include provisions to safeguard the members' right to participate in the affairs of their local Association. Often a minimum period of notice is required for meetings, and members have both the right to call meetings and to receive notice of meetings called by others. The Conservatives do not seem to offer such safeguards either in theory or practice. The suggested model rules contain the following interesting passage:

Notice of General Meetings

16. (1) Notice of the annual general meeting and of any other general meeting of the Association shall be given by written notification to every individual member.

    (2) Whilst every member of the Association is entitled to attend all general meetings, the fact that any member of the Association has not for any reason whatsoever been notified of a general meeting shall not invalidate such meeting or any resolution passed or any election or appointment made at such meeting.

Government

Only the largest parties, Conservative, Labour, Liberal and Ulster Unionist, have party leaders as part of the formal structure. Those parties which grew from within Parliament, that is, those which began as parliamentary groups and set up their mass organization outside Parliament in order to facilitate re-election, initially developed a formal structure dominated by the leader. On the other hand, the remaining parties, which were set up outside Parliament in order to secure representation inside, have attempted to produce a 'democratic' structure with the annual conference as the supreme body. The two nationalist parties are, in a formal sense, leaderless and are dominated by their National Committees and their Executives, with the annual conference acting as the supreme governing body, though the President of Plaid Cymru is responsible for the government and organization of the party between meetings of Conferences, Council and the Executive Committee. The Labour Party is in a somewhat ambivalent position, being formally similar to the nationalists, with the conference as ultimate arbiter, while in practice its leaders have been trying to establish the parliamentary leadership as the arbiter of party policy.

In the Conservative Party, policy is the prerogative of the Leader, advised by a committee. Resolutions passed at the conference are also only advisory (until 1965 the Leader did not even attend the conference, but merely addressed a rally held after the end). In its formal arrangements the party leaves itself as much room for manœuvre as possible. The rules of the National Union are mostly definitions of the composition of the various bodies comprising the Union.

The new Liberal structure emphasizes the powerlessness of the conference (Assembly) by allocating the task of policy formulation to the Council and the Standing Committee, bodies which comprise only the active elite of the party, and placing the overall direction of the work of the party in the hands of the National Executive Committee, a relatively small body of people, and party administration with a five-member Finance and Administration Board. The Constitution adds a slightly 'Gaullist' touch in stating that 'the President shall be the guardian of the party's constitution'.

The basic structure of the parties is presented in the following diagrams. They are intended as summaries of the formal arrangements within the parties and should be studied in conjunction with the party constitutions printed at the end of the study. It is worth noting that in the National Union organizations or committees are frequently represented by their chairmen, *ex officio*. This is particularly the case with representation on the smaller bodies, such as the

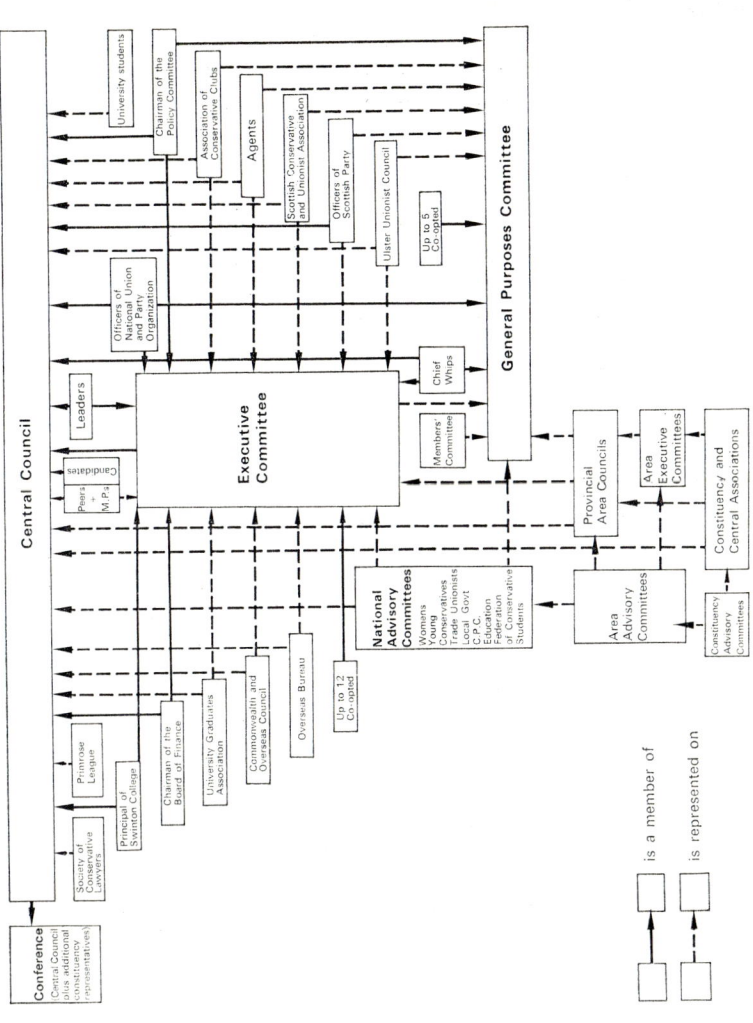

Figure 1 The National Union of Conservative and Unionist Associations

Central Council

Conference
(Central Council
plus additional
constituency
representatives)

Society of
Conservative
Lawyers

Primrose
League

Principal of
Swinton College

Chairman of the
Board of Finance

University Graduates
Association

Commonwealth and
Overseas Council

Overseas Bureau

Up to 12
Co-opted

University students

Chairman of the
Policy Committee

Association of
Conservative Clubs

Agents

Scottish Conservative
and Unionist Association

Officers of
Scottish Party

Ulster Unionist Council

Up to 5
Co-opted

Officers of
National Union
and Party
Organization

Leaders

Candidates

Peers +
M.P.s

Executive Committee

Chief
Whips

Members'
Committee

General Purposes Committee

National Advisory Committees
Womens
Young
Conservatives
Trade Unionists
Local Govt.
C.P.C.
Education
Federation
of Conservative
Students

Provincial
Area Councils

Area
Executive
Committees

Constituency and
Central Associations

Area
Advisory
Committees

Constituency
Advisory
Committees

is a member of

is represented on

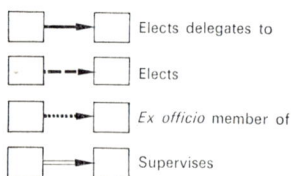

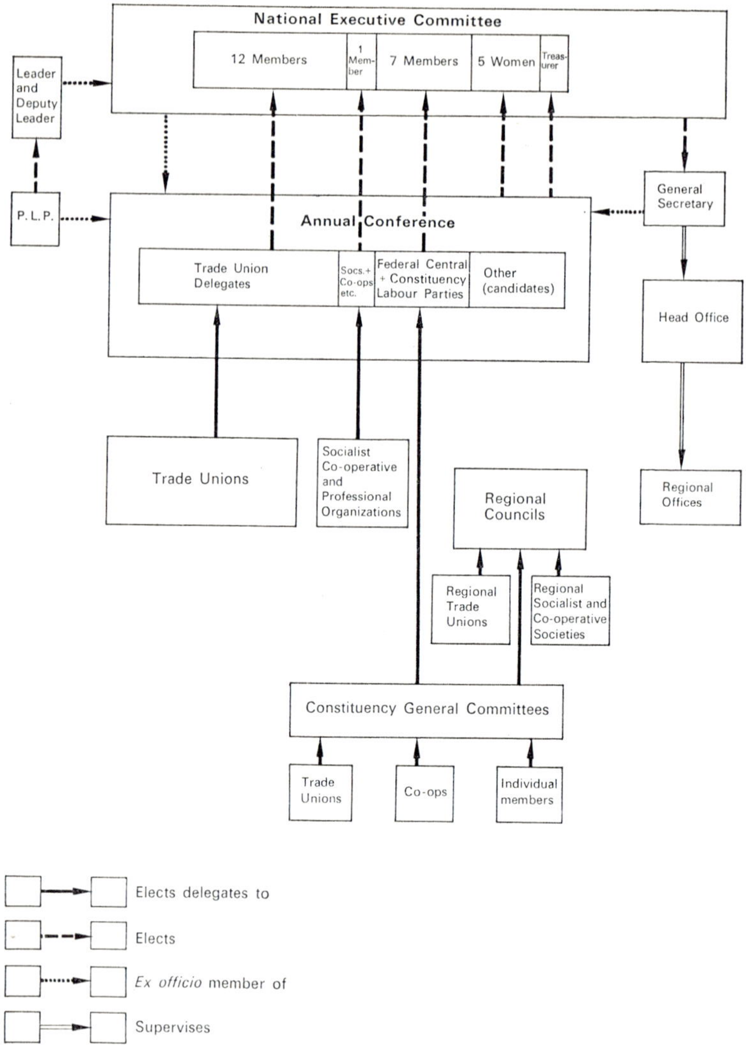

Figure 2 The Labour Party

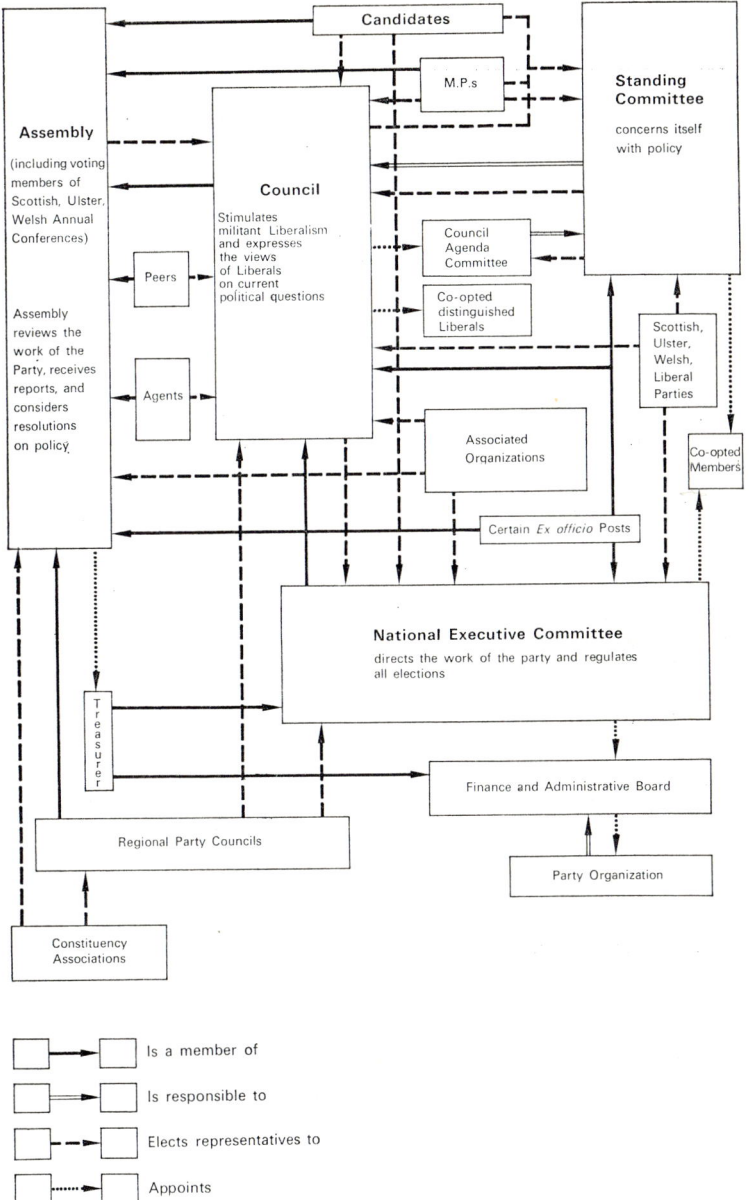

Candidates

M.P.s

Standing Committee
concerns itself with policy

Assembly
(including voting members of Scottish, Ulster, Welsh Annual Conferences)

Assembly reviews the work of the Party, receives reports, and considers resolutions on policy

Council
Stimulates militant Liberalism and expresses the views of Liberals on current political questions

Peers

Agents

Council Agenda Committee

Co-opted distinguished Liberals

Scottish, Ulster, Welsh, Liberal Parties

Co-opted Members

Associated Organizations

Certain *Ex officio* Posts

National Executive Committee
directs the work of the party and regulates all elections

Treasurer

Finance and Administrative Board

Regional Party Councils

Party Organization

Constituency Associations

Is a member of

Is responsible to

Elects representatives to

Appoints

Figure 3 **The Liberal Party**

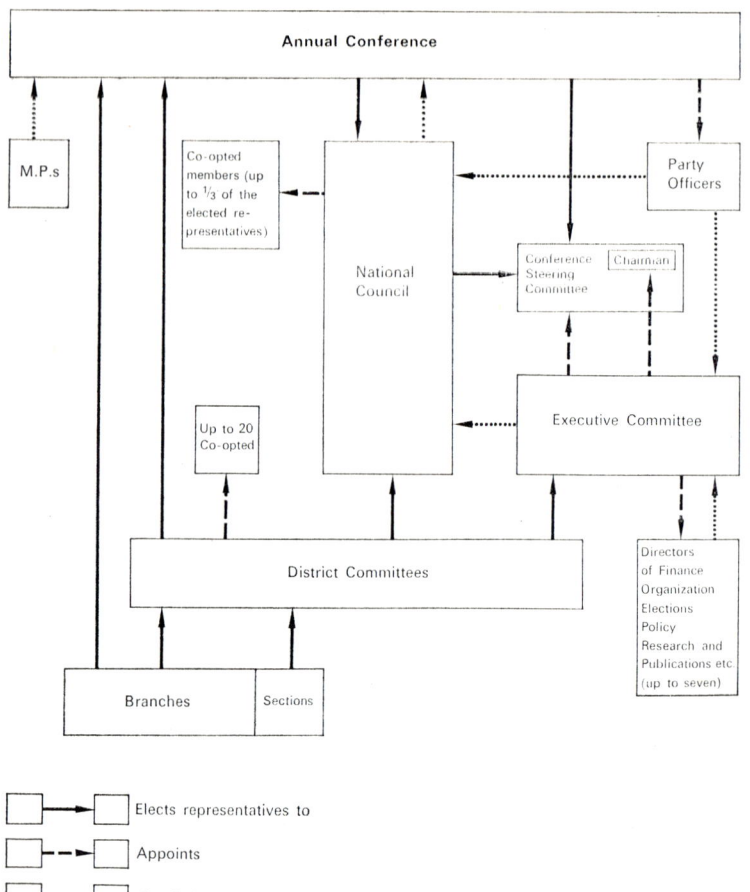

Annual Conference

M.P.s

Co-opted members (up to ⅓ of the elected representatives)

Party Officers

National Council

Conference Steering Committee   Chairman

Executive Committee

Up to 20 Co-opted

District Committees

Directors of Finance Organization Elections Policy Research and Publications etc. (up to seven)

Branches   Sections

☐—▶☐ Elects representatives to

☐--▶☐ Appoints

☐······▶☐ *Ex officio* member of

Figure 4 **Plaid Cymru**

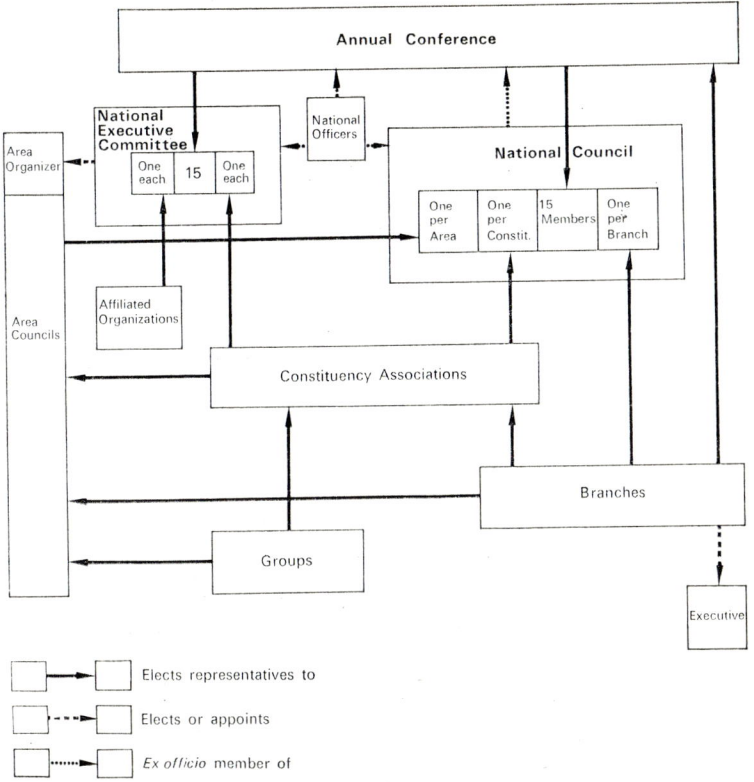

Annual Conference

National Executive Committee
One each 15 One each

National Officers

National Council
One per Area | One per Constit. | 15 Members | One per Branch

Area Organizer

Area Councils

Affiliated Organizations

Constituency Associations

Branches

Groups

Executive

Elects representatives to

Elects or appoints

Ex officio member of

Figure 5 Scottish National Party

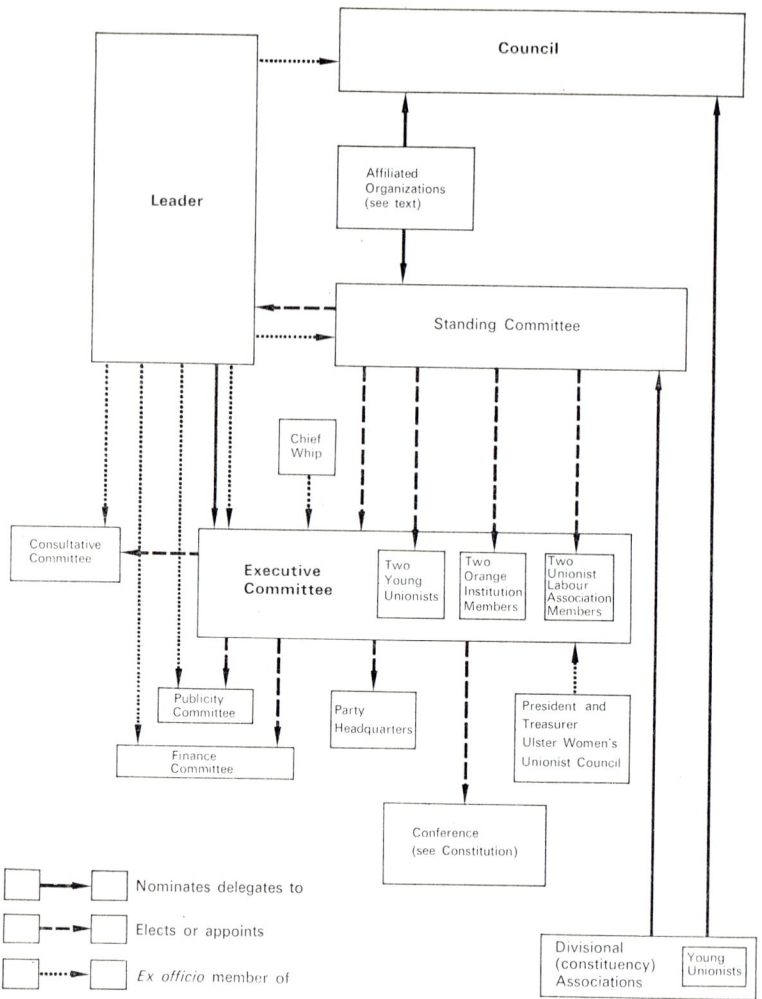

Figure 6 The Ulster Unionist Party

General Purposes Committee. On larger bodies, such as the Central Council, such representation is supplemented with other officers (*ex officio*), or elected representatives, or both.

In some cases, at the lower levels of the structure, the diagrams may be somewhat imprecise, or may not correspond even to the actual formal structure. This is partly because the structural details of the lower levels depend upon the nature of the area concerned (e.g. it will depend upon whether a borough is divided into two or more constituencies). It is also partly due to the fact that, at the lowest levels of organization, the informal structure often seems to take precedence over the formal structure to the extent that some bodies which might exist theoretically are never created in practice. One might cite as examples here the position of the Constituency Advisory Committees in the National Union. These bodies are intended to mirror similar bodies at the national level, yet it is clear that they do not exist in all constituencies.

It should be emphasized that the relative size of the boxes in the diagrams should not be regarded as indicating anything definitive about the bodies they represent. No attempt has been made to relate box sizes directly to any factor ('importance', membership size, etc.). The diagrams depict relationships.

Party conferences

The diagrams in the previous section illustrate the position of the party conference in each organization.

With the exception of that of the Ulster Unionists (who are entirely at the mercy of their executive committee), all the constitutions have lengthy and detailed provisions concerning the nature of representation at the conference. These are included in the appendices.

Much of the discussion of the role of the conference in the affairs of the party turns on the question of the extent to which conference determines party policy, and exercises effective control over the party. This topic is considered in Chapter 8 with reference to certain parties. It is, however, worth noting at this stage certain formal provisions relating to conferences.

The conference of Plaid Cymru is unique in that any member may attend and speak though they may not vote. The order of business is laid down in the standing orders; the only power which the Executive Committee appears to have is that of deciding the order of discussion of motions submitted, and of the time to be spent on each. They do not seem to have the power to conflate resolutions or otherwise modify motions submitted to them.

29

In contrast, the S.N.P. conference is carefully specified, with the National Council having the power:

Part two. 8. Preparation of Agenda, etc., for Annual Conferences

The National Council shall be responsible for the preparation of the Agenda for the Annual Conferences of the National Party and they shall have the power:

    (a) to decide whether resolutions, etc., nominations and other matters pertaining to the Annual Conference are in accordance with the Constitution and Rules of the National Party

    (b) to revise and amend resolutions or incorporate in one resolution a number of similar resolutions from several Branches or Constituency Associations, or to rewrite resolutions received provided always that the principles underlying the resolutions shall not be infringed

    (c) to decide the order of business to be transacted, the placing of items on the Agenda, and the approximate time to be allocated to each item.

Should, however, any Branch or Constituency Association consider that any such decision of the National Council infringes the principle of the resolutions or is against the expressed wishes of the Branch or Constituency Association concerned, it may as provided by 6(d) of Part Two hereof give notice of an amendment to rectify the matter. Unless a Branch or Constituency Association gives such notice of amendment, the matter shall not be raised at the Annual Conference.

In the Liberal Party it is the Standing Committee and the Council which seem to be in the strongest position to make party policy. Council is given the responsibility of determining the procedure of the Assembly and of classifying and arranging the business to be brought before the Assembly 'in such a way as to avoid repetition or overlapping and to ensure that adequate time is allowed for the discussion of important subjects'. As the supreme governing body, it is the Central Council of the National Union which determines conference procedure, though the much smaller General Purposes Committee decides and arranges the agenda. In fact the Conservative Conference is little more than the Central Council plus additional constituency representatives including agents and organizers. The Labour Party Constitution provides for a Party Conference Arrangements Committee of five delegates, elected by the Conference, who are responsible for arranging the agenda.

Documentation

The Rules and Standing Orders of the National Union of Conservative and Unionist Associations. Revised 1970.
The Constitution and Standing Orders of the Labour Party. Revised 1969.
The Constitution of the Liberal Party. 1969.
The Constitution and Standing Orders of Plaid Cymru. Revised 1970.
The Scottish National Party Constitution and Rules. 1967.
The Constitution and Rules of the Ulster Unionist Council. 1970.

Some parties produce documents which provide useful guides to party organization. In particular, the Conservative and Unionist Central Office publishes an *Organisation Series* which contains pamphlets on aspects of party organization, the following being of particular interest:

The Party Organisation (revised 1964).
Model Rules for Constituency and Branch (1967).
The Voluntary Worker and Party Organisation (revised 1961).

The Labour Party publishes *Party Organisation* (Eleventh Edition, 1966), and a useful study is Sarah Barker, *How the Labour Party Works* (1955). The Liberal Party has produced *Effective Organising: A Guide for Members of the Liberal Party* (1963), while the Ulster Unionist Council produces a *Year Book*.

Addresses of Party Headquarters (1970)

Conservative: 32, Smith Square, Westminster, S.W.1.
Labour: Transport House, Smith Square, S.W.1.
Liberal: 7, Exchange Court, Strand, W.C.2.
Plaid Cymru: 8, Heol y Frenhines, Cardiff.
Scottish National: 59, Elmbank Street, Glasgow, C.2.
Ulster Unionist: 3, Glengall Street, Belfast 12.

2 Parties and party reorganization

Introduction

As voluntary associations and organizations, political parties in Britain vary considerably in their formal structure, and such structures are affected by a range of factors. Party structures which may appear monolithic in practice may still be susceptible to change, and such changes may be the consequence of rank and file as well as leadership initiatives. Demands for structural changes by parties have not always followed severe electoral setbacks, as the case-study of the Simpson Committee demonstrates, though deficiencies evident to some for many years may become more apparent at that time and can serve as useful scapegoats to rationalize away such setbacks.

Changes in the structure of major party organization often come by formal action, though important changes can also follow informal individual or group action which serve to modify existing practices without leading to formal structural changes. Though there is frequent criticism of structural attributes which are felt to affect adversely the electoral success or the public image of particular parties, formal structural change is not always easy to achieve. In this chapter the emphasis is on formal demands for party reorganization, and structural and constitutional changes within parties with well-defined structures. However, it is clear also that parties such as the S.N.P. and Plaid Cymru face problems in their efforts to create a formal party structure, and adjust that structure to political change over time. Changes in response to evidence of increased party membership and electoral support may be easiest to achieve, but it remains a major task to create and maintain a stable and efficient national organization in order to capitalize on rising popular support or remain competitive in the face of election setbacks.

The constitutional framework of a political party is an important indicator to the locus of power and authority within that party. Moreover, constitutional changes may in themselves have important political and policy implications. The impetus for structural reorganization may come from several sources, but is likely to involve more than mere questions of efficiency or cohesion. It may be instigated by the party leadership in response to rank and file constituency pressure, or may take place in one of the quasi-autonomous sections of a party without affecting the central party organization. Even the major parties have something akin to a federal structure, as is shown in the case-study of the Scottish Conservative Party by Derek Urwin, while leaders of the Liberal Party in 1970 sought to make their Constitution more federal in practice. Demands for constitutional change can also produce internal conflict, since their effect may be to change the balance of power within a party, or the role of particular groups or organizations.

In discussing questions of internal party organization, it is difficult to distinguish between changes intended to improve electoral efficiency, communications and participation, and changes whose effects would be to alter internal patterns of influence over questions of policies, electoral strategy or leadership. The constitutional framework of a party determines who participates formally and in what way, yet parties have to create organizations to make decisions on election tactics, finance, the allocation of manpower and resources for day-to-day administrative housekeeping activities and the minutiae of election campaigns, as well as policy-making or leadership selection. While the electoral success of a party may not depend solely on the efficient running of the party machine, it is vital to study the processes of internal structural change in order to gain a full understanding of the dynamics of party activity. As Medding suggests:[1]

Because a party may consist of a number of ideological, socioeconomic, generational, regional, ethnic or religious groups, each with outlooks, interests, leaderships and rank and file memberships of their own, the only way in which the process of party decision-making can be properly understood is by closely following their activities as they operate within the party's constitutional structure.

Attempts at formal reorganization and internal party reform provide valuable glimpses of the internal conflicts and compromises which have an important bearing on the political success of any political party.

Notes

1 P. Y. Medding, 'A Framework for the Analysis of Political Power in Political Parties', *Political Studies*, 1970, p. 16.

Further reading

Major documentary sources relating to party reorganization by the Labour and Conservative parties since 1945, excluding the Simpson Committee reports, include the following:
Interim Report of the Sub-committee on Party Organisation, 1955 (Wilson Report), Transport House, 1955.
Interim and Final Reports of the Committee on Party Organisation (Maxwell-Fyfe Report), Conservative Central Office, 1949.
The Selwyn Lloyd Report, 1963, Conservative Party, 1963.
A detailed analysis of the efforts of Lord Woolton to reorganize the Conservative party is given in J. D. Hoffman, *The Conservative Party in Opposition 1945–51,* London, 1964, and general discussion of party reorganization in R. T. McKenzie, *British Political Parties.*

Articles

D. Clarke, 'The Organisation of Political Parties', *Political Quarterly,* 1950, pp. 79–90.
W. Fienburgh, 'The Future of Labour's Organisation', *Fabian Journal,* November 1955, pp. 10–14.
H. J. Hanham, 'The Local Organisation of the Labour Party', *Western Political Quarterly,* 1956, pp. 376–88.
R. L. Leonard, 'Goodbye to Labour's Penny Farthing?', *New Society,* 14 September 1967, pp. 358–9.
G. Loewenberg, 'The British Constitution and the Structure of the Labour Party', *American Political Science Review,* 1958, pp. 771–90.
R. T. McKenzie, 'The Wilson Report and the Future of the Labour Party Organisation', *Political Studies,* 1956, pp. 93–7.
'Labour Party Organisation: A Note on its Future', *Fabian Journal,* July 1955.
'Our Penny Farthing Machine', special supplement to *Socialist Commentary,* October 1965.
M. Steed, 'How Not to Reform a Constitution', *New Outlook,* April/May 1968, pp. 35–40.

Scottish Conservatism: a party organization in transition*
by Derek W. Urwin

In April 1965 the annual conference of the Scottish Unionist Association approved of plans proposed by the party leaders which would not only change the party's name back to 'Conservative' after an interval of fifty-three years, but also radically reform the organizational structure of the party. The object of this article is to offer an exploratory study of the structure of Scottish Conservatism in the twentieth century, the reasons for its rather distinctive organization as well as those reasons underlying the pressure for change, and the problems faced by the reformers.

Scottish Conservatism, although seemingly conforming to the generalized picture of British Conservatism, has its roots in a different social setting and political history: modern Scottish Toryism took shape in the nineteenth century against a background of the complete dominance of Scotland by a great Liberal alliance, which had its moral and ethical basis in almost total commitment to Scottish Presbyterianism and to the doctrines of free trade. The rather different social setting meant that certain structural features were adapted into the Scottish Conservative party organization which were designed to meet these different social characteristics and which hence differentiated party organization in Scotland from that in England.[1] These differences remained in existence until 1965 when pressure for reform eventually succeeded in its attempt to pattern the Scottish party structure after the English model.

Scottish Conservatism, in theory, claims to be 'independent' of its English counterpart in structure, if not in general aims and policy.[2] The outstanding illustration has been the insistence of the party in retaining until 1965 the title, 'Scottish Unionist Association'—long after the original justification for this nomenclature had disappeared. A better word would probably be 'autonomous', for there have always been several important ties with the English party.

The Scottish party's attitude towards its 'independence' has been curiously ambivalent. Autonomy and independence are treasured values throughout the Scottish party. During the campaign in the Glasgow Woodside by-election in 1962, Iain Macleod, then Chairman of the Conservative Party Organization, took care to placate local sentiment by emphasizing that the by-election was not his concern, but that of the Scottish Unionists.[3] Yet on the other hand, the belief in a completely independent association has been dropped when it is thought that London can help in some way. Much of the

* Reprinted by permission of the Clarendon Press, Oxford, from *Political Studies*, 1966, pp. 145–62, with footnotes abridged.

energy of the Scottish Conservatives, in fact, has in the past been devoted to the defence of 'independence'. It has been, however, essentially an unreal struggle. The nature of their own attitudes and of their organization have not been commensurate with the responsibilities which 'independence' implies.

The Unionist party structure before 1965

The Conservative party structure that developed in Scotland during the late nineteenth and early twentieth centuries was that introduced previously in England: that is, the structure was hierarchical, with a distinction between 'voluntary' and 'professional' organizations and members.[4] However, there were several differences which gave the Scottish party some peculiar characteristics.

At the apex of the 'voluntary' hierarchy was the representative Central Council of the Scottish Unionist Association. It was an unwieldy and ineffective body, being essentially a meeting place of the two Divisional Councils, the representative bodies of local associations in the East and West of Scotland. These Councils were composed almost entirely of delegates from the local Associations which are of considerable strength in this relatively decentralized party. Since the sentiment of localism is extremely strong within the party, some stress must be laid upon the word 'delegate', which has been the term used in party literature.

The bulk of the work of the Divisions fell upon the permanent staff employed by the Divisional Councils, of whom the most influential were the two permanent divisional secretaries, who were in direct contact with the London Central Office. In fact, all the functions which in England are performed by the Central Office were in Scotland, apart from a few negligible tasks, performed by the Divisional Councils. The nearest English equivalent to these permanent secretaries are the area agents. However, the permanent secretaries were appointed by and were answerable to their respective Divisional Council. Furthermore, it must be emphasized that each Council raised its own fund, and that these were separate from those of the Chairman's Office (the 'professional' side of the Scottish organization), which in fact received 'allowances' from the Councils, and the London Central Office. There was no one central Scottish fund.

Below the Eastern Divisional Council were four Area Groups. These were not at all equivalent to the English area organizations, being without any 'professional' staff. They merely provided a forum where member constituency associations could discuss local problems. They were without any power, and on the whole gave little justification for their existence. The only active area was the Number Four Group, covering the Highland region. In that case the constituencies formed a reasonably coherent group with a set of common problems. Resolutions on Highland questions have often been presented collectively to the annual conference by the Highland associations under their group title.

In its broad outlines the annual conference has followed the English pattern. Debates at conferences reveal the intense local feelings that sometimes exist in the constituencies. Delegates are often less inhibited than their English confreres in their criticisms of Conservative governments and policies.

Since 1918 Scotland has been a 'problem child' of the British economy. Although an 'orthodox' Conservative policy often emerges from the Scottish conferences, the most intense debates have been concerned with specific Scottish interests. The following selection of quotations from resolutions and debates is indicative of the resentment felt at times against the English leadership: 'the dead hand of officialdom' (on the Conservative government's house-building programme);[5] 'the present economic situation of this country is due mainly to the inertia of the present Government';[6] 'sheer, muddled thinking' (on Mr Marples's Highland road-building policy).[7] It has also been claimed at Scottish conferences that Labour governments seem to do more for agriculture than Conservative governments,[8] and that Conservative governments seem to be doing everything possible within their power to depopulate the Highlands.[9] Since the Conservative government's decision in 1959 to withdraw the marginal land aid production grants, the discontent of Highland Conservatives has increased. During the 1965 Conference inquest on the loss of three Highland seats, speakers from the area were particularly scathing about the party leadership, as the following selection of quotations indicates: 'the slogan last October about life being better under the Conservatives seemed to Highlanders like a sick joke'; 'a top Tory attitude of sycophantic complacency'; 'the party's magic circle of leadership would remain as remote from the mood and hopes and aspirations of the people of Scotland as the Government of Vietnam is from the people of Vietcong'.[10]

In theory the structure and defined objectives of the local constituency Associations are the same in Scotland as in England. The basic feature of the Scottish Association is the great emphasis placed on local autonomy and complete freedom of action. It is perhaps significant that one of the objects specifically included in the English Model Rules as an essential duty of local Associations,

[that a local Association should] co-operate with the Area Council

> and with Party Headquarters in the common aim of establishing in power a Conservative and Unionist Government

is mentioned in the Scottish Association's manual only as an object for which it is desirable for local Associations to work.[11]

The representative structure of the English National Union is paralleled by a similar hierarchical structure of 'professional' paid party workers, with the Central Office at its apex.[12] The two pyramids are close together at all levels, assisting the process of integration. Such a parallel structure did not exist in Scotland. The only Scottish 'professionals', the workers in the Chairman's Office in Edinburgh, formed an apex without any base. The Chairman's Office was created in 1950 after a reorganization of the old Scottish Whip's Office. The Chairman is appointed, like his English counter-part, by the British party Leader. In theory the Office was the link between the Scottish Unionists and the national leaders.[13] The implication is that the Leader of the British Conservative Party was also Leader of the Scottish Unionist Association.

But in reality the Office provided little more than an information service. The position of Chairman possessed potentialities which were never fully realized because of the power of the Divisional Councils and local Associations. In contrast to the situation in England, where the area agents are the direct employees of the Central Office,[14] the Scottish divisional secretaries were employed and remunerated by the Divisional Councils themselves. Moreover, recruitment of constituency agents is fully the prerogative of the local Associations. Consequently the Chairman's Office possessed a relationship with the rest of the party which was essentially one of limited guidance and co-operation. Its internal structure was reorganized in 1960, but party reformers failed to gain it any extra powers.

The structural framework of the party was therefore based upon the English model. It was, however, much more decentralized than the English pattern. Much more power within the party lay with the 'volunteers' of the local Association.

The yearning for local autonomy permeates every local Association, but is particularly strong in the rural areas removed from the centres of 'control' in Glasgow and Edinburgh. Local and regional sentiments have affected the activities of political parties in Scotland. Scottish Unionism, faced with the problem of operating the English party structure in different social conditions, probably went more than halfway in trying to accommodate the party to these social conditions.

The social setting

Within Scottish Conservatism one can discern different attitudes in the rural constituencies from those in urban areas. In the rural areas a more traditional atmosphere is retained. The social structure in the cities and 'commuting counties' is rather different. Here the party has emphasized organization, and the pattern of party behaviour is similar to that in England. The 'enemy' is also clearly recognizable. Furthermore, the urban constituencies are more compact and the local Associations more susceptible to unified direction and control.

In the more rural areas, however, the party gives the impression of being rather fragmented and somewhat more susceptible to internal squabbles than constituency Associations elsewhere in Britain. No doubt the opportunities for dissension within the Conservative ranks are strengthened by the fact that the Labour Party here has had no or very little formal organization.

Some stress must probably also be laid upon the nature of the terrain and the vagaries of the climate in the more rural areas. The largest constituencies in area in the United Kingdom are to be found in Scotland. Quite apart from the peculiar organizational problems of the islands, the bad roads and scattered population give party candidates and organizers a particularly trying time. In the Highlands, apart from Inverness-shire where the existence of a large town might blur the pattern, the winter months tend to enforce political idleness. All this means that greater emphasis is put upon the effectiveness of branch organizations:

> This constituency is quite large and scattered. Kinross and West Perthshire Unionist Association is, therefore, largely dependent upon its various Branches to maintain an effective organization throughout the whole constituency.[15]

For the rural Scot, the political choice, when Scottish Liberalism was largely dormant or defunct, lay between Toryism and the Labour Party, and he did not seem to be particularly enamoured of either. Unionist propaganda constantly emphasized that Labour principles ran counter to the Scottish tradition of 'independence'. The party image is therefore of great importance here, as elsewhere, in determining voting affiliation. But it is not so much that the Tory image is advantageous, but that the Labour image is even more disadvantageous (the Labour Party has succeeded in winning only one seat in rural Scotland). This point was well illustrated by the Liberal victories in the Highlands and Borders in 1964.

Much of the extreme radical element of the Highlands has by now disappeared. The landless have moved over the decades to the industrial areas. Among those who remain, the fear that the 'lairds' will refuse to invest money in their localities, if opposed politically, has at times been strong. As one small farmer put it: 'I daena like the Tories but we maun vote wi' the folk wi' the money else they'll send it a' out o' the country.'[16] Of course, the likelihood and importance of such behaviour by the lairds is negligible. Their greatest political weapon has been the widespread attitude of deference and the semi-feudal nature of the society. No matter what people's opinions may be, the social standing of the man in the 'big house' can remain as high as it ever was.[17] The geographical and social dominance of the 'castle' is transferred to politics. This influence, however, is usually implicitly felt rather than explicitly stated. Bochel, for example, describes how the Earl of Cawdor stood at his castle gates to see how many people in the village attended a Labour Party meeting: only two turned up.[18]

The strength of Conservatism in the countryside is explained also by the emergence of a new class of farmer, the owner-occupier, and by a renewed interest in the land. In this respect the cycle has come full circle. Towards the end of the eighteenth century Scottish land-lords were noted for their agricultural experiments. Within the next century the Highlands had become virtually one huge shooting-box. But after 1918 there was a return to the land. This was emphasized by the increased number of owner-occupiers who rose to prominence through the break-up of the old estates under their financial burdens. Moreover, much of the land was offered to the original tenants, who thus became landowners in their own right.[19] The emigration of many of the landless and the increase in the number of landowners created a fairly solid basis for Conservative recruitment of voters and supporters.

Local Associations: intra-party disputes

The social situation and the decentralized nature of the party organization conduced to leave much power within the party with the local Associations. Any attempts by the central party organs to interfere in constituency affairs have been hesitating and sporadic. When allegations of interference were made, the central organs hastened to deny the charges. The Scottish party seems to be troubled by more disputes than the English party. Throughout this century there have been numerous instances of Associations overruling their Executive Committees on important questions. Other examples reveal that, although the executive decision may have been vindicated, a substantial minority in the Association was prepared to take its dissatisfaction to the point of open rebellion. The central bodies of the party were usually helpless bystanders.

Broadly speaking, intra-Association disputes can be divided into three categories: those caused by differences over issues; those caused by micro-regional differences; and those caused by very local or personal differences. Usually disputes involve more than one of these factors. Two classic examples in the first category are the disputes in Greenock in 1910 over Free Trade,[20] and in Kinross and West Perthshire in 1938 over the 'Red Duchess'.[21]

Marked regional differences occur in many rural Associations, owing, in some cases, to the large size of the constituencies. The great emphasis in party literature and organization upon the need to improve branch effectiveness, giving the branches a sense of increased importance and independence, may help to generate this type of internal dissension. In Inverness-shire the position of Fort William provides a rival centre around which opposition to the town of Inverness can coalesce. This was the basic cleavage in the county Association in the early fifties over its Unionist Member, Lord Malcolm Douglas-Hamilton.[22] The strong sentiment of localism may give rise to feelings of jealousy and discontent in small areas or among particular families. In Inverness-shire, for example, dissentients to the Association's choice of candidate in 1922 were confined to one influential family.[23] Similar personal discontent was behind the efforts to dislodge Mackie in Galloway in 1945,[24] and also seems to be the cause of the recent controversies in Caithness and Sutherland, although here the dispute began over issues of Conservative Highland policy.[25]

The most serious dispute of recent years has been that in East Aberdeenshire. The trouble partly began with Patrick Wolrige-Gordon's involvement with Moral Rearmament, but it seems clear that many participants in the dispute used their opposition to his participation in this religious movement as a cover for more obscure personal objections. The dispute completely divided the Association into two camps. Attempts at compromise were 'nothing more than wasted Saturday afternoons'.[26] However, 'petty' local and family reasons were behind the warfare, with one of the principal battles occurring within the Wolrige-Gordon family itself. This type of bickering in a rural constituency can be regarded as a modern equivalent of the personal and family feuds characteristic of eighteenth-century Scottish politics. Both sides in the dispute sought to enlist the aid of the central party organs. When Mr Wolrige-Gordon claimed that Michael Noble, then Chairman of the Party, was intervening in the East Aberdeenshire dispute to help him retain his seat, Mr Noble declared that he had no intention or authority to interfere

41

with a constituency Association's right to select its own candidate.[27]

However, it seems that the Chairman's Office did not remain aloof from the proceedings. For example, Major Gordon, the local chairman, said of the executive meeting which rejected Mr Wolrige-Gordon:

> This meeting was prompted from several sources—disquiet among the branches . . . adverse reports from Westminster on our member, *and also from the Headquarters of the Unionist Party in Scotland*, and many other independent sources.[28]

This action by the central party organs only assisted in making the impasse much worse. They were unable to do anything but stand by and watch the local factions struggle on in their long war of attrition.

In part disputes arise because the 'gentry', with their long tradition of possessing a definite social status demanding deference from their locality, are entrenched firmly in local positions of power within the party. Many have been able to take the time to consolidate their own position in the Associations, without seeming eager or capable of improving party organization and efficiency. They have come in for much criticism from more 'progressive' party members, of which the following quotation is a good example:

> I submit that the fault is not with the chief officials, who do know their job, and who, despite their long service, or rather because of it, are of great value to the party, but that the people who need a shaking are those in charge of the local Associations—round pegs in square holes—whose prime desire seems to be to attend 'at homes' and conferences, to adorn platforms at big meetings, and whose greatest activity is criticism.[29]

Local Associations: candidates and agents

Another aspect of the localization of Scottish Unionist politics can be seen in the selection of parliamentary candidates. Theoretically the central bodies possess a supervisory function over selection. The choice of the local Association could be ratified only if the candidate had been placed upon the approved list of candidates, compiled by the Chairman's Office after consultations with the Divisional Convenors and Secretaries. But in the light of the constituency Associations' very real desire for non-interference it is difficult to see how their choices could be vetoed effectively by a central organization virtually powerless owing to local sentiments and the decentralized party structure.

Although the electorate may vote upon national issues and national party programmes, politics in Scotland retain a strong local flavour. It is considered useful if the candidate is a local man, or can at least claim some local connection. However, this 'unwritten law' is perhaps more honoured in the breach than in the observance. An M.P. is expected to pay greater attention to constituency affairs and grievances than is normally the case in England. If these are ignored, his chances of re-adoption may be seriously affected. But by paying assiduous attention to this aspect of Scottish rural politics, it is possible for a Member to create for himself, consciously or unconsciously, a position possessing something of the quality of the clan chief.

Unionist candidates selected for safe seats tend to be all of one mould. A definite type of social background is, if not necessary, definitely advantageous. Discontent is thus generated among people who possess the ambition to sit in Parliament, but not the desirable social and residential qualifications. A sense of frustration is especially marked among Unionists who are advocates or solicitors. Many of these, being Lowlanders and without pretensions to Highland connections, are virtually confined to winning a candidacy in one of the very few safe Unionist seats in the Lowlands. Banffshire Association, for example, refused to adopt Donald Anderson, the Solicitor-General, despite his being supported by the popular sitting member, Sir William Duthie. Instead they selected a local farmer.[30] At the 1957 Conference, D. M. H. Smith, twice unsuccessful in South Ayrshire (a safe miners' seat), vented his frustration in the following outburst (which was entirely unrelated to the motion under discussion):[31]

There is an invisible and impenetrable barrier which separates Non-U Unionist from U Unionist candidates . . . We woke up one morning and found there was a candidate [in North Ayrshire, a safe Unionist seat] where we did not know a vacancy existed. We have had quite a few people who fought seats that they had no hope of winning—many of you know who I mean—and they were well qualified to be in Parliament.

I think the author of the book *Eastern Approaches* [Sir Fitzroy Maclean, the selected candidate], should write another one called 'Northern Approaches' and explain how it was done.

It was revealed at this Conference that a committee had already been formed to consider this problem and the consequent grievances.

However, it was dominated by members of the Divisional Councils, rendering it impotent.

The nature of local Unionist politics, especially in the rural areas, has also been illustrated by the reluctance of Associations to employ professional agents. Until recently the fully qualified agent was almost unknown. Many Associations have for long employed 'agents', but usually the latter have not held any professional qualifications, often being local gentlemen operating in a part-time capacity on the basis of the little experience gained from their participation in local politics. Party headquarters have had no control and little influence in this matter. The situation has been improving slowly since the 1959 General Election and discussions on the subject of party agents at the 1960 Conference. The agent and his position is the only aspect of party organization and activity in which persistent efforts at re-organization have been made. But many local Associations are still reluctant to employ full-time agents; to them this is too radical a change.[32]

It is significant that the training of potential agents had to be financed by the Chairman's Office fund. In theory, salaries and conditions of service are now more or less on a par with those in England, and there is an increasing tendency to advertise for qualified agents when posts become vacant. However, the problem had another aspect. The scope of agents' ambitions was very limited in Scotland. In England agents can hope for advancement to area agents and eventually to the Central Office itself. This hierarchical ladder of promotion did not exist in Scotland. The divisional secretaries usually served a long apprenticeship within the divisional offices, and the Chairman's Office had no official link with local party agents.

The state of party organization

A common attitude nowadays among Scottish, as well as among English, Conservatives is the belief that they constitute the only opposition to Socialism. This has placed great strains upon their relationship with local National Liberal Associations.[33] The position has changed greatly from the inter-war period when Unionist leaders, such as Sir Robert Horne and Sir John Gilmour, never tired of stressing that local Associations should co-operate with the Liberals.[34] They feared that the Tories were not yet a mass party in Scotland, but the 1924 General Election proved that the party could break the radical grip on Scotland. Later elections, notably that of 1945, showed that it could hold its ground.

Scottish Conservatism as a strong political force, however, is reflected in the relatively undeveloped state of the local Associations as electoral organizations. Many Associations are of recent origin, and have not as yet settled the *modus vivendi* of their operations. The prevalence of Liberal–Unionist co-operation between the wars had not been due entirely to the eagerness of local Unionists to win new adherents: Unionist local organization was intermittent, or even non-existent, particularly in the more rural areas. A network of constituency Associations had come into being only after 1918. Before that they had been largely confined to the Lowland belt, especially around Glasgow, where the Central Office worked very closely with local Associations. The success of Unionist candidates in parliamentary elections often took local Unionists by surprise. Attempts to create effective constituency Associations occurred only after such individual electoral victories. Throughout the period of the expansion and consolidation of Unionist strength at the polls during the 'twenties and 'thirties, local Unionist organizations remained relatively weak and disorganized. The hierarchical structure was complete in name only.

Most of the rural constituencies still rely upon a network of social contacts. This social network is the basis of attempts to create or enlarge branch Associations. It is the laird, the solicitor, the doctor, and perhaps the minister and the schoolteacher—people possessing definite roles with a definite social status—who provide the nucleus of any such branch. In many instances this social network is used to achieve ends usually done elsewhere by more formal party methods.

Attempts to reorganize the Scottish Unionist Party have all been concerned with bringing the party into conformity with its English counterpart. However, they came up against resistance to change which was, as it were, built into the Scottish party organization. The division of the party into what amounted to two distinct organizations produced a somewhat rigid, ossifying structure. Many active party members felt that the two divisions had little common ground. In a very large measure this was a reflection of the localism and conservatism described above. The usual argument for the retention of the two divisions with the same form and same powers was that the problems of the two regions are quite different. Although the system of Divisional Councils cannot be blamed for the failures of 1959 and 1964 or for the relatively disorganized state of the party, it cannot have had a salutary effect on the party.

Furthermore, the Chairman's Office was in a peculiarly difficult position. Constitutionally deprived of any authority, it had still to attempt the task of co-ordinating party activities. In the last resort, its sole means of commanding the authority expected of it rested upon the personality of its occupant.

The main organizational differences between the English and

45

Scottish parties lay in the power of the Divisional Councils and the impotence of the Scottish Chairman's Office. If the Scottish structure was to conform to the English model, the structure and powers of these bodies had to be altered. Because Scottish Unionism emerged relatively unscathed from the 1945 General Election, the agitation for organizational reform in England after 1945 did not have its counterpart in Scotland.

The few suggestions for change got nowhere. 'Soul-searching' in Scotland appeared only after the failures of 1959, but until the 1964 General Election produced further setbacks, efforts designed at producing overall radical changes failed, either because of determined resistance or through sheer lack of interest.

Attempts at reform

Attempts to reform the Scottish Unionist Party focused not only on party organization, but also on the party's name as symbolic of the out-of-date character of the party machine, and on the refusal of the party to contest local government elections openly. Since the arguments employed against proposals for reform illustrate some deep-rooted attitudes characteristic of Scottish Unionism, it will be profitable to discuss these debates before moving on to comment on the successful reforms of 1965.

Before 1965 the only attempt to change the party's name to 'Conservative and Unionist' which came anywhere near to success arose at the 1956 Scottish Unionist Conference. After a heated debate the Conference decided by a narrow majority that the matter should be considered, although the platform was overwhelmingly in opposition. Sir Colin Thornton-Kemsley summed up the 'old guard' attitude when he claimed, 'The word "Conservative" conveys a sense of an excessive fondness for the past, a reluctance to change, and a disharmony with ideas of progress!'[35] Until 1965 the matter seems to have been quietly buried.

One recurring theme at recent annual conferences has been the vexed question of party nomenclature in local government elections. In England the Central Office now campaigns for the adoption of the Conservative party label in local elections, and its wishes have been largely obeyed. In Scotland, however, Unionists persistently took the line that the use of national party labels by anti-socialist groups in local elections is to be avoided. The 1950 Conference declared that it was the duty of all local Associations to work for the return of any 'progressive', non-Socialist candidate.

The nearest those wishing to reverse this policy have come to success was in 1957, when a committee was appointed to consider the question. It reported the following year, recommending that the official sponsoring of candidates in local elections should be left to the discretion of the individual Associations.[36] Few local Associations have made use of the recommendation, though where a separate local 'Progressive' party organization exists (usually only in the larger burghs) there is a clear but unofficial link between Unionist and Progressive organizations.[37] The general fear has been that the introduction of party politics in local elections would split the anti-Socialist vote, and that many moderates would refuse to vote for Unionist candidates. This fear is an expression of the widely held belief that the party does not yet possess a firm mass allegiance. It also expresses the fear of the loss of local freedom in the party and of an increase in centralized party control. It has been claimed that the party would then be ruled 'from Whitehall to town hall'.[38]

The relatively poor performance by the Unionists in the 1959 General Election meant that reorganization became a major topic of discussion within the party. At the 1960 Conference a committee appointed by the Divisional Councils presented a report on the situation.[39] Its recommendations were as follows: improvements in the status, remuneration and conditions of service of constituency agents; improvements in the salary and conditions of service of trainee agents; the introduction of political education for party workers and the general public; an increase in subscriptions; greater representation of Young Unionists at higher levels; reorganization of the Chairman's Office. It was also argued that the party should make sterner efforts to secure the best possible office bearers at all levels, since 'that was where the party failed'.

The motion from the floor for party reform came from the East Perthshire Association, led by its M.P., Ian McArthur. He repeated the proposals put forward in the report mentioned above, and also suggested that, since many party facilities were highly developed in the South, they should make more use of them. He then approached the crux of his argument:

> We believe it is desirable to place at the centre of our organization the responsibility for general direction or guidance, the formulation of policy and the control of party finance. . . . A single central body responsible for these matters would facilitate the creation and operation of a third administrative area in Scotland. At present there are two, but it might be that the formulation of the third, or even a fourth, would improve our efficiency.

Although there were only ten dissentients to the two resolutions, the recommendations for reform, excepting those dealing with party

47

agents and the Chairman's Office, were not taken up by the party. In particular, Mr McArthur's veiled attack on the role and powers of the Divisional Councils was resisted. The conference could only recommend; any decision lay with the Central Council, which in effect meant the two Divisional Councils. And it is here that opposition to change found a firm basis from which to operate. Arguments at the 1960 Conference against the East Perthshire resolution attempted to deprive the Conference of even the right to consider such questions of reorganization. It was argued by opponents of change that 'the divisional councils are the places where we can examine the question very carefully indeed, and if they are in any doubt about it, we can remit it to the constituencies', and that 'the present divisional councils were complementary to each other and the perfect link between them was the present chairman of the party'. It was further claimed that changes would mean the replacement of the existing flexibility by a party machine akin to that possessed by the Labour Party. These were attempts to give any decision on reform to people who were fundamentally hostile to reorganization with its accompanying central control (but who would have the final decision in any case).

The loss of still more Scottish constituencies in the 1964 General Election placed opponents of change in an extremely disadvantageous position. Reformers, headed by the Chairman, Sir John George, and most of the Scottish Unionist M.P.s, had prepared their plans for reorganization some time before the election.[40] Since the 1964 Election had proved their point, they immediately took up the offensive, although it was still feared that strong opposition would come from the Divisional Councils.[41] Sir John George announced his proposals in January 1965, and at special private meetings of the Divisional Councils and of delegates from all the local Associations, they were accepted in principle with very little dissent.[42] The proposals were accepted by the Annual Conference, meeting at Ayr in April, although it can perhaps be said that the Conference's hand had been forced, since the Chairman had already appointed individuals to the most important posts in the proposed structure.

This is not to say that opposition was not vocal. There were proposals from local branches that the reorganization should be postponed—presumably indefinitely—and that the plan was being 'forced upon the members' by the reformers who were 'acting undemocratically'.[43] Moreover, the Vice-Chairman of the party, Sir John Gilmour, took care to emphasize that 'the basic unit is still the constituency',[44] although it was obvious that the purpose of the reorganization was greater central control.

First, the reformers persuaded the party to drop its parochial attitude over nomenclature. The party is now known as the Scottish

Conservative and Unionist Association, a title which younger party members had long been urging. Now posters would no longer have to be changed from Conservative to Unionist at great expense. Second, an attempt was made to make the party compete as a Conservative Party in local elections. A Chairman's Office spokesman said before the Conference that strong opposition to this move still existed among the 'older school', who wished to divorce national politics from local issues. Reformers, however, did have the satisfaction of seeing the party agree that Conservative candidates should stand for local elective office in areas controlled by the Labour Party.[45]

The most important changes, however, were those creating a more-or-less total reorganization of the party structure. On the 'voluntary' side, the two Divisional Councils were disbanded. In their place the reorganization established five regional councils: City of Glasgow; Highland; North-Eastern; Central and Southern; South-Western. It was hoped that this structure would be less expensive to operate, more co-ordinated, and would offer more effective central direction, particularly as the Chairman's Office would be able to have stronger authority over the Regional Councils than it had over the Divisional Councils.

The most interesting reforms, however, concerned the 'professional' side of the organization. The design was to create a pyramid of paid workers with the Chairman's Office at the apex, in line with the English model. Each regional council was given an agent who is appointed by and answerable to the Chairman of the party. The old financial system was abolished and a single Scottish fund established, which would be controlled by the Chairman, while the National Treasurer, like the Chairman, is to be appointed by and responsible to the British party Leader. In addition the staff and research department of the Chairman's Office has been greatly expanded and an overall policy committee created. Moreover, a Conservative Political Centre Officer for Scotland has been established for the first time.[46] Thus it can be seen that the changes introduced by Sir John George had two purposes: first, to link the Scottish organization more closely with the English leadership, and second, to impose some form of central direction and control on the Scottish party. The only flaw in the scheme is that, unlike the situation in England, the Chairman's Office still does not possess any direct authority over constituency agents who are still principally accountable to their local Association.

Conclusion

During the nineteenth century, Conservatism was a minor political force in Scotland. The growth of Scottish Conservative strength began

49

only with the disintegration of the old Liberal alliance. The intrusion into politics of the Labour Party was only one factor affecting the control of Scotland by the Liberal Party. The decline in Liberal support was occasioned by the slowly changing nature of Scottish society, in particular by the gradual unification of the Scottish churches through the lessening of religious polemic and sharply differentiated dogmas. The 'de-Christianization' of the populace was one of the most crucial factors in the realignment of Scottish party allegiance; the political faith lost the moral and ethical values with which it had been invested. The final breach in the former homogeneity of Scottish society occurred with the arrival of the Labour Party. This breach had perhaps been long delayed by the intrusion of religious excitement and Irish Home Rule. As the Labour Party rapidly established itself as the leading party in the industrial areas, the middle classes swung to the Unionist Party, which they believed could offer the best opposition to the Labour Party. Since 1918 there has been a sharp division between the working classes of the industrial regions and the rest of Scotland.

Scottish politicians have never been so open as their English colleagues to the charge of Butskellism. A certain air of feudalism and high unemployment figures reinforce party division for them.[47]

From this description of the structure and problems of Scottish Conservatism and from a comparison with its English counterpart, it would appear that the Scottish party is in an earlier stage of development. 'Modernization' has been retarded by the traditionalism which shows itself continuously in the history of Scottish politics. This is especially true of Scottish nationalist groups, which tend to look back to a pre-1707 'golden age'. Since the present Conservative organization is of a fairly recent origin, it is not surprising that many problems still exist.

Given this situation, the important question has always been how and when the party will correspond more fully to the English pattern, which is the direction in which it is moving. The theme of 'dependent politics' is constant throughout Scottish history. A realization of this fact has always been manifest in London, which, however, finds it convenient at times to pay lip-service to the concept of Scottish independence. A reluctance to be too closely related to or assimilated by the English party is another reason why opposition to change has existed in Unionist circles. The alteration of the Scottish party's name to 'Conservative and Unionist' was continuously opposed by the Northern and North-Eastern constituency Associations partly because of this reason.[48]

Reformers saw the focal point of attack as being the need to reduce the autonomy of the local Associations to a more systematic control and conformity. Such reorganization necessitated changes in the balance of power between the Chairman's Office and the Divisional Councils. The battle to reform Scottish Toryism began, in essence, after the 1959 election. The first attempts were successfully blocked by the many established interests which feared that their influence and prestige would be diminished or would disappear under such centralization. The defence of the *status quo* has been tenacious, and it is debatable whether reform would have succeeded without the further stimulus of losing several Scottish constituencies usually regarded as 'safe' for the party. At any rate, the loss of three Highland seats and the near escapes in several others meant that a mood of self-criticism and 'soul-searching' was created, during which determined efforts to achieve some kind of reorganization stood an excellent chance of succeeding. The alternative would seem to have been a slow and unsatisfactory process of piecemeal change.

Compared with other party organizations in Scotland, however, the Conservative structure has always been impressive. Since it already helps greatly in such mechanical tasks as transporting people to the polls, one doubts whether the reorganization will give the party more effect with the electorate.

Indeed, it is doubtful whether reorganization will bring to an end the intra-Association disputes seemingly endemic in rural Scotland. The social character and needs of these areas are undergoing a change, which was, perhaps, illustrated by the success of the Liberals in rural Scotland in 1964. Scottish Conservatism now seems to be out of touch with these needs. It is a new identification of Conservatism with these needs, rather than structural reform, which will enable the party to recover the ground lost very largely through complacency. The day-to-day responsibility thus rests with the local Associations, which are perhaps still the determining factor in the party. Unless a majority of them accept the need for a revision of attitudes and internal policies and structure, it can legitimately be suggested that the structural reforms of 1965 will not have much serious effect on the relationship of the party with the electorate, and consequently that the problems which have faced Scottish Conservatism in the past will remain largely unsolved.

Notes

1 See D. W. Urwin, 'The Development of the Conservative Party Organization in Scotland until 1912', *Scottish Historical Review*, 1965, pp. 89–111.

2 See, for example, the statement by an official of the Scottish Chairman's Office in the *Glasgow Herald*, 5 April 1965, in which he emphasized that 'the two parties are completely separate'.
3 See the *Guardian*, 23 November 1962.
4 See, for example, R. T. McKenzie, *British Political Parties*, *op. cit.*, pp. 146–293.
5 Quoted in the *Glasgow Herald*, 17 May 1952.
6 *Scotsman*, 11 May 1956. The motion received unanimous approval.
7 *Glasgow Herald*, 11 May 1962.
8 *Scotsman*, 19 May 1949.
9 *Glasgow Herald*, 11 May 1962.
10 *Glasgow Herald*, 23 April 1965.
11 *The Year Book for Scotland*, pp. 21–2 (the Association's manual).
12 R. T. McKenzie, *op. cit.*, pp. 272–93.
13 *The Year Book for Scotland*, p. 18.
14 R. T. McKenzie, *op. cit.*, p. 293.
15 *The Unionist*, No. 1 (September 1962) (the journal of the constituency Association).
16 Quoted in *The Third Statistical Account of Scotland: The County of Aberdeen*, H. Hamilton, ed. (Glasgow, 1960), p. 109.
17 See J. Bochel, 'The Organisation of a County Constituency Labour Party Before and During a Parliamentary Election', unpublished B.A.(Econ.) dissertation, University of Manchester, 1956, pp. 18–19.
18. *Ibid.*
19 See, for example, *The Third Statistical Account of Scotland*, *op. cit.*, p. 110, and in the same series, *The County of Banff*, H. Hamilton, ed. (Glasgow, 1961), p. 193.
20 See J. Donald, *Past Parliamentary Elections in Greenock 1832–1931*, Greenock, 1933, p. 53.
21 See Duchess of Atholl, *Working Partnership*, London, 1958, pp. 221–8, *passim*. See also the *Scotsman*, 20 November 1938.
22 See reports in the *Scotsman*, 18 November 1952, 1 May 1953, 2 May 1953; *Glasgow Herald*, 25 April, 2 May 1953.
23 See the *Scotsman*, 6 March 1922.
24 See *ibid.*, 7 June 1945, 30 December 1958.
25 See *ibid.*, 23 November 1963, 16 August 1965; *Glasgow Herald*, 23 November 1963.
26 Although expressing distaste at the attention accorded them, both sides nevertheless seemed eager to have their views recorded by the press. See the *Scotsman*, 17 October 1958, 13 April 1962, 28 January, 14 May 1963.
27 See *ibid.*, 16 May 1962.
28 Quoted in *ibid.*, 14 April 1962. The author's italics.
29 *Glasgow Herald*, 25 September 1930, from a letter by a Unionist worker during a correspondence occasioned by a reader's criticism of the party leadership.
30 See the *Glasgow Herald*, 10 December 1962; *Scotsman*, 6 February 1963.
31 Quoted in the *Scotsman*, 13 April 1957.
32 See *The Year Book for Scotland, 1954–64* for the gradual increase in the

number of full-time agents. Part-time agents are often known as 'organizing secretaries'.

33 The best example was the dispute in Leith. See reports in the *Glasgow Herald*, 30 October 1951; *Scotsman*, 2 November 1953, 13 December 1954, 5, 9 May 1955.

34 This can be seen by looking at any campaign reports of the period. The Scottish Unionists, for example, did not wish to leave the Lloyd George Coalition. Bonar Law was practically a lone figure in Scotland on this issue.

35 Quoted in the *Scotsman*, 12 May 1956.

36 See *ibid.*, 12 April 1957, 9 May 1958.

37 See, for example, *The Third Statistical Account of Scotland: The City of Aberdeen*, H. Mackenzie, Edinburgh, 1953, pp. 529–30, for comments on the situation in Aberdeen. See also readers' comments on the situation in Glasgow in the *Glasgow Herald*, 30 October 1963; 1, 2, 4, 5, 6, 12 November 1963; 19–21 May 1964.

38 Quoted in the *Glasgow Herald*, 18 April 1953. See also *ibid.*, 21 May 1964.

39 The following account is taken from the *Scotsman*, 14 May 1960. In fact two committees were originally created—in the East and West. They later collaborated to construct a joint report.

40 *Scotsman*, 16 September 1965.

41 *Ibid.*, 7 December 1964.

42 *Glasgow Herald*, 6, 9 January, 6 March 1965.

43 *Ibid.*, 23 February, 6 March 1965.

44 *Ibid.*, 9 January 1965.

45 *Scotsman*, 15, 24 April 1965.

46 *Glasgow Herald*, 6 January, 27 March, 1 April 1965; *Scotsman*, 24 April, 16 September 1965. Throughout these months it was suggested by the Chairman's Office that the standard of electoral candidates could be improved by a policy of recruitment covering a much wider catchment area. More than most, this suggestion is unlikely to have any great effect.

47 *Scotsman*, 16 July 1960.

48 The opposition came originally from Orangemen in the West of Scotland.

The Simpson Committee and Labour Party reform 1966-9

It is unusual for major parties to embark on substantial efforts at internal party organization after having won a convincing General Election victory. Yet this is precisely what did occur in October 1966 at the Labour Party Annual Conference, when Richard Crossman announced that the National Executive Committee had decided to set up a Committee of Enquiry into the Party Constitution and Organization. The N.E.C. appointed five of its members to serve on the committee, under the chairmanship of William Simpson of the Foundry Workers Union. Its terms of reference were to examine the present organization in all its aspects and at all levels, and propose reforms necessary to equip the organization to meet the challenge of modern-day politics, review the party constitution and propose detailed reforms for bringing it into line with the contemporary needs of the party. There was considerable rank-and-file doubt as to the efficacy as well as the impartiality of this committee. Such doubt was not merely based on the fact that the committee was a sub-committee of the N.E.C., which many in the Labour movement believed was itself responsible for the defects in the existing party organization, or to the fact that three of the five members were trade unionists, who as a group have been less anxious to change the central party organization and unwilling to question the continuing preponderance of trade-union voting power inside the party as a whole. It was also the result of a decade or more of talk about the need for reform with little to show by way of change.

However, there was some measure of agreement as to the major defects in party organization. Agents were poorly paid, as were many of the Transport House staff responsible for important tasks such as research or publicity, and there was an air of amateurism about much of the National Headquarters organization in comparison with their rivals in Conservative Central Office. The need for reform was recognized as early as 1955, and a Committee on Party Organization chaired by Harold Wilson was set up after the General Election defeat of that year (see R. T. McKenzie, 1956, *op. cit.*). The terms of reference of the Committee instructed it to enquire into all aspects of party organization directly affecting the efficiency of electoral machinery at all levels, and though the committee did make some scathing comments on the state of party organization as a whole, its specific proposals were related to improving electoral machinery rather than the basic party structure. Thus Transport House was not, and had not since, been subject to the sort of overhaul of Conservative Central Office undertaken by Lord Woolton between 1946 and 1950, or the changes that took place in the mid-1960s instigated by Edward Du Cann. After the 1959 election defeat the Labour Party became immersed in doctrinal policy disputes, but after the 1964 election victory there was increasing pressure from within Transport House itself for reforms. Salary rises were turned down in an effort to emphasize the necessity for major reorganization. A pressure group known as the Plan for an Efficient Party, led by Jim Northcott, pressed for changes, and the announcement by Richard Crossman marked the belated response of the N.E.C. to this pressure.

The Committee decided initially to make definite proposals within a year on priority matters of party finance, the party secretaryship, a national agency service, political education, and regional organization in Greater London. Special working parties, which included co-opted members, were set up to study the last three matters. The Committee presented an Interim Report to the N.E.C. in September 1967, which was later published and presented for debate at the Annual Conference a month later, the N.E.C. promising to give detailed consideration to it in the light of the debate.

Labour Party—Interim Report of the Committee of Enquiry into Party Organization, 1967

Summary of main recommendations

Party Finance

1. That the National Executive Committee approach affiliated unions to increase the per capita affiliation fee to the maximum possible sum, and to increase the actual number of members affiliated to the Party (para. 14).
2. That steps be taken to bring unions not affiliated into affiliation (para. 14).
3. That the Annual Conference be recommended to restore to members of affiliated unions the right to enrol as members of ward committees and be delegates to the Annual Conference and to local party General Committees without the necessity of being individual members of the Party (para. 14).
4. That the Party should be asked to decide on an individual membership contribution based upon a minimum flat rate contribution; or a contribution graduated according to the personal income of the member, and that the National Executive be urged to support a graduated scheme (para. 17).

55

5. That the scales of contributions should be:

Annual Income	Annual Contribution		
	£	s.	d.
Below £1,000		12	0
Above £1,000 but below £2,000	1	0	0
Above £2,000 but below £3,000	2	10	0
Above £3,000 but below £4,000	5	0	0
Above £4,000	10	0	0

(para. 18).

6. That Members of Parliament should not be asked to pay a separate or additional contribution, but that the P.L.P. be approached for a voluntary contribution by their members towards the cost of servicing the P.L.P. (para. 19).
7. That constituency parties be encouraged to supplement any national scheme of contributions by local voluntary schemes (para. 20).
8. That before launching a nation wide scheme of graduated contributions pilot schemes be introduced in a few constituencies and that special full time staff be employed to get the scheme established (para. 21).
9. That constituency parties be urged to make a determined effort to persuade as many of their members as possible to pay their contributions annually, and by banker's order, or by the G.P.O. Giro system when introduced (para. 23).
10. That no further consideration be given to the possibility of an Associate Membership (para. 25).
11. That the National Executive Committee ask the Annual Conference to include payment of all levies on constituency parties for some national effort or scheme as a condition of representation at the Annual Conference (para. 26).

Government and Party

12. That there is need for improved communications between the Government and the National Executive and that the top link should be between the Prime Minister and the Secretary. That the Secretary should play a more prominent political role and to assist him a Deputy Secretary be appointed to deal with political aspects of Party policy (para. 35).
13. That the National Executive be recommended to reconstruct its sub-committee system and to establish not more than three sub-committees to cover its main functions, i.e. policy formulation, organization, administration, publicity (paras 36, 37, and 38).

14. That the main business of National Executive Committee meetings should be the presentation of a report by the General Secretary (para. 39).

Constitution, Rules and Standing Orders

15. That the procedure for dealing with amendments to the Party Constitution, Rules and Standing Orders be revised so that amendments proposed one year should be referred to the National Executive Committee and should be the subject of a report presented to the following year's Conference (para. 43).

A National Agency Service

16. That the principle of the employment by the National Executive Committee of agents for service in selected constituencies be adopted (para. 46).

17. That the money needed to finance this form of employment be supplied from a national fund established by the National Executive Committee and to which each of the constituency parties receiving the service shall contribute an agreed amount (para. 47).

18. That the National Executive Committee shall transfer for the next three years £50,000 a year to the fund from the General Election Fund (para. 47).

19. That there shall be no contracting out by any constituency party selected by the National Executive Committee to participate in the scheme (para. 47).

20. That in the case of a constituency whose Parliamentary candidate is sponsored by an affiliated organization the contribution shall be not less than the amount the sponsoring organisation is permitted to pay under the Hastings Agreement (para. 47).

21. That a special appeal be made to the whole movement for contributions to the fund to start it off (para. 47). (An alternative proposal is referred to in the same paragraph.)

22. That the National Executive Committee shall select the constituencies to have the services of the nationally employed agents and that the selection shall be decided by the degree of marginality of the constituencies (para. 50).

23. That the regional organising staff be redeployed so as to integrate as far as possible their activities with those of the nationally employed agents, it being understood that any alteration of the regional structure towards district or more local organisation for example would affect the whole question of the agency service (para. 51).

Political Education

24. That a Political Education Section be established at Head Office which would co-ordinate and develop all political education activity in accordance with a plan designed to meet the various educational needs of the membership (para. 60).

25. That a Political Education Officer be appointed as the head of the Section, who shall be directly responsible to the General Secretary (paras 60 and 62).

26. That high priority shall be given to the training of those who are to be teachers, discussion leaders and organisers of educational courses in modern teaching methods, with special emphasis on student participation and the use of visual aids (paras 58 and 64).

27. That political education sub-committees be established at all levels of party organisation to direct and develop educational activities concerned with the training of members to undertake administrative, organisational and election duties, and with arranging political studies and discussions at party meetings and organising conferences, schools and discussion groups of various kinds (paras 63 and 64).

28. That Head Office shall undertake the provision of the necessary material for those participating in the scheme, including visual aids, manuals and guides, and information on political, economic and social matters (para. 65).

Co-ordinating Machinery for Greater London

29. That there shall be an effective Regional Council for the whole of Greater London (paras 74 and 75).

30. That the National Executive Committee shall appoint a General Secretary to the Regional Council with overall authority within the region, at a salary commensurate with the heavy responsibilities of the office; an Assistant Secretary, having special responsibility for publicity; four area organisers, each to be responsible for a clearly defined area and to work under the immediate direction of the Regional Council Secretary (para. 76).

31. That the clerical staff needed to service these officers be employees of the National Executive Committee (para. 76).

(For the basis of representation at the Regional Council Annual Conference, the number of officers and members of the Regional Executive Committee and the method of their election, as well as the Council's financial arrangements, see appendix.)

32. That a standing Local Government Advisory Committee,

responsible to, and acting under, the direction of the Regional Executive Committee, be established to help to co-ordinate the work of the whole of the Council Labour Groups in Greater London and to deal with matters relating to the Inner London Education Authority (para. 80).

The Interim Report and its recommendations provoked considerable discussion at the Annual Conference and among party activists in the constituencies. At the Conference, the General Secretary of the Labour Agents Union and several agents testified to the need for improvements in the pay and working conditions of agents, and hoped for changes if a National Agency Service was created. Robert Maxwell accused the N.E.C. of being responsible for the inefficient, underfinanced and badly organized state of the party, attacked the Committees' scheme to improve party finance, and suggested alternative schemes. Others, including Frank Cousins, attacked the recommendations that M.P.s might make contributions towards the cost of servicing the Parliamentary Labour Party, and that union members be allowed to enrol as ward committee members, Annual Conference delegates and constituency general committee members without being individual members of the party. A very controversial recommendation was the strengthening of the political role of the General Secretary, especially his link with the party Leader in order to strengthen the position of the N.E.C. as the custodian of Conference decisions and representative of the party in the country. There was also controversy and opposition to recommendations for a new Greater London Regional Council of the Labour Party.

In November 1967 the N.E.C. considered the latter recommendations, and accepted them in principle. After consultations between N.E.C. representatives and the Executive Committees of the London Labour Party and the Southern and Eastern Regional Councils regarding the recommendations, a Consultative Conference attended by delegates representing 123 party and affiliated organizations was held at Congress House in January 1968. In February 1968 the N.E.C. considered the proposals put forward at the consultations, and a number of them were embodied in the provisional rules for the new Regional Council.

On 31 March 1968 a conference was held in Camden Town Hall to establish a Greater London Regional Council of the Labour Party attended by delegates representing party and affiliated organizations, and presided over by a member of the N.E.C. The National Agent presented the final proposals of the N.E.C., and a resolution to establish a Greater London Regional Council of the Labour Party based on the provisional rules (see Appendix 1, pp. 320–6, *Report of the 67th Annual Conference of the Labour Party, Blackpool 1968*) was carried by 799 to 240 votes. The conference elected a provisional committee chaired by Robert Mellish, M.P., and the N.E.C. appointed an Assistant National Agent as its Acting General Secretary pending the appointment of a General Secretary.

In January 1968 the N.E.C. considered the recommendations concerned with the setting up of a National Agency Service. The proposal was accepted in principle, and it was agreed that a partial scheme should be introduced as soon as possible, £50,000 was to be set aside from the General Election Fund for the next three years to launch the Service, and the General Secretary would issue an appeal throughout the Labour movement to subscribe to the National Agency Service Fund. Agents entering this service would be employed by the National Executive Committee. Negotiations were begun with constituencies interested in the scheme, but existing financial resources were unlikely to allow more than thirty-five agents to be recruited initially.

The National Executive also agreed to accept sections of the Report concerned with amendments to the party constitution, rules and standing orders, whereby resolutions to amend these would be invited annually by the N.E.C., which would submit a report to the next Annual Conference making recommendations about accepting or rejecting amendments and giving reasons for their recommendations. Debate could take place on the report and votes taken by the Conference. Amendments to the party constitution and standing orders to provide for these procedures were accepted at the 1968 Annual Conference.

The National Executive also considered the recommendations on party finance and decided to make a specific proposal for higher affiliation fees to the 1969 Annual Conference. It was also agreed to discuss with the P.L.P. the proposal that their members should make voluntary contributions towards the cost of servicing the P.L.P., and the P.L.P. later did make such a contribution. The 1968 Annual Conference also accepted an amendment to the party constitution making payment of all levies on affiliated organizations a condition of representation at Annual Conferences. The N.E.C. decided not to support the proposal for a graduated scheme of individual membership contributions, and also decided not to ask for acceptance of the recommendation that members of affiliated unions be given the right to enrol as members of ward committees and be delegates to Conference or general committees without the necessity of being individual members of the party.

The N.E.C. also agreed to accept the recommendations relating to the role of the General Secretary, the appointment of a Deputy

Secretary, the establishment of a Political Education Section, and the recommendation to reconstruct the National Executive sub-committee system.

In July 1968 the Committee presented its second and final report to the N.E.C., who decided that it be published and presented to the Annual Conference for debate, and then be considered in detail by the N.E.C. and any major departures from present practice or action would be brought before the 1969 Annual Conference. Among the recommendations was a major reorganization of the women's section of the party, advocating the setting up of councils in each constituency to co-ordinate drives to attract younger women, run campaigns on local problems and important policy issues, and train younger women in leadership, public speaking and to run as candidates in local elections. The size of the women's annual conference should also be doubled. They also recommended the abolition of the special five-member women's section of the National Executive Committee, redistributing these seats, three to the trade unions and two to the constituency parties. Another major recommendation sought to give the Young Socialists more autonomy, while other recommendations involved regional boundary changes and the re-designing of N.E.C. sub-committees into three separate bodies dealing with policy, organization and propaganda, and publicity and political education respectively. It was also recommended that assistant regional secretaries attend special weekend training courses in publicity (for the full text of the report, see *Report of the 67th Annual Conference of the Labour Party, Blackpool 1968*, pp. 362–80; Summary of Recommendations, pp. 379–80).

These recommendations were debated at the 1968 Annual Conference at Blackpool. A further technical recommendation set out a plan for the party to set up a property company to take care of constituency party properties. In 1969, Labour Party Properties, Ltd., was created, and was designed to develop commercially the land and buildings owned by local parties in order to produce additional capital and income, as well as providing premises for their political activities.

At the 1969 Annual Conference in Brighton appropriate amendments to the party constitution and rules were recommended by the N.E.C., following their acceptance of most of the recommendations in the second report of the Simpson Committee. The N.E.C. did not, however, accept the recommendation on changing the composition of the N.E.C., but agreed to give further consideration to the matter after the Conference and report to the 1970 Conference. The N.E.C. accepted a recommendation entitling a constituency party to appoint an additional woman and/or Young Socialist delegate to the Annual

Conference, and proposals relating to women's organizations, the Young Socialists, and regional boundary changes. In February 1969 eight assistant regional organizers attended a two-week course in public relations at Transport House, and weekend refresher courses were later held at Derby.

Amendments to the party constitution and rules were proposed and accepted at the private session of the 1969 Conference to allow most of the above recommendations to be implemented. This concluded the formal action on the recommendations of the Simpson Committee.

In considering the work of the Simpson Committee, in the light of Labour's defeat at the 1970 General Election, it seems fair to assert that the Committee tried hard to live up to its wide terms of reference, though it may also be argued that it was set a near-impossible task. It is clear that the effects of many of its accepted recommendations have yet to be seen, but it is also clear that it should have gone even further in its recommendations regarding the creation and funding of the National Agency Service, the improvement of Transport House's fund-raising activities, the educational activities of the party, and the strengthening of the Young Socialist movement and women's wing of the party. Despite the improvements in agents' salaries, the new scheme was unable to increase substantially the number of full-time agents, which had fallen since the 1966 Election, while lack of money and effective constituency organization continued to hamper election campaign activities and was an important factor in Labour's defeat in 1970. Many of these points were made in a report by the national agent, Ron Hayward, to the N.E.C. outlining and analysing the possible causes of the 1970 Election defeat, and were reiterated at the 1970 Annual Conference.[1]

Action to implement many of the recommendations of the Simpson Committee may have come too late to have had any real effect on the fortunes of the Labour Party in 1970. However, it seems clear that much remains to be done to bring the party machine to the standard required by the terms of reference of the Committee. The recommendations of the Committee, controversial as they were, may have done little more than oil the wheels of the penny-farthing rather than constructing a new jet machine.

Notes

1 For other criticism, see R. L. Leonard, 'That Old Penny Farthing Again', *Socialist Commentary*, November 1968.

3 Parties and party finance

Introduction

A major responsibility of party organizations at all levels is to obtain the necessary financial resources to perform their own functions in a manner which will provide maximum aid to the electoral fortunes of party candidates. The larger the party organization the more important is the matter of raising funds. Broadly speaking there are two main ways in which political parties raise money nationally. The first is to obtain large sums from a small number of wealthy supporters and/or collect small sums of money from many people, while the second is to develop large- and small-scale fund-raising schemes through either national or local party organizations. Party funds are both collected and spent at three levels, nationally, regionally and in the constituencies.

Finance is important for all aspects of party activity in Britain, but analysis and evaluation of its influence on party competition is not easy. It is difficult to obtain accurate and comprehensive information on how much money individual parties receive and how such money is spent, and any statements about total sums raised and spent can only be estimates.[1] No political party is obliged legally to publish its accounts, but the Companies Act of 1967 does require the disclosure of company contributions to political funds and activities. All party candidates are required by law to submit a return of election campaign expenses to the local returning officer, since candidates are subject to a legal maximum expenditure which depends in part on the size of the electorate in individual constituencies, and this information is available for public inspection for twelve months, but it is very difficult to gain any accurate estimate of the annual expenditures of individual constituency party organizations.[2]

The costs of political party activity at elections in Britain is small by American standards, and is affected by a variety of legal and other factors. At the constituency level all candidates are required by law to put up a deposit of £150 which is lost if they fail to get one-eighth of the total votes polled. Minor parties are most affected by this, since they often have the most difficulty in raising the deposit and are most likely to lose it. Each candidate does, however, get one free delivery of election material, and no party or candidate can buy television time for campaign purposes. Broadcasting time for party political broadcasts is allotted in terms of the proportion of party membership in the House of Commons, and in 1969 the Liberal Party took advantage of this to make a direct appeal for funds. While the two major parties possess obvious advantages in terms of their ability to obtain finance, they also complain about the lack of adequate funds to compete effectively, and also accuse each other of not revealing accurate information as to just how much money they obtain, spend or have in reserve. The trade unions have always been the financial mainstay of the Labour Party nationally, and individual unions also sponsor financially candidates in particular constituencies, while business and financial organizations provide the backbone of the national finances of the Conservative Party.

When a General Election is in the offing, special fund-raising appeals are often made by parties. In 1967, the Conservative Party also launched a public appeal for £2m., and, for the first time in 1968, Conservative Central Office published details of its income and expenditure for the calendar year ending 31 December 1967. The information provided indicated an estimated deficit for the year of £443,000 and a consequent decline in reserves to £796,000 (it was alleged that the Labour Party had over £2¼m. available to it in reserves held either by itself, or in the political fund of the unions). Early in 1969 the then Chairman of the Conservative Party organization, Anthony Barber, announced to constituency party chairmen the implementation of certain economies including the dismissal of several full-time party officials, mainly at the regional level. The income and expenditure account of the Central Funds of the party for the year ending 31 March showed a marked improvement, with a substantial increase in contributions from constituency Associations, and an excess of income over expenditure which allowed reserves to increase to a figure of just under £2m.

At about this time the General Secretary of the Labour Party was also concerned at the parlous state of party finances, and launched a national appeal for £1m., aiming for the first time at professional middle-class people, and asking them to contribute £5 annually, but the response was disappointing. Yet at this very time both parties were planning extensive advertising campaigns costing at least £200,000 as preliminaries to the coming General Election.

Explanation of these apparent paradoxes testifies to the real problem of getting an accurate method of comparing the financial positions of the major parties at any time. Neither party lacks substantial resources, but deliberate distinctions are made between four types of funds: (1) current running costs of the national party organization, (2) reserve funds, (3) election-campaign costs, (4) local constituency funds. Only under the first category, and in a few local constituencies, do the major parties appear to be in anything like the type of financial difficulties which are a daily reality for the Liberal Party.

It is the scope and size of money collected and spent on political activities that distinguishes the two major parties from other parties in Britain. In particular it is the ability to operate large-scale national party headquarters financed principally by large contributions from 'vested interests' (business and the trade unions) that give the major parties a significant organizational advantage. The sad experiences of the Liberal Party in trying to return to 'big-league' status in the mid-1960s with headquarters in Smith Square, financed on the strength of donations from individual sympathizers and quota payments from constituencies, is adequate testimony to the utility of 'institutional' sources of funds. As Martin Harrison suggests, 'Labour's penury is undreamt riches to the Liberals',[3] and one might add to this that the problems of fund-raising for other parties seem even greater. Thus it is not surprising that in 1969–70 the National Front should avidly pursue the possibility of inheriting a fortune reported to exceed £1m.!

Yet it is easy to forget that while the two major parties possess major advantages in terms of financial resources for national party headquarters and national election campaigns, their quasi-autonomous organizations may be weaker. For parties like the S.N.P., campaigning on a narrow front in a particular area and heavily emphasizing constituency efforts to recruit card-carrying members in order to bolster finance and membership figures, it is more realistic to compare them organizationally and financially with the Scottish Conservative and Unionist Association or the Scottish Liberal Party, if such information is available. Total S.N.P. income was estimated at about £200,000 in 1967–8, and S.N.P. headquarters' accounts for 1967 showed an £8,000 surplus. In this respect the financial assets of a party gaining members and electoral support may mean that in the short-term they can maintain a viable national organization, but the experiences of the Liberal Party in the late 1960s illustrate the danger of over-expanding a national organization in the hope that it will generate additional support which will incidentally produce the necessary funds to maintain such expansion.

The location of party finance is also extremely important, and can affect the work of a party. There is often tension between the central and constituency organizations, and if the latter control the purse-strings they can also control party decision-making. Fund-raising schemes are initiated by national party organizations to help finance the work of the national headquarters and to fight national elections at all levels, while some funds collected at the local level are used to finance national party activities (some form of quota system of payments by constituencies to the national party organization generally exists in those parties with a national headquarters).

Though the Conservative and Labour Parties rely heavily on funds provided by companies and trade unions respectively, and such financial help is considerable, the funds are not simply handed over to the parties as a stable annual source of income, nor is such money guaranteed in advance to be available at the most opportune time. The arrangements by which the unions pay the Labour Party are more automatic, and they involve decisions made by individual unions to give money from their political funds to the party at all levels, including the sponsoring of candidates in particular constituencies, in return gaining considerable influence over many aspects of Labour Party activity. Co-operative societies also provide a small but stable source of income for Labour politics. This finance is only a part of the total political funds of the unions, and at times certain unions have threatened to withhold general fund or funds to sponsor candidates. Trade unions are also required to make a statutory return of certain types of political expenditure. Extra money is usually given to Transport House election funds when a General Election seems imminent (in 1970 the unions promised the Labour Party £350,000 to fight the Election), but it is often intended as much to tide the party over nationally, following the Election. The relative frugality of attitude shown by the unions tends also to permeate Transport House attitudes towards the spending of funds, a matter which has been a source of contention within the party, especially since Transport House has generally not been active in raising large sums of money on its own behalf.

Equally, the amount received by Conservative Central Office from companies is only a part of the money spent by them on 'political' activities, and is not a fixed amount, though it is usually a larger amount annually than that received by Transport House from the unions in affiliation fees (in 1968 it was estimated at over £400,000, as opposed to some £270,000 to Transport House, and constituency and other contributions are also usually considerably higher annually). Evidence provided by the legal requirements of the 1967 Companies Act suggest that these direct payments came largely from the City and from a number of large companies. There is also some apparent connection between company generosity and company employment of senior Conservative M.P.s and prominent party officials. In both parties industrial donations greatly outweigh the money contributed by constituencies, some of whom may be an actual liability on national party funds. In 1967, the Conservative Party income was estimated at £642,000 of which less than a third came from constituency organizations. Expenditure was over £1m., of which £437,000 went on Central Office administration, publicity and education activities, and close to £400,000 was spent on assistance to area and constituency organizations.

National party organizations are therefore concerned with ensuring that constituency party organizations maintain effective fundraising schemes. Conservative Central Office puts out a special pamphlet on this (*Constituency Finance, Fundraising Supplement No. 1*, Conservative Central Office, 1968), spelling out in detail a variety of schemes for raising money to supplement the basis of constituency income; a strong subscribing branch membership backed by direct subscriptions and contributions. This, along with a general pamphlet on constituency finance (see the selections which follow), indicates the thoroughness with which the Conservative national organization seeks to generate and maintain constituency fund-raising as an integral part of total party effectiveness and electoral success, especially as the Maxwell-Fyfe reforms meant constituencies could no longer expect their candidates to make substantial financial contributions to election expenditures.

National party organizations are also responsible for spending a major part of party funds, and the judicial use of such funds both at and between elections is of crucial importance, as is indicated by a series of party reforms intended to provide more efficient ways of collecting and spending money (see for example the discussion of the Simpson Committee recommendations in Chapter 2). The position of party treasurer is of importance in that he has formal responsibilities for these matters, and the position is usually held formally by a senior member of the party, probably in Parliament. The financing of the activities of the national party headquarters is a major expense at all times, and the Conservative Party in particular seeks to maintain a well-organized and well-remunerated staff at Central Office, providing a range of services for all parts of the party. Of particular importance are the services provided to the parliamentary party (Conservative Central Office spent £37,000 on this in 1968). This was shown in 1969 when Labour M.P.s voted a £10 yearly levy on themselves to help finance the running costs of the P.L.P., estimated at £20,000 annually, all of which had been previously paid out of national party funds.

Though it is extremely difficult to obtain and present valid comparative evidence about the collection and use of money by British political parties, some broad general points can be made. The Conservative Party as a whole raises, retains and spends more money

67

annually than any other party, and lays particular emphasis on the importance of finance to provide effective organizational and other supports to constituencies and candidates at elections. The Conservative Party has also been more successful than the Labour Party in making constituencies assume financial responsibilities. For very different reasons both the Labour and Liberal parties find it more difficult to maintain a stable overall financial base, the former because of its heavy reliance on the unions and the reluctance or inability of rank-and-file supporters to give financially, and the latter because of an inability to maintain a permanent broad-based source of finance. Though finance in itself is not sufficient to win elections for political parties, the lack of adequate finance may have an adverse effect on election performances. Equally, while it may not be necessary in 'safe' seats to have a constituency Association with ample funds at its disposal (as many Labour constituency parties demonstrate), the ability of a constituency Association to maintain a viable permanent organization, with a full-time paid agent, able to finance effective election campaigns and also able to make substantial quota payments to the party nationally, can help substantially in the achievement and maintenance of electoral success.[4] Emphasis on, and concern for, this aspect of party activity, as indicated in the documentary material which follows, can at times help to maximize swings of popular support for a party such as occurred in the 1970 General Election.

Notes

1 For a range of estimated financial returns and expenditures of different sections of the Conservative, Labour and Liberal parties, see R. Rose, *Influencing Voters*, Appendix, pp. 248–77.
2 For an attempt to provide estimated figures of the income and expenditure of a range of Conservative and Labour constituency organizations, see M. Harrison, 'Comparative Political Finance—Britain', *Journal of Politics*, 1963, pp. 665–78.
3 *Ibid.*, p. 678.
4 See 'The Orpington Story', *New Outlook*, March 1963, pp. 3–18, 27–42.

Further reading

Documentary sources are scattered. Information on the annual accounts of the Labour Party are contained in the annual reports of the N.E.C. to the Annual Conference printed in the *Labour Party Annual Conference Reports*, and of the Liberal Party in the *Annual Report and Accounts* published by the Liberal Party Organization and presented to their Annual Assembly. For information on the political funds of registered trade unions, see the

Report of the Chief Registrar of Friendly Societies, Part 4: Trade Unions (London, H.M. Stationery Office, annually). For evidence on the size and range of expenditure on political activities by corporations and companies, see *Economic Brief*, February 1970 (Labour Party, 1970). Information on the political finances of the Co-operative Party is contained in the *Annual Report of the Co-operative Party* (London, Co-operative Union Ltd).

For historical information on the role of finance in party politics in the nineteenth century, see W. B. Gwyn, *Democracy and the Cost of Politics in Britain*, London, 1962, and H. J. Hanham, *Elections and Party Management*, London, 1959, Chapter 17. For general surveys of party finance in the Conservative, Labour and Liberal parties in the 1960s, see M. Harrison, 'Comparative Political Finance—Britain', *Journal of Politics*, 1963, pp. 664–85, and R. Rose, *Influencing Voters*, London, 1967, Appendix, pp. 248–77. For general details of trades-union political finance, see M. Harrison, *Trade Unions and the Labour Party Since 1945*, London, 1960, Chapters 1 and 2. Some discussion of local constituency party financing is contained in A. H. Birch, *Small-Town Politics*, London, 1959, especially pp. 45–53, and there is a brief discussion of party finance in the Conservative and Labour parties in R. T. McKenzie, *British Political Parties*, Appendix B.

Attempts by Conservative Central Office to provide financial guidance to constituency organizations include *Constituency Finance*, London, 1969, and a fund-raising supplement, and the Liberal Party has a section on finance in *Effective Organising*, London, 1963. For discussion of party expenditure in pre-election advertising, see the contribution by R. Rose in D. E. Butler and A. King, *The British General Election of 1964*, London, 1965, Appendix IV, pp. 369–80. For a useful comparison with party expenditure on elections in the U.S.A., see H. E. Alexander and H. B. Meyers, 'A Financial Landslide for the G.O.P.', *Fortune*, March 1970, pp. 104–6. The initial efforts of a group called the Labour Party National Fund Raising Foundation, headed by Robert Maxwell, to stimulate concern within the Labour Party for fund-raising at constituency and national level is shown in the study *Ideas from Scandinavia*, by Clive Bradley (London, 1967).

Articles

F. C. Newman, 'Money and Elections in Britain—a Guide for America', *Western Political Quarterly*, 1957, pp. 582–603.
'Reflections on Money and Party Politics in Britain', *Parliamentary Affairs*, 1957, pp. 308–32.
R. Rose, 'Money and Election Law', *Political Studies*, 1961, pp. 1–15.
'Lotteries are Aiding Funds of Local Labour Parties', *The Times*, 13 October 1964.

National party funds
The central funds of the Conservative Party

Section reprinted from *Constituency Finance*, a booklet put out in 1969 in the Conservative Central Office Organization Series, pp. 7–8.

The Central Funds of the Party

The Party Treasurers rely on two main sources:
The Constituency Quota system
The Central Board of Finance

The quota system

The quota system is an arrangement, originally approved at the Brighton Conference of 1947, under which constituencies in England and Wales contribute voluntarily to the Central Funds of the Party. The purpose is to help provide the income which the Party needs at the centre if all the essential tasks are to be carried out. A committee on the Party Organisation under Sir David Maxwell-Fyfe estimated in 1948 that £200,000 was required. To meet this situation they had to devise a system which would be voluntary, related to a principle that could be readily understood, and be capable of adjustment according to the local circumstances. These conditions, met by the Maxwell-Fyfe formula, still apply. The basis on which contributions are assessed is the Conservative vote at the last general election, ignoring by-elections. A flat rate equally applicable to all constituencies would tend, however, to favour the successful against the unsuccessful constituencies. The Maxwell-Fyfe formula is therefore the fairest means of relating contributions to the capacity to pay. Thus where the Conservative was successful at the last general election, the basic figure per vote is varied according to the ratio of the Conservative vote to that of the runner-up, i.e.:

	Ratio	Amount payable per Conservative vote
Below	7 to 6	9 d.
Exceeds	7 to 6	10½d.
..	8 to 6	12 d.
..	9 to 6	13½d.
..	10 to 6	15 d.
..	11 to 6	16½d.
..	12 to 6 and over	18 d.

Where the Conservative was defeated the scale would be based on the ratio of the Conservative vote to that of the winner:

Ratio		Amount payable per Conservative vote
Exceeds	5 to 6	7½d.
..	4 to 6	6 d.
..	3 to 6	4½d.
..	2 to 6	5 d.
Is below	2	1½d.

This formula, under which the most securely-held Conservative seats make the greatest contribution to the Central Funds, is an application to the Party Organisation of the Conservative principle that the strong should help the weak.

Each year the treasurers of the Party decide, in consultation with the area treasurers, what the national target shall be. This means that a figure of so much per vote is decided on as a basic figure. Provisional area quotas are then worked out on this basic rate for acceptance by area treasurers.

Area treasurers then agree individual quotas with each association. Where necessary, they have discretion to vary the Maxwell-Fyfe formula to take account of exceptional circumstances.

The quota is the contribution made by the constituency to central funds. The Maxwell-Fyfe plan ensures that it is given voluntarily and on a basis which takes account of local circumstances.

The Conservative Party Board of Finance

The Central Board of Finance consists of the Party treasurers and the area treasurers. It has the task of raising funds for the Party from sources not usually tapped by the constituency association. The Board employs representatives to make personal approaches to donors. New approaches are initiated after consultation and in agreement with constituency associations and representatives are constantly in touch with constituency officials who can give them invaluable assistance.

The first £50 of any donation received by the Central Board of Finance is credited towards the quota contribution of the donor's constituency. The Board of Finance is not a competing agency, and particular care is taken to keep local interests to the forefront and not to divert local money from the constituency to the centre. Experience, however, has shown that some donors will give substantially more to central funds than to local funds and that the quota credit given to a local association may exceed what a donor would be willing to give locally. Constituency associations can assist representatives by suggesting suitable approaches and, where appropriate, giving them letters of introduction.

The constituency is represented on the Board by the area treasurer and the work of the Board is often of great help to constituencies in achieving their quotas.

Note: The annual quotas set for each constituency and the actual payments made are printed in the official reports of the annual conferences of the Conservative Party.

Local party organization and finance
The Conservative Constituency Association

Section reprinted from *Constituency Finance, op. cit.*, pp. 9–11.

The Constituency Association and its own Funds

How the money is raised

There are four main sources:
  Membership, subscriptions and contributions
  bazaars, fetes, social activities
  small lotteries, draws and sweepstakes
  special appeals.

Membership, subscriptions and contributions
The strength of a constituency association stems from its membership. The target should be one third of the Conservative vote, but like all such targets this is to be exceeded if possible. Members must be sought in all sections of the community and, though money is important, a high proportion of active members is essential. It is not enough to have only subscribers; a strong body of men and women helpers from all walks of life, sustained by the support of many others participating in its affairs, is the only sure foundation for a financially and politically successful association. This is primarily a branch commitment since subscribers direct to the centre will probably not exceed one fifth of the total membership and they are automatically also members of the branches where they reside.

There is no minimum or maximum subscription but regard must be had to the cost of 'servicing' each membership, e.g. every member is entitled to receive a notice of the association annual general meeting, and expects to be kept informed from time to time of the various branch and association activities. Members expect, rightly, to receive the Party's literature so, unless they subscribe additionally to the C.P.C. Literature Service, this is another charge against the membership subscription. With postage and printing costs the servicing of a membership will cost not less than 5s. a year. Clearly, Conservatives can expect from the Party, at every level from branch to Westminster, only as much as they pay for and it is suggested that only in exceptional cases can less than 10s. be regarded as a realistic amount to subscribe.

Thus the maintenance of a high level of subscription is the first responsibility of branch and constituency treasurers. In achieving this they must not only guide subscribers as to the amount, but also make collection and payment as easy as possible. For the latter purpose the Banker's Order offers the greatest scope; it ensures continuity, eliminates the labour of collection and by facilitating 'spread-over' makes a higher subscription easier to meet. Subscribers who have G.P.O. Giro Accounts may find this an easy way to make regular payments into branch or association funds. The potential advantage in having a G.P.O. Giro Account should, therefore, not be overlooked by branch and constituency treasurers. It is important to establish a higher subscription rate than has been achieved hitherto. This is most likely to follow from a personal face to face approach. Intending subscribers often ask for guidance and it is helpful if an amount for the year's subscription can be stated as a monthly figure. There are many subscribers able to give as much each month as sometimes they are asked to contribute each year. For example, £1 a year is only 1s. 8d. a month.

5s. a month is £3 a year	
10s.	(£6)
£1	(£12)
£2	(£24)
£5	(£60)
£10	(£120)

If these figures are kept in mind the advice given to potential subscribers should have the desired effect. The use of a banker's order, making quarterly or even monthly payments possible, could be an added advantage.

Subscription Collection

The 'Block System' described in other Manuals is the basis on which collection is organised.

Aids to collection include envelope schemes, the use of individual collecting boxes and approaches through the book scheme. Details of these can be obtained from the Organisation Department (Finance) at Central Office and particulars of membership and subscription drives which from time to time are found to succeed in various constituencies are also available. Experience shows that some methods succeed in some places but fail in others. Therefore, the question of suitability is clearly one to be decided locally. Nevertheless there is evidence that Survey Canvassing described in 'The Key to Success: The District Committee Room' provides a very sound guide to potential subscribers. Thus, a by-product of a survey canvass could be information showing districts in which membership drives might most advantageously be conducted.

Bazaars, fetes, social activities
While these events can be run primarily to raise money, they also keep the association in the public eye and often provide a platform for the Member of Parliament or Party front bench speakers. They are valuable, too, in keeping Party workers together, exercising them between elections, and holding the interest of supporters less inclined to take part in more serious day to day political activities.

'Briefs' for the organisation of some events of this kind are included in Fund Raising Supplement No. 1; advice and information is available from Organisation (Finance) at Central Office and from the provincial area offices.

Small lotteries, draws and sweepstakes
Sweepstakes and lotteries should not be regarded as a main source of income but they can be used from time to time within the limitations imposed by the Betting, Gaming & Lotteries Act 1963. These are outlined in Fund Raising Supplement No. 1 and should be strictly observed.

Raffles (at fetes, bazaars and similar social activities) can be run provided the quite elementary requirements of the Act are observed. The same applies to Bingo as part of another entertainment but Bingo on its own is subject to a number of restrictions which should be studied with very great care before a decision to use this form of fund raising is made.

Similar care must be taken in the promotion of football pools.

Special Appeals
Appeals for 'Fighting Funds' are a major source of income, especially when made at the time of a general election or by-election. Otherwise, special appeals, e.g. for funds for the acquisition of property or equipment, should be resorted to only sparingly; it is better to build up a regular and sufficient income backed by adequate, though not excessive, reserves.

Part two The role of parties in the political process

4 Candidate selection and leadership recruitment

Introduction

A major rationale for the existence of a political party is to compete for and hold political office at all levels of government. To do this, party procedures are set up whereby individuals are recruited and selected to compete for political office, and party Leaders chosen who are acceptable to all sections of the party. In performing these necessary party functions, political parties also incidentally help to maintain the legitimacy of the political system as a whole. In general they provide orderly and open electoral competition for governmental positions at all levels, and in particular provide the major source for the recruitment of political decision-makers. However, for those parties in Britain likely to be able to obtain a majority in Parliament, the selection of a party Leader has more significant implications, since they are in effect choosing the next Prime Minister or the Leader of the Opposition. In the same way, party organizations selecting a candidate in constituencies normally won by their party are in effect choosing an M.P., who may later become a member of the Cabinet or even party Leader (or for that matter the Chairman of the Prices and Incomes Board or the Betting Levy Board!). Thus what are essentially internal party procedures and activities do in many instances have an important effect on the nature of political leadership and governmental decision-making in the political process as a whole.

The process of candidate selection is an important feature of constituency party activity, as Michael Rush demonstrates. However, unlike the United States, there are no electoral laws in Britain to inhibit parties from determining for themselves their methods of selecting candidates to fight elections. In the early days of parties, the selection of Leaders and party candidates was made by party caucus, and this tradition remains substantially for the Conservative, Labour and Liberal parties, the prime responsibility for choosing the party Leader resting with the party members in Parliament, and the selection of candidates with party activists and members in the local constituency. Candidates are therefore normally selected by small groups not necessarily representative of the attitudes of all constituency supporters of the party. The autonomy of parliamentary party and local constituency organization is not absolute, as Michael Rush indicates, but their dominance of the respective procedures has been criticized both by academics and party members.

Certain Conservative constituency organizations, beginning at Hampstead in 1949 and Brighton Kemptown in 1959, have sought to introduce their own particular variations of 'primaries' in order to make selection more 'open',[1] including one at Reigate in 1969 being held at a meeting open to the press and television, and the wives of candidates were also asked to make a speech.[2] Following the 1966 Election, there were reports of demands for the use of a postal ballot of members by the Caithness and Sutherland constituency Conservative Association to reconcile differences about the acceptability for adoption of a local candidate, and a similar dispute over the adoption of a prospective Conservative candidate for the Thirsk and Malton constituency also led to demands for a secret ballot of members. The Conservative Association in Wells sent out a massive eight-page questionnaire, along with voting particulars of every election since 1900, a map of the polling districts and local electoral districts in the constituency, plus information of the procedure for selecting a candidate, to the large number of potential candidates anxious to become their standard-bearer in this safe Conservative seat. In 1969 the party agent of the Knutsford constituency Conservative Association devised a complicated selection scheme which involved a large number of individuals representing different party groups in the screening of applicants, their top choices going before a selection committee whose short list would be given to the Executive Council who would make the final selection, and the person chosen would then have to appear before a special general meeting of the whole Association for final adoption as prospective parliamentary candidate. Most of these variations in general procedure have taken place in 'safe' Conservative seats where the constituency Association is, in effect, choosing the next M.P. However, perhaps a more typical example of the range of factors affecting the selection of a Conservative candidate is the case-study by Julian Critchley on the manner in which Julian Amery came to be chosen in the Brighton Pavilion constituency in 1967.

Academic analysis of candidate selection testifies to the wide diversities in the manner of selection, within as well as between the two major parties, and has been critical of their effects on the political process as a whole as well as the parties themselves. Janosik[3] analysed data gathered from Labour Party leaders in a stratified random sample of thirty-six constituencies, and concluded that the selection processes used by many constituency Labour parties did not operate in the best interests of the party. The virtual autonomy of local constituency party organizations over candidate selection also has important implications for party discipline. On several occasions M.P.s have succeeded in combating attempts to discipline them, such as taking the party Whip away or expelling them, when they have the strong backing of their local Association. In 1968 Desmond Donnelly, Labour M.P. for Pembroke, was expelled from the party yet retained the support of officers of his constituency Association (eighteen members of the local Executive Committee initially resigning from the Labour Party in support of him), who were successful in obtaining a legal decision invalidating a resolution of the National Executive of the Labour Party suspending the activities of the Pembroke Labour Party, and depriving the officers of the right to use funds. Later Donnelly formed a new party, the Democrats, selecting candidates who fought by-elections against official Labour candidates. Donnelly himself sought re-election in Pembroke as a Democrat in 1970 but was defeated. In 1970, S. O. Davies, having been refused renomination as the Labour candidate for Merthyr Tydfil because of his age, ran as an Independent Labour candidate and won, beating the official Labour candidate and two others. At the 1970 Annual Conference of the Labour Party a rules amendment was accepted allowing the National Executive to be the final arbiter on candidate selection in constituencies.

As Michael Rush indicates, the rationale for becoming a minor candidate is often quite distinctive, and there is less competition for such candidacies. Selection procedures differ from those of the two major parties, though not fundamentally. In some respects it is possible for minor parties to exercise more central control, while making specific demands that candidates chosen be local and 'emerge' from local Associations. Factors of size and tradition make it clear that neither Transport House nor Conservative Central Office can impose their candidate on a local constituency Association, though they may exert covert influence in this and other matters,[4] and help local Associations by providing lists of approved candidates. In safe seats the views of the retiring members are usually highly respected, and this can be a channel of national party influence. There was evidence of such activity in July 1969 by the retiring Labour M.P. for Manchester Ardwick, Leslie Lever, in favour of Gerald Kaufman, the current Labour Party parliamentary press liaison officer, who was ultimately selected, but not before a good deal of local ill-feeling was voiced publicly. Some Labour constituency Associations may also be influenced in final selection by the fact that a candidate has union sponsorship (which means financial help). Transport House maintains two separate lists of approved candidates, List A which includes persons nominated by trade unions and approved by the National Executive, and List B consisting of persons not sponsored by trade unions or the Co-operative Party but whom the National Executive considers suitable for parliamentary candidature.

The selection of party Leader is of great importance to the success and unity of the party as a whole. Michael Rush argues that the exigencies of the parliamentary situation lead those parties with at least a modest representation in Parliament to select their Leaders by methods in which the parliamentary party is dominant. This does not apply for parties whose parliamentary representation is nil or negligible. The Leader of such a party is not necessarily a person holding elected office, for the election of Winifred Ewing to Westminster in 1967 did not make her the formal Leader of the Scottish National Party.

The protests made within the Liberal Party following the selection of Jeremy Thorpe in 1967 reflect the dilemmas of a former major party whose parliamentary influence has declined, with a substantial rank and file who feel that the role and influence of the parliamentary party should be less great than in the past in determining the activities of the party. New procedures were also introduced in 1965 for the selection of the Conservative Party Leader, following controversy and criticism over the manner in which Leaders 'emerged' in 1957 and 1963.[5] The result is that though there remain important formal differences between the two major parties over their methods of selection and the status of their Leader in or out of office, practices have tended to become similar in response to practical political considerations within Parliament. Formal differences between the parties, for example with regard to security of tenure, no longer seem to be reflected in practice.[6]

The choice of party Leader by the two major parties is important also because like candidate selection it affects the selection of members of the government. For all parties it is of crucial importance because the Leader has a significant influence on the image and future fortunes of the party.[7] This influence may be important in maintaining the loyalty of party workers and members as well as attracting electoral support, and can also affect the type of party candidates chosen. After the Conservative defeat in 1966 the Central Office list of approved candidates was subjected to a thorough review by the Chairman and Vice-Chairman of the party with the avowed intention of providing a choice of candidates reflecting a broader cross-section of the community and more consistent with the image of the Leader, Edward Heath. The Vice-Chairman of the party later claimed that more candidates were being adopted from business and industry below the rank of director, and from the teaching profession and with local ties. All this without lessening the numbers of old Etonians among the ranks of Conservative M.P.s elected at by-elections and in the 1970 General Election.

Notes

1 See L. W. Martin, 'The Bournemouth Affair: Britain's First Primary Election', *Journal of Politics*, 1960, pp. 654–81, also P. Paterson, *The Selectorate*, London, 1967, pp. 129–31.
2 See also a report of the selection meeting in 1969 of the Wimbledon Conservative Association, *The Times*, 9 July 1969.
3 E. Janosik, *Constituency Labour Parties in Britain*, London, 1968, pp. 113–55.
4 See M. G. Clarke, 'National Organisation and the Constituency Association in the Conservative Party: The Case of the Huddersfield Pact', *Political Studies*, 1969, pp. 345–7.
5 See R. Churchill, *The Fight for the Tory Leadership*, London, 1964.
6 See A. H. Birch, *The British System of Government*, London, 1967, pp. 116–23.
7 See D. Butler and D. Stokes, *op. cit.*, Chapter 17.

Further reading

For comprehensive surveys of candidate selection by the Conservative, Labour and Liberal parties, see A. Ranney, *Pathways to Parliament*, London, 1965, and M. Rush, *The Selection of Parliamentary Candidates*, London, 1969. For analysis of candidate selection with an emphasis on the social background of candidates, see P. G. Richards, *Honourable Members*, London, 1959, Chapter 1. For a general analysis of the social background of candidates and leaders in Parliament, see J. Blondel, *Voters, Parties and Leaders*, London, 1969. For evidence of British procedures in a comparative context, see L. Epstein, *Political Parties in Western Democracies*, London, 1967, Chapter 8. For a general statement on candidates and their selection, see R. L. Leonard, *Elections in Britain*, London, 1968, Chapter 7, and on the selection of Liberal candidates in particular, see J. S. Rasmussen, *The Liberal Party: A Study of Retrenchment and Revival*, London, 1965, Chapter 10. For an amusing novel on the personal aspects of candidate selection, see D. Walder, *The Short List*, London, 1964. On leadership recruitment in general, see W. L. Guttsman, *The British Political Elite*, London, 1963.

Articles

J. Biffen, 'The Constituency Leaders', *Crossbow*, 1960, pp. 27–32.

J. Bonnor, 'The Four Labour Cabinets', *Sociological Review*, 1958, pp. 37–48.

A. M. Potter, 'The English Conservative Constituency Association', *Western Political Quarterly*, 1956, pp. 363–75.

A. Ranney, 'Inter-Constituency Movement of British Parliamentary Candidates 1951–9', *American Political Science Review*, 1964, pp. 36–45, also articles in *New Society*, 16, 23 September 1965, on candidate selection.

Candidate selection and its impact on leadership recruitment [1]
by Michael Rush

It has become a commonplace in studies of British politics to draw attention to the prominent role of the public schools in general, and of Eton in particular, in such spheres as the Civil Service, Parliament and various administrations. Indeed the politicians themselves have drawn attention to it: Harold Macmillan once boasted that he had more old Etonians in his Cabinet than Attlee had had in his, whilst in November 1964 Harold Wilson was seeking to disassociate his government from any stigma of an establishment aura when he said: 'The day of dynasty and the era of nepotism is over.' [2] Nevertheless, several members of Wilson's first Cabinet were ex-public schoolboys, together with no less than 18 per cent of the Labour M.P.s elected in 1966.[3] Whilst it is true that the proportion of Labour M.P.s with a public-school education pales beside the corresponding portion of Conservative Members elected in 1966, of whom no less than 80 per cent had attended public schools,[4] the fact remains that it is substantially above the national average of less than 6 per cent.

Similarly, if another common educational criterion is used, that of university education in general, and graduation from Oxford or Cambridge in particular, a picture again emerges of a Civil Service, a Conservative Party, Labour Party, and of Cabinets in which individuals with such backgrounds either predominate or form substantial minorities. In comparing the backgrounds of M.P.s elected in 1951 with those elected in 1966, Butler and King conclude that the difference between the two is that 1966 resulted in 'an intellectually livelier Parliament but *not necessarily a more representative one*'.[5]

The extent to which Parliament is and should be representative of the nation, or more properly the electorate, concerns not only the background of those elected to Parliament but also the extent to which these men and women are *politically* representative of those who elect them. Whilst it is not intended to argue or even examine here the case for microcosmic representation in the House of Commons, our concern is with the process by which candidates, and therefore, party Leaders, ministers and Prime Ministers are selected, because those who hold high political office in Britain are drawn largely from the House of Commons. F. M. G. Willson pointed out that of the 173 persons appointed to the Cabinet between 1916 and 1958 only 28, or 16·2 per cent, could be described as 'unorthodox' in that they entered the Cabinet with at the most only nominal parliamentary experience, whilst a further 5, or 2·9 per cent, had served only in the House of Lords.[6] This means that no less than four-fifths of the

Cabinet ministers appointed during this period had first served a political apprenticeship in Parliament, mostly in the House of Commons, although a few had been members of both houses, having received or succeeded to peerage after serving in the lower house.

This is a clear indication of the decline of importance of the House of Lords. No serious consideration has been given to the appointment of a peer as Prime Minister since 1940, so much so that in 1957 Lord Salisbury and Lord Kilmuir were considered sufficiently neutral to conduct soundings of the Conservative Party in its search for a successor to Sir Anthony Eden. Similarly, it has become increasingly rare for peers to be appointed heads of *major* government departments, notwithstanding the appointment of Lord Home as Foreign Secretary in 1960 (which was the subject of considerable criticism on constitutional grounds) and Lord Carrington as Secretary of State for Defence in 1970. The House of Commons is, therefore, the principal source of ministerial material, the more so under any Labour administration, which normally has fewer ministers in the Lords than their Conservative opponents and which seeks to minimize the role of the upper house.

Quite apart from the fact that the majority of Cabinet ministers are drawn from the House of Commons, the apprenticeship they serve there is far from nominal: excluding those whose Parliamentary experience was entirely in the House of Lords (and, of course, the 'unorthodox' entrants) the Cabinet ministers appointed between 1916 and 1958 had served an average of sixteen years in the Commons before their appointment.[7] Moreover, they had also spent an average of four and a half years as ministers outside the Cabinet before entering the latter body.[8]

There is, in fact, a well-marked path to high office: the first step for the majority of ministers is appointment as a Parliamentary Private Secretary, a position which is unpaid, has no official status in the ministerial hierarchy and in which the M.P. fulfils the role of aide or assistant to the minister concerned. For a substantial minority, however, the first step is appointment as a junior minister, but only a small proportion are made senior non-Cabinet ministers, whilst very few indeed go straight into the Cabinet with no ministerial experience or with its opposition equivalent of having been a front-bench spokesman. If a party has been in opposition for a long period, covering several Parliaments, then it is quite likely that when it does eventually achieve office a number of the ensuing Cabinet appointments will include men who have had no previous ministerial experience, as was indeed the case with the Labour administration formed in 1964. Nevertheless, all but two of the ten Cabinet ministers without ministerial experience then appointed had been Opposition Front

Bench spokesmen, and all except two had served in Parliament for eleven or more years. It is interesting to note that, although Wilson did appoint three non-Parliamentarians as Ministers of State and another three as junior ministers, the overwhelming majority of those to whom he gave office were M.P.s who had been elected in 1959 or earlier.

Philip Buck has calculated that, even *including* the position of P.P.S., only a quarter of the Members of Parliament elected between 1918 and 1955 achieved any kind of office. If the P.P.S.s are excluded the proportion falls to less than 16 per cent.[9] The chances of achieving office are not therefore very high, but the fact remains that membership of the House of Commons is the initial step towards ministerial office. Furthermore, the dominance of Parliament by the two major parties makes it extremely unlikely that a member of any other party, even assuming that he can secure election to Parliament, will ever achieve office. Even during the period 1918–58, which did include several years of coalition government, 93·5 per cent of the members of the House of Commons who held ministerial office and 98·4 per cent of those who held Cabinet office were members of the Conservative and Labour parties.[10]

The extent to which the Conservative and Labour parties dominate Parliament can be shown by analysing the relative marginality or safeness of constituencies,[11] which reveals that two-thirds of the latter may be regarded as being firmly in the hands of one or other of these two parties. Put another way this means that more than two-thirds of the seats which changed hands between 1950 and 1966 could be described as marginal, and nearly 96 per cent as either marginal or semi-marginal.

In two-thirds of the constituencies, therefore, selection by the incumbent party is tantamount to election, whilst in the remaining seats the fate of most Labour and Conservative candidates depends upon the electoral swing. It is true, of course, that the Liberal Party won twelve seats in 1966, but only one could be considered safe or impregnable. Moreover, the impact of the electoral system on the Liberals is severe: in 1966 the party secured 8·5 per cent of the total national vote but only 1·9 per cent of the seats, and it is further testimony of the inexactitude of the simple plurality that in 1964 the Liberals secured 765,000 *more* votes than in 1966 and three *fewer* seats. The extent to which the party owes its success in these constituencies as much to the quality, personality and persistence of its candidates as to any firm and continuing support for the Liberal Party is worth considering. Between 1950 and 1966 only one Liberal-held seat has survived a change of candidate and this was Montgomery, which was retained for the Liberals by Emlyn Hooson in 1962, following

87

the death of Clement Davies, the former Liberal Leader. Every other Liberal constituency was a gain from Conservative or Labour, and it is not unreasonable to suggest that the initial winning of these seats and possibly their subsequent retention owes a great deal to the Liberal candidates concerned.

If the impact of the electoral system is severe on the Liberal Party, however, its impact on other minor parties is devastating. Very few minor party candidates have successfully challenged the major parties. Most of those who have were candidates representing various nationalist or other groups in Wales, Scotland and Northern Ireland. Others, such as parties on the extreme left like the Communists or the Socialist Party of Great Britain, or on the extreme right, like the British National Party or the Union Movement, have completely failed to secure a single electoral success since 1950, when the last Communist M.P. was defeated.

Although minor parties are penalized by the electoral system, this is not a total explanation of their lack of success. The majority of the electorate appears to subscribe to the view that, at general elections at least, the real choice is between the Conservative and Labour parties and that a vote for any one of the minor parties is a wasted vote. The success of minor parties depends on creating a viable electoral base. This is, for example, what the Democratic Labour Party in Australia has managed to achieve with Catholic support, what Social Credit has achieved in Canada with provincial bases, and what the Labour Party in Britain achieved with trade-union and working-class support. It is also what the Irish Nationalists achieved during the later part of the nineteenth and early part of the twentieth centuries, and it is what the Welsh and Scottish Nationalists hope to achieve in the future. Other fringe parties such as the British National Party, or the Union Movement, or the Patriotic Party, or the Socialist Party of Great Britain have never succeeded in establishing substantial electoral bases. Only the Communist Party has succeeded in securing the election of any M.P.s, but its support is too widely scattered to challenge the Labour Party which robs it of its natural supporters.

Most minor parties nominate only a handful of candidates at each General Election: some, such as the National Socialist Movement and the Greater Britain Movement, shun electoral tactics altogether, but others, like the National Front, put up candidates only in one or two selected constituencies. The Communist Party, however, has always sought to maintain a fairly widespread challenge, and, after nominating 100 candidates in 1950 and only a tenth of this number in 1951, has been gradually building up the proportion of constituencies it contests until in 1966 and 1970 it reached around 9 per cent. Similarly, the two nationalist parties in Britain have been increasing the proportion of Welsh and Scottish seats they fight so that in 1970 Plaid Cymru contested all thirty-six Welsh constituencies and the Scottish Nationalists all but six of the seats in Scotland.

The success of the Communist and the two nationalist parties in securing the election of Members of Parliament has been very limited. The Communists' greatest success was in 1945 when they secured 0·4 per cent of the vote and two M.P.s. Previously the party had secured the election of solitary candidates in 1922, 1924 and 1935. Prior to 1966, when Gwynfor Evans won the Carmarthen by-election, the sole nationalist victory had been that of Dr R. D. McIntyre in the Motherwell by-election of April, 1945.[12] In 1967, however, the Scottish Nationalists won a victory of considerable proportions at Hamilton, overturning a substantial Labour majority. Both nationalist parties have been increasing their support in post-war general elections. Despite their by-election success of 1945 the Scottish Nationalists were unable to win more than 1 per cent of the Scottish vote until 1964 when they secured 2·4 per cent and then went on to double this in 1966. Similarly, Plaid Cymru secured approximately 1 per cent of the Welsh vote in 1950 and 1951, but in 1955 they exceeded 3 per cent and in 1959 5 per cent. In 1964 and 1966 they experienced a slight fall, but this was more than offset by their by-election success at Carmarthen and the drastic reduction of Labour majorities at Rhondda West and Caerphilly. In 1970 the nationalist parties raised their share of the vote in Wales and Scotland to over 11 per cent, but failed to increase their representation at Westminster: the S.N.P. lost Hamilton but gained the Western Isles, while Plaid Cymru lost Carmarthen.

Neither nationalist party has yet succeeded in becoming *the* major electoral rorce in their respective areas, though both can be regarded as a challenger to the hegemony of the two major parties in Wales and Scotland, particularly at by-elections. It is important to note, however, that much of their success in securing the election of M.P.s had been limited to by-elections and, in spite of winning an increasing share of the Welsh and Scottish votes and a considerable increase in party membership, support for third or minor parties tends to fall at general elections compared with by-elections. Both Plaid Cymru and the Scottish National Party have a long road to travel before either has the dominance achieved by the Irish Nationalists between 1874 and 1916.

None the less, both nationalist parties and the Communist Party aspire to parliamentary representation to a degree far beyond that of other minor parties. It is interesting to note, therefore, that the greater the electoral effort mounted by these parties the more they conform in the selection of their parliamentary candidates to the methods followed by the major parties. The basic control most parties have over the selection of candidates is that of whether a particular constituency will be contested in the name of the party. In so far as this relates directly to the size of a party's effort it is a positive control, but in so far as it relates to the selection of particular individuals as party candidates it is a negative control since the party may refuse to recognize a candidate, but cannot normally impose an alternative nominee against the wishes of the local branch.

The Conservative and Labour parties normally contest all but a handful of the constituencies, but for the other parties the decision is limited to factors of finance and strategy. Finance covers not only the cost of the electoral campaign, which can often be minimized with voluntary help, but the willingness to risk the loss of the £150 deposit on failing to secure an eighth of the votes cast in any constituency. This is an important consideration because minor parties can normally expect to lose a substantial proportion of their deposits: in 1966, for instance, the Communists lost all fifty-seven of their deposits, the Welsh Nationalists saved three out of twenty, whilst their Scottish compatriots, further demonstrating their growing electoral support, saved over half their twenty-three deposits. Financial considerations will therefore normally dictate the number of seats a minor party can contest, but strategic considerations will determine which constituencies are contested within the financial limit. The most important factor, of course, is the distribution of party support, and efforts are made to build up support in particular constituencies by contesting them as often as possible:[13] nearly 90 per cent of the seats contested by Plaid Cymru between 1950 and 1966 were fought at more than one of the six general elections; similarly over four-fifths of the seats contested by the Scottish Nationalists were fought more than once in the same period; and a similar figure applies to the Communist Party. Thus the main strength of Plaid Cymru is found in North Wales, in seats like Carmarthen and Merioneth, and in particular constituencies in South Wales which have been consistently contested over several elections. Scottish Nationalist support tends to be more diffuse, whilst Communist strength is inevitably concentrated in industrial areas, of which the two most important are London and Central Scotland.

A number of other factors play a significant part in the selection of constituencies to be contested, of which one of the most important is finding a suitable local candidate rather than an outsider. Such candidates may already have the advantage of being known locally and the cost of 'nursing' the seat is reduced considerably. A local candidate, moreover, may also be compared favourably with any outsider adopted by one of the other parties. In 1966 over three-quarters of the Communist and Scottish Nationalist candidates and over two-thirds of the Plaid Cymru candidates had direct local connections with their constituencies.

The Communist Party also adopts a number of other criteria in deciding which seats to contest. Since its main strength lies in industrial areas it seldom contests Conservative- or Liberal-held constituencies, but some care is exercised in selecting those Labour seats it wishes to fight. For example, in 1950, 1966 and 1970, when Labour governments were seeking re-election, the Communists nominated candidates in the constituencies of various Labour ministers, and at every general election Communist candidates oppose a number of the trade-union-sponsored Labour candidates.

The nationalist parties experienced a period of growing electoral support in the late 1960s which it seemed could assume proportions beyond the significance of by-election victories, even given the failure to improve their parliamentary representation in 1970. In such circumstances the minor parties, aspiring as they do to major party status, and no matter how justified these aspirations may be, tend to select candidates in ways which are markedly similar to those of the Conservative, Labour and Liberal parties. Like their larger rivals, both the Communist Party and the Scottish Nationalists retain the right to veto any candidate chosen by a local party, but this is an essentially negative control and selection is basically in the hands of local parties. The Scottish Nationalists also maintain a list of available candidates, who have previously been vetted at national level. At the local level the procedures again tend to be similar, with the initial steps being taken by small Selection Committees, subject to later approval by wider bodies representative of the local membership. The Communist Party does exercise more central control through its district committees, but the essential national decision is whether to contest the seat rather than impose a candidate upon the local rank and file, with whom there is close liaison.

The selection of candidates in the Liberal Party follows a similar pattern. In a sense the Liberal Party is neither a minor nor a major party since it refuses to sink to the former status and continues to aspire to the latter. After a disastrous election in 1950, when it fought three-quarters of the seats and lost two-thirds of its deposits, the Liberal Party experienced a limited revival. The party has tended to make its greatest impact at by-elections, but it still nominates a substantial number of candidates at each general election: in 1964 and 1966 nearly four-fifths and nearly half the constituencies respectively had Liberal candidates. It was the hope of the Liberal Party, especially in 1964, that it would achieve a position of balance between the two major parties and become the key factor in the formation of a coalition or minority government. The party came close to achieving this aim, but the whims of the electoral system left the Liberals in a stronger electoral position, with three more M.P.s, only to deprive them of the role of political arbitrators. It is ironical that had the Liberal-Conservative electoral pacts in Bolton and Huddersfield been maintained it is quite possible that the Liberal Party would have found itself in a situation in which it held the political balance, since the retention of Bolton East by the Conservatives and of Bolton West and Huddersfield West by the Liberals would have deprived Labour of its absolute majority. It was not to be, however, and in 1966 the Liberal Party was again as far from the centre of political power as ever, in spite of the fact that it increased its membership in the Commons to twelve. In 1970 this representation was reduced to six, though the total votes cast for Liberal candidates remained over two million.

For those candidates who wish to become Members of Parliament then, the normal vehicle of their ambition must be one of the two major parties, because it is only in these parties that anything approaching a guarantee of election to Parliament can be made. A recent study makes it quite clear that the Liberal leadership is fully aware of this: 'the secretary of the Liberal Central Association *discourages* any potential candidate who indicates he is interested in standing *because he hopes to get into Parliament*.'[14] Nevertheless, the Liberal Party maintains a selection procedure which is substantially similar to that of the Conservative and Labour parties. At the national level the party organization maintains a list of available candidates and applicants for the list are screened on behalf of the party headquarters by regional committees. Unlike the minor parties, the national organization does not decide which constituencies will be contested, although this is usually a matter for discussion between the local Association and party headquarters. Nor does there appear to be any formal procedure to veto selections by disaffiliating a local Association from the national organizations. Since the veto powers of other parties are essentially negative in character, and cannot be used to place candidates in particular constituencies, these differences are of less significance than might at first appear. The crucial point is that in all political parties, the Liberals included, the selection of candidates is primarily a local responsibility. In the Liberal Party the process of selection at local level is likely to begin informally when potential candidates are invited to meet local party activists or a sub-committee of the constituency Executive Committee. Those candidates who have made a favourable impression will then be interviewed by the Association's Executive Committee, and a recommendation on adoption will be made to a special meeting of the general membership of the Association. This final stage of adoption is usually a formality, as it is in other parties.

What distinguishes the selection of Liberal candidates most of all from the selection of their Conservative and Labour rivals is that it is as much a process of *search* as of selection. Though this applies in many respects to the minor parties, it is especially applicable to the Liberals because they seek to contest so many constituencies.

Local Conservative Associations and Constituency Labour Parties (C.L.P.s) are far more likely to have a choice of possible candidates than their rivals, except in all but the most hopeless seats. It is important to realize, however, that the majority of Conservative and Labour candidates selected at each election are destined for defeat, since most of the candidates who are elected, regardless of the electoral swing, are M.P.s *seeking re-election*. This accounts for over two-fifths of the Conservative and Labour candidates nominated at the five general elections between 1951 and 1966. This therefore limits the number of Conservative- and Labour-held seats which become available for the would-be M.P.s. Ostensibly every seat in the House of Commons is subject to open competition at a General Election, but in practice the vast majority of seats are pre-empted by the two major parties and the majority of these seats by sitting M.P.s. Only a small proportion of M.P.s retire at a General Election (7·6 per cent between 1951 and 1966) and, whilst an average Parliament may see as many as fifty or more by-election vacancies, the total number of vacancies in Conservative- and Labour-held constituencies between 1950 (excluding the General Election) and 1966 (including the General Election) was only 469. A candidate may, of course, wrest a marginal seat from the incumbent party and this method secured the election of 210 Conservative and Labour M.P.s between 1950 and 1966, but it is not easy to effect the necessary electoral swing, even though it is comparatively simple to predict which constituencies are vulnerable. In these cases the fate of the candidate is in the hands of his party and he will normally benefit or suffer under the relative homogeneity of the electoral swing.

The fortunate few candidates who inherit favourable majorities contrast sharply with the many less fortunate, who can hope to be little more than standard-bearers for their respective parties. Even so the machinery of selection is common to all local Conservative and Labour parties, the principal difference between selection by the incumbent party and the non-incumbent party in a safe seat being the fierceness of the competition for the vacancy; the more hopeless the constituency the more likely it is that selection will take the form of a search for a candidate. In other words, Conservative and Labour selectors in safe seats are fully aware that, barring an electoral disaster, they are selecting the constituency's next Member of Parliament; selectors in marginal seats are normally aware that they *may* be selecting an M.P., and those in hopeless seats are only too well aware that they are selecting a standard-bearer.

Selection, in fact, is a moment of real power for the local activists, one of the few occasions when a decision of importance is taken at local rather than national level. The manner in which these decisions are taken and the criteria applied are therefore of considerable importance, since they are central to the composition of Parliament from which the national leaders are drawn. In spite of this the role of the national party organization tends to be peripheral. Although there are a number of differences between the Conservative and Labour parties the basic process is similar. The national organizations of both parties maintain lists of candidates which are available to local parties seeking candidates and both keep a watching brief over every selection. This surveillance, however, is designed to ensure that the proper procedures are followed, rather than forcing any national choice upon the local selectors. Any attempt to foist a candidate on a local party is likely to result in his summary rejection: if the party headquarters wishes to secure the selection of a particular individual then this can only be achieved with the full co-operation of the local party concerned.

One of the principal differences between the two parties is the practice among the Conservatives of allowing interested persons to *apply* for the candidature, whereas a would-be Labour candidate must be nominated by a local party organization.[15] For this reason alone a safe Conservative constituency will normally have a larger numerical choice, since the number of Labour nominees is limited to the number of local party organizations, although this is somewhat offset by the growing Labour practice of encouraging local organizations to hold preliminary interviews of possible candidates before making an actual nomination to the C.L.P. Because of this larger choice a Conservative Association will usually appoint a small Selection Committee which interviews as many as twenty or thirty of the applicants and then draws up a short list of two or three, who subsequently appear before the Association's Executive Council. This latter body, normally numbering at least forty persons and often more than 100, hears the applicants make short speeches and answer questions. After an exhaustive ballot, the council then recommends one applicant to a general meeting of the Association. This final stage is usually a formality, although from time to time there are attempts to oppose the adoption of the council's nominee, and very occasionally such attempts are successful.[16] Finally, at the beginning of the election campaign itself, a second adoption meeting is held, but again this is usually a formality, since the rejection of a candidate at this stage would be the height of foolishness.[17]

The Labour Party follows a similar method, except that the short-list is normally drawn up without the candidates first being interviewed, and Labour short-lists are invariably longer: at least four candidates and possibly as many as six or eight. This is partly a reflection of the federative nature of the party in that the various sections of each C.L.P. compete fiercely for the candidature, and partly a reflection of the desire to give the General Management Committee (G.M.C.) of the C.L.P., which makes the final selection, as wide a choice as possible. At the subsequent selection conference the candidates make their speeches and answer questions, then the G.M.C. makes its choice by means of an exhaustive ballot. Unlike his Conservative counterpart, a Labour candidate's selection is not subject to the approval of a general meeting, except shortly before the actual election campaign, when rejection is unthinkable.

Both parties retain the right to reject candidates selected by their local organizations. In the Labour Party this takes the form of making the selection of every candidate subject to endorsement by the National Executive Committee and from time to time such endorsement is refused.[18] In the Conservative Party, local Associations are asked to seek the approval of the party's Standing Advisory Committee on Candidates in respect of any candidate who is not already on the list of available candidates, and that this should be done before the formal adoption of the candidate. Failure to comply with this request may result in the non-recognition of the individual as an official Conservative candidate.[19] A similar, but alternative, method is for the National Union of Conservative & Unionist Associations to withdraw recognition of a local Association and to establish a rival body whose candidate it subsequently recognizes.[20] Such cases are very rare, however, and the powers they give the national organizations are purely negative, ridding the party of a candidate to whom it objects, rather than securing the selection of a candidate it favours.

The two parties differ more sharply on the criteria which they apply to selection, however. Whilst the personal qualities of potential candidates are by no means ignored, political factors tend to play a much greater part in Labour selections. Conservative selectors lay considerable stress on the personality of the candidate and attach relatively little importance to a candidate's position in the political spectrum, whereas Labour selectors pay more attention to a candidate's attitude on various political matters and many selections are decided on a left-right basis.[21]

The federative nature of the Labour Party also plays an important part in selection, since in any Labour-held seat there will normally be competition for the candidacy among the various trade unions, the local ward parties and, possibly, the Co-operative Party,[22] and this competition can be both fierce and bitter. Some trade unions adopt a proprietary attitude towards particular constituencies and resent any attempt to wrest the nomination from them. At the same time the unions are primarily interested in securing parliamentary representation and are therefore reluctant to contest non-Labour seats. Those they do contest are, for the most part, marginal or semi-marginal constituencies which Labour could be expected to win given a favourable electoral swing. From the point of view of the C.L.P., a union or Co-operative candidate has the advantage of being financially sponsored by his nominating organization and if he is selected the C.L.P. will usually receive not only some assistance towards election expenses but also an annual grant. The non-federative nature of local Conservative Associations and the party rules concerning finance means that neither of these factors, sectional competition and financial considerations, plays any part in the selection of Conservative candidates.

The main result of these differences is that there tends to be much greater uniformity in the type of candidate selected by Conservative Associations than in the type selected by C.L.P.s. For example, the majority of the working-class Labour M.P.s are trade-union candidates and these candidates contrast sharply with their non-sponsored colleagues in terms of age and education. In these two respects, in fact, non-sponsored Labour Members have more in common with Conservative M.P.s than with their sponsored colleagues.

There is also an important contrast between the candidates selected by incumbent and non-incumbent parties: the candidates who become M.P.s tend to be even less representative of the nation than those who are defeated.[23] This being so, it is inevitable that the nation's leaders, drawn as they are mainly from the House of Commons, will be at least as unrepresentative of the population. As long as Prime Ministers continue to feel bound by the convention that ministers from outside Parliament in general, and outside the Commons in particular, are the exception rather than the rule, then their choice of ministerial colleagues remains relatively limited. The fact, therefore, that Conservative selectors tend to express a preference for candidates with a public-school background, or that Labour selectors increasingly prefer middle-class candidates, is crucial to leadership recruitment. In this sense leadership recruitment is subject to the law of demand, but it is also subject to the law of supply, whether it concerns the selection of a candidate or a minister, or, for that matter, a Prime Minister.

Equally crucial to the candidate selection and to leadership recruitment are the pressures imposed by the political system: parties concede local autonomy in selection because it is the price of effective local organization; the nature of local party organization leads different parties to adopt similar methods of selection; the conventions of parliamentary government limit the choice of ministers and the political pressures of parliamentary government dictate the methods by which party leaders are chosen. Despite their differing origins, aims, policies and traditions it is noticeable that all three parties with sizeable parliamentary representation select their leaders in a basically similar fashion. Robert McKenzie has suggested that the distribution of power within British political parties is primarily a function of Cabinet government and the British parliamentary system,[24] but it can further be argued that the pressures of the political system impose a degree of conformity on British political parties in general, and this has been the major argument here in respect of candidate selection and its impact on leadership recruitment.

Notes

1 The research into the selection of Conservative and Labour parliamentary candidates was carried out by the author in preparation for a Ph.D. awarded by the University of Sheffield in 1966. The author also acknowledges the assistance received from the Research Fund of the University of Sheffield. See also M. Rush, *Selection of Parliamentary Candidates*.

2 Anthony Sampson, *Anatomy of Britain Today*, London, 1965, p. 3.

3 D. E. Butler and A. King, *The British General Election of 1966*, London, 1966, p. 211.

4 *Ibid.*, p. 211.

5 *Ibid.*, p. 212. Author's italics.

6 'Routes of Entry of New Members to the British Cabinet, 1868–1958', *Political Studies*, 1959, pp. 222–32, also 'Entry to the Cabinet 1959–68', *Political Studies*, 1970, pp. 236–8.

7 *Ibid.*

8 *Ibid.*

9 P. W. Buck, *Amateurs and Professionals in British Politics, 1918–59*, Chicago, 1963, pp. 47–8.

10 *Ibid.*, pp. 84–5.

11 See the definitions devised by S. E. Finer *et al.*, in *Backbench Opinion in the House of Commons, 1955–59*, London, 1959.

12 Dr McIntyre was defeated three months later at the General Election of 1945.

13 This is invariably linked with building up support for local elections.

14 Jorgen S. Rasmussen, *The Liberal Party: A Study of Retrenchment and*

Revival, London, 1965, p. 212. Author's italics. For further discussion
of Liberal Party selection, see Austin Ranney, *Pathways to Parliament*,
London, 1965, Chapter 9.

15 E.g. Ward parties, local Labour Parties, trade unions, women's sections,
Co-operative Parties, Young Socialists, etc.

16 E.g. Southport, 1952, and the by-election at Nelson and Colne in 1968.

17 However, in 1966 at the adoption meeting of the South Fylde constituency Conservative Association an unsuccessful attempt was made to
oppose the adoption of the incumbent M.P., some forty people finally
voting against his adoption.

18 A recent case is that of John Palmer at Croydon North-West, prior to
the General Election of 1966.

19 This has only happened once since the war, at Chorley in 1950.

20 This also has occurred only once since 1945, at Newcastle upon Tyne
North in 1951.

21 This was particularly the case during the struggle in the Labour Party
over unilateral nuclear disarmament.

22 Members of the Co-operative Party stand as Labour and Co-operative
candidates under a series of electoral agreements between the Labour
and Co-operative Parties.

23 See Butler and King, *op. cit.*, Chapter 12.

24 R. T. McKenzie, *British Political Parties*, *op. cit.*, p. 635.

How Julian Amery and Brighton got each other*
by Julian Critchley

[In the spring of 1967, Sir William Teeling, Conservative M.P. for Brighton Pavilion, announced that he did not wish to seek re-nomination at the next General Election because of his age. The consequences of this statement are recounted in the following report.]

The report in *The Times* of 4 April (though it had already appeared in the *Brighton Argus*) was just what a West Country farmer, a London barrister, a director of a leading electronics firm and a good many more besides had been waiting for. Those on the candidates' list at the Conservative Central Office lost no time in intimating to its keeper, Geoffrey Johnson-Smith, that when he sent along a selection list to Brighton, they would like to be on it. The same ones, and others who shared the ambition if not the pedigree, took the first opportunity to get off a little note to the Brighton Conservative Association which they prepared to follow up in person at the first opportunity.

They were wise to act in haste. By the closing date, 30 June, no fewer than 124 men and women (most of them on the Central Office list) were seeking to be Sir William's successor. The description is exact: with the seat's present majority, and even without the current pro-Tory swing at by-elections, whoever gained the winning ticket in the lottery of candidate selection was also plainly homing on the Palace of Westminster—age permitting, probably for the next twenty years, a span that can also be measured as, at the very least, £65,000.

Six souls applied too late, and, whoever they were, the Pavilion Tories scrupulously ruled them out. The wise 124, however, would have been wiser still had they kept—but why should they?—a close eye on the social life of Brighton.

In December 1966, three full months before Sir William's announcement, Brighton Conservatives gave their Winter Ball in the Metropole Hotel. The guest of honour was the former Conservative Secretary of State for Air, Mr Julian Amery. He was no longer an M.P.; his seat at Preston, held by a majority of only twelve, had gone to Labour in the last General Election. He attended the ball at the personal invitation of Sir William Teeling.

That night Mr Amery met the Brighton Tories. He met them again soon after the turn of the year, when he accepted an invitation to address the elegantly styled Burke Supper Club. Most of the more

* Reprinted from *The Sunday Times*, 5 November 1967, with the permission of Times Newspapers Limited.

99

influential local Tories are members and so Mr Amery met them again.

When the list closed at the end of June, Julian Amery's name was on it, and Sir William Teeling had already been heard to remark, and indeed was to be heard again, if not again, that 'the Chief Whip wants Amery back in the House'.

A list of 124 is by no means unprecedented, but still formidable. To cope with it, the chairman of the association, Mr Frank Edmonds (who is a former leading Young Conservative, and an accountant, and who—like so many more in Brighton—works in London) set up a Selection Committee. It had twenty-seven members: two from each of the constituency's nine wards, two Y.C.s, and the seven elected constituency officers. They were divided into six syndicates, each of which was dealt twenty or so names for consideration; they were told, however, that they could endorse any number.

Edmonds laid down a number of criteria for their guidance. The age should be between thirty and fifty-five. Ex-ministers should have preference, as should any local candidate. No one should be disqualified on grounds of sex or religion. Candidates should be so established in their professional or business careers as to be independent of their parliamentary salary.

The syndicates met four times, and came up with thirty-nine names. These were then reduced to a 'short list' of seventeen, who were invited to attend for interview in batches of about four during September.

Three of the seventeen later withdrew, Mr Christopher Soames, the former Minister of Agriculture (who, like Mr Amery, had been turned down at Honiton earlier in the year) wrote that he would prefer to try for the impending by-election at South Kensington. Mr Paul Williams also an ex-M.P., explicitly declared that he was not prepared to compete against Mr Amery. Mr Winston Churchill preferred the opportunity of Gorton, Manchester (which he narrowly missed taking); the candidates department at Smith Square felt, not unreasonably, that Mr Churchill should be allowed to win his spurs elsewhere.

That left fourteen, and in turn they attended a series of little sherry parties given by the chairman's wife, after which they were interviewed. The atmosphere at the interview was described (admittedly by an unsuccessful contender) as being 'like a People's Court'.

They were marked as follows: 15 per cent for 'manner, impression and personality'; 15 per cent for political record; 10 per cent for career outside politics; 40 per cent for answers to questions; and 20 per cent for their political views.

Every one was asked eight questions (not necessarily in this order):

Why do you want to represent Brighton?

Are you prepared to live within twenty-five miles of the constituency?

What role will your wife play?

Britain's status in the world has declined: what would you do to rectify it?

What part should the constituency play in the life of the member?

How would you define the difference between Conservatism, Socialism and Liberalism?

How would you describe yourself: left, centre or right of the party?

At the last party conference we put forward a resolution to the effect that the party Leader should submit himself for re-election every two years: do you agree?

They presented few problems to Julian Amery. His country cottage at Chelwood Gate is twenty-five miles away in the grounds of Birch Grove, the home of his father-in-law, Mr Harold Macmillan. His position within the party was not really a hurdle at all, but Mr Amery was leaping superbly: 'If you mean by Right-wing, pro-British, then I am Right-wing; but in home affairs I am a Disraelian Tory.' He stumbled, however, over the question of biennial election of the leader. It is a fairly radical idea, which has been interpreted as oblique criticism of Edward Heath and, it is believed, upset Central Office who regarded the proposal as inadmissible. When Amery answered that he was much against any such idea he did so ignorant of the fact that the idea came from the chairman of the Association himself.

It was not, of course, all sherry and selection. Indeed, over the sherry it was suggested to the contenders—in one case 'insistently'— that they should buy tickets at £3 10s. each for a lunch to be given to Sir Alec Douglas Home during the Brighton Conference. Some refused, but others accepted, including four of the eventual finalists. At the lunch, however, they found to their dismay that they were all put on the same table, instead of being seated next to some local alderman whose ear they might catch.

Mr Amery who, as we have seen, already knew a little of Brighton social life, was there; his wife had helped to sell tickets. So were four people from Preston, his old seat: the chairman, the agent, and two devoted supporters. He had invited them, and they, of course, were free to mingle, unsegregated, with the Brighton 'selectorate'. It was described by some as his trump card.

With the Conference out of the way, the percentage marks of the selection committee were taken from their safe, and opened. The markings were anonymous, but once re-related to the appropriate names produced the following order: Mr Amery, Mr Dudley Smith,

Mr Edward Gardner, Mr John Lovill and Mr Ronald Bates, Mayor of Brighton. It was decided that these five would be the finalists. The inclusion of two local men, Lovill and Bates, is seen by some as a device for splitting the anti-Amery vote—three is the more usual number—but it is an arguable point. The nine who were passed over included six ex-M.P.s, of whom Mr David James had sat until 1964 as member for Brighton, Kemptown: the others were Sir John Arbuthnot (Dover), Mr Alan Glyn (Clapham), Mr Graeme Finlay (Epping), Mr William Compton Carr (Barons Court), and Mr Martin McLaren (Bristol North-West), again in that order.

The final was arranged for Wednesday, 1 November, to take place before the fifty members of the Executive Council of the Association. Contenders would speak for fifteen minutes, there would be time for questions, and then the wives were to be asked to speak for three minutes.

Candidate selection is a process hugely enjoyed by the selectorate, who regard it as a just reward for so many years of canvassing on wet nights and addressing envelopes. There is no reason at all to suppose that the Brighton executive, predominantly lower-middle-class, among them insurance agents, housewives, salesmen, small business men, retired people, relish it any less than their fellows in, say, Leicester or Gorton or Hamilton who the very next evening were to experience the other end of the process.

The fact of the wives speaking added a new dimension. It is more usual for wives to be vetted discreetly, over sherry or tea. Whatever their participation did for the audience, it caused resentment among the finalists: 'An impertinence,' said one, 'but I suppose the whole thing was an impertinence.'

Mr Bates spoke first. He attacked all the others as 'one-time losers', hawking themselves from constituency to constituency. This did not go down well. He got five votes and was eliminated. Next came Mr Gardner, a Q.C. and the former Member for Billericay, but even so he only got six.

Third was Julian Amery. His speech was the performance of the evening. Alone among the contenders he had held office: 'You need someone as an M.P. who knows his way around the corridors of power,' he told fifty pairs of waiting ears and eyes. 'I have done my country some service, in war as a guerrilla leader, in peace as a Secretary of State.' He mentioned Disraeli; he is one of the few select Tories under seventy who always do. Withdrawal East of Suez was 'to fail in our duty to our friends. We must recover our national honour—and with George Brown as our Foreign Secretary, our national dignity. I refuse to believe that our mission in the world has ended: our greatness lies ahead of us.'

His peroration—'the message of Disraeli, Joseph Chamberlain and Winston Spencer Churchill: patriotism and progress'—was rapturously received. He did not go on much about Brighton, apart from an opening reference to 'its Regency tradition, grave and gay . . .', or even mention his plans for nursing the constituency. Some of the others did, but he pitched his speech on a different plane altogether. He got twenty-three votes.

Dudley Smith, ex-M.P. for Brentford and Chiswick, who followed him, had all along been regarded as his principal challenger. He concentrated on Brighton—he has the reputation of being a first-class constituency member—and answered questions calling for a stronger line with the trade unions and stricter control of immigration. His efforts won him nine votes.

John Lovill was last in. He spoke on economic affairs, but as a former local Young Conservative Chairman gave most of his time to local problems. As the 'favourite son' of (evidently) only a few, he got seven votes. His best point may well have been his call for closer co-operation with local business: the Treasurer is a local hotelier, but all the other officers work outside Brighton, so that the executive does not really represent the town's employers. He may also have suffered, as local aspirants frequently do anywhere, from being too well-known.

Among the wives Mrs Amery, by general consent, made one of the two best speeches and the best personal impression. Her taste alone had led her to see the occasion as not one for dressing up, and she appeared before her audience in a simple pink buttoned dress with knitted roll-neck collar and sleeves, and a single brooch by the right shoulder.

Mr Bates was eliminated, and there was a second ballot: Amery 27, Smith 10, Lovill 8, Gardner 5. Mr Amery's name was then put to the meeting and received general support. He was in.

Why was he chosen?

'He has put Brighton back on the map,' said one of the fifty afterwards. Another said: 'We were fed up with the standard pattern'— the Identikit Tory candidate, middle-class, middle-thirties, middle-minded (i.e., reflecting whatever Central Office opinions are current), married with two children, who has lately been winning all the seats.

Was his victory inevitable? Probably. Mr Amery, at forty-eight, was the most senior and best-known candidate. He enjoyed the support of Sir William Teeling, the sympathy of the Chairman and the good wishes of many of the more influential local Tories. Sir William's part is interesting: while his influence at Brighton is certainly greater than at Westminster, his advocacy of Mr Amery's candidature was not, of itself, so important. The invitation to the Winter Ball was more significant. From then on, Julian Amery took his chances as they came.

There may also have been an element of desire for reflected glory. A former minister is a possible future one, and 'Amery knows everybody', as one of the executive put it on Wednesday night, somehow aware that the next candidate had come to them straight from having drinks with King Hussein of Jordan.

And, of course, and not unreasonably, there is politics in its broadest sense. Amery's speech gave voice to the anxiety of his unsophisticated fundamentalist audience over the state of Britain and also offered some temporary comfort. It was all 'splendid stuff' and typical of the causes that the one-time Suez rebel has espoused. It is not simply that the Brighton Tories are 'right-wing', rather that Amery and Brighton Pavilion are compatible. As one of the defeated contenders put it, 'They deserve each other.' Whether or not that is true, there are lessons to be learned from a close look at the workings among the grass-roots of Sussex.

[Postscript

Following the resignation of Sir William Teeling, at a by-election on 27 March 1969 Julian Amery retained the seat for the Conservatives, with a majority of 12,982, and returned to the House of Commons. At the 1970 General Election he retained the seat with a slightly reduced majority (10,594).]

The selection of party leaders

Party	Leader	Method
Conservative	*Edward Heath* July 1965	First under new procedures—a ballot of party in Commons, supervised by 1922 Committee Chairman. Three candidates (Heath, Maudling and Powell). On first ballot Heath had overall majority but not 15 per cent more than second candidate, Maudling, as required. No second ballot as other two withdrew. Heath chosen and duly approved by the Party Meeting (Conservative M.P.s, Peers, prospective candidates and National Union Executive Committee members).
Labour	*Harold Wilson* February 1964	Ballot of P.L.P. Three candidates (Brown, Callaghan and Wilson). Wilson ahead on first ballot, but not an absolute majority. Callaghan dropped out as required, and Wilson won on second ballot a week later. Procedure for election of Leader while in office allows as many ballots of P.L.P. as necessary in a day.
Liberal	*Jeremy Thorpe* January 1967	Ballot of Liberal M.P.s. Three candidates (Hooson, Lubbock and Thorpe). Lord Wade in charge of election and alternative vote system used. On first ballot Thorpe 6 votes, others 3 each. Others withdrew and Thorpe elected unanimously.
S.N.P.	*Tom Wolfe* May 1969	Chosen by simple majority vote of annual conference.

Party	Leader	Method
Ulster Unionist	James Chichester-Clark April 1969	Chosen by ballot of Ulster Unionist M.P.s at Stormont. Two candidates—Chichester-Clark 17 votes, Faulkner 16. Motion carried to make vote for Chichester-Clark unanimous. Decision endorsed by standing committee of Ulster Unionist Council.

The selection of parliamentary candidates— formal procedures

Procedures for selecting Labour, Liberal and S.N.P. candidates are contained in the party Constitutions (see Appendices—the Labour Party in Clause IX, the Liberal Party in Section H, and the S.N.P. in Part 2, Section 17). The model rules of the Conservative and Ulster Unionist parties contain sections setting out recommended procedures for selecting both parliamentary and local government candidates, and are reproduced below.

Conservative Party

Selection of candidates

21. (1) *Parliamentary candidates*
    (a) Whenever it may be necessary to select a parliamentary candidate to contest the constituency in the interests of the Party, the executive council shall appoint a selection committee which shall interview possible candidates and recommend those whom it may approve to the executive council. The selection committee shall act in consultation with the Standing Advisory Committee on Candidates of the National Union of Conservative and Unionist Associations, and shall not recommend for adoption any candidate who has not obtained the approval of the Standing Advisory Committee.
    (b) In the event of a by-election, the finance and general purposes committee shall act as the selection committee unless a selection committee has already been appointed.
    (c) Any person recommended as a prospective candidate by the executive council must be presented to a general meeting of the Association for adoption.

    (2) *Local government candidates*
    (a) Whenever it may be necessary to select for support a local government candidate for a ward or electoral division, the branch committee concerned shall recommend a candidate to the executive council and if he (or she) is approved by the executive council shall present him (or her) to a general meeting of the branch for adoption.
    (b) If the local government area extends beyond the area of a branch the foregoing procedure shall be carried out by the branches concerned, acting jointly.

Ulster Unionist Party

Selection of candidates

12. (*a*) *Imperial Parliament:*

Each Divisional Association at its Annual Meeting shall elect to the Central Selection Committee one delegate for each 500 electors, or part thereof, on the Electoral Register for the purpose of acting in conjunction with the delegates from each of the other Associations of . . . Belfast Division regarding the selection of a candidate for the Imperial Parliament, such delegates to include representatives of the Women's Unionist Associations and the Young Unionist Associations.

(*b*) *Northern Ireland Parliament:*

The Selection Committee for the Northern Ireland Parliament shall consist of the Members of the Executive Committee.

(*c*) *Local Government:*

The Selection Committee for Local Government shall be formed from the Officers of the Association and the six delegates from each Polling District within the Boundary of the Ward or area of representation, together with representatives of the Women's Unionist Association and the Young Unionist Association as agreed between the Associations concerned.

(*d*) The Proposer of any name must have the full authority in writing from such person before submitting that name. All intending candidates must sign an undertaking agreeing to abide by the decision of the Selection Committee and to support loyally the candidate finally selected. Selection of candidates must be confirmed at a General Meeting of the members of the Association. In the event of the Meeting not confirming the selection of a candidate, the Chairman shall not have power to receive any further nominations, but shall refer the matter back to the Committee.

(*e*) Members may be required to present their Membership Card or other proof of membership before admission to any meeting.

5 Parties in Parliament

Introduction

Political parties in Britain have as a primary objective the gaining of legislative representation in order to have some direct influence on political debate and an indirect influence on governmental decision-making. Consequently, elections apart, the most visible aspects of political-party activity and competition are found in their functioning in Parliament, be it Stormont or Westminster. Parliamentary debates are reported extensively by the mass media, the behaviour of parties in the legislative arena is open to considerable public scrutiny, and public assessment of parties in Parliament may have a significant effect on electoral fortunes.

Overshadowing all aspects of major party activity in the House of Commons is the influence of party discipline as exercised by the Leaders of the Conservative and Labour parties on their parliamentary colleagues. Much academic study of parliamentary-party activity has centred on the effects of this discipline, and has revealed that it is a complex as well as a ritualistic process.[1] Hugh Berrington explores the historical complexities of party cohesion, and Anthony King demonstrates that rebellion can take distinctive forms in a party with a tradition of avoiding public disagreements.

There are, however, other aspects of party activity in Parliament which are significant. Unity is an essential prerequisite for the success of a political party, yet internal stresses within a party in Parliament may often be severe. Therefore, while the need for cohesion requires the creation of disciplinary procedures, efforts must also be made to allow M.P.s to exercise their traditional responsibilities. Thus there are important procedures which allow M.P.s to become informed, to express opinions, and to ventilate opinions in order to perform what many observers believe to be the major function of the House of Commons, the legitimization of the work of government, or in Samuel Beer's phrase, the 'mobilization of consent'.[2] This is done both by Parliament and by the parties, through arrangements for the presentation of Private Members Bills, the formal questioning of members of the government, and the establishment of party committees and committees of the House of Commons. Backbenchers can and do play important roles in the work of the P.L.P. and the 1922 Committee respectively, and on party committees, the range of which is shown in the material explaining the organization of the P.L.P. Such party committees are informal in nature and designed as much to put backbench pressure on the party leadership as determining parliamentary party policy. They can, however, have an important effect on the pattern of parliamentary debate and are major channels of group influence by backbench M.P.s within their parties. The 1922 Committee is essentially a political discussion group, where no votes are taken or resolutions prepared, and Conservative backbench committees are likely to be more influential when the party is in opposition. The P.L.P. has a more important formal role in the determination of party policy, especially when the Labour Party is in opposition, and its Code of Conduct is also intended as a support to the Whips in maintaining party discipline. When a party is in control of government, Cabinet members and even the Prime Minister may sometimes feel the need to attend backbench party meetings either to debate or to present arguments justifying a particular line of policy.

Representation in Parliament for the Liberal Party, the S.N.P. or Plaid Cymru is important, and it involves the playing of a different type of role by such M.P.s. Useful work can be done on Commons committees, questioning members of the government, and exploiting the limited opportunity to present a Private Members' Bill, but the main concern is to ventilate particular policies and points of view which are distinctive to the parties concerned or appear to be ignored by the two major parties. This aspect of party activity and its significance in terms of policy innovations is discussed in a later chapter.

It is important to all parties that their activities in Parliament appear consistent with the expectations of those who give them electoral support. In practice the parties, and especially their leaders, have a good deal of freedom to determine for themselves how they will act in Parliament, and this can lead to debate and disagreements within parties, especially by cohesive groups.[3] Such disagreements can lead to individuals or groups of M.P.s abstaining from voting on particular issues, or even voting against their own party in Parliament, with the party having to decide whether or not to take disciplinary action. As Richard Rose has suggested: 'The surface cohesion of British parties reflects an equilibrium between forces pulling in different directions, not a unity obtained by a single, united thrust',[4] and this fact is no more evident than in study of the elected members of political parties in Parliament.

Notes

1 See especially R. J. Jackson, *Rebels and Whips*, London, 1968.
2 See S. Beer, 'The British Legislature and the Problem of Mobilising Consent', in B. Crick, ed., *Essays on Reform, 1967: A Centenary Tribute*, London, 1967, pp. 81–100.
3 See the case-study of the Campaign for Democratic Socialism, in Lord Windlesham, *Communications and Political Power*, London, 1966, pp. 81–150.
4 R. Rose, ed., *Studies in British Politics*, London, 1966, p. 328.

Further reading

There has been a good deal written on aspects of party cohesion and discipline in Parliament, as the titles of many of the articles recommended below indicate. R. J. Jackson, *Rebels and Whips*, London, 1968, provides both a comprehensive analysis and bibliography on all aspects of this question, while an excellent case-study of the impact of a policy issue on party cohesion is L. Epstein, *British Politics in the Suez Crisis*, London, 1964, and for analysis of the implications of individual rebellion against party and constituency, see N. Nicolson, *People and Parliament*, London, 1958. For detailed studies of Private Members' Bills and Question Time respectively, see P. Bromhead, *Private Members' Bills in the British Parliament*, London, 1956, and D. N. Chester and N. Bowring, *Questions in Parliament*, Oxford, 1962. For general discussion of the impact of parties on individual M.P.s, see P. G. Richards, *Honourable Members: A Study of the British Backbencher*, London, 1959, and the work of party committees in a particular policy area, see P. G. Richards, *Parliament and Foreign Affairs*, London, 1967, especially pp. 133–7. For an analysis of the make-up and opinions of backbenchers, see S. E. Finer *et al.*, *Backbench Opinion in the House of Commons 1955–9*, London, 1961, and their relations with the party, see R. K. Alderman and J. A. Cross, *The Tactics of Resignation*, London, 1967. See also H. Mitchell and P. Birt, *Who Does What in Parliament*, London, 1971.

Articles

R. K. Alderman, 'Discipline in the PLP, 1945–51', *Parliamentary Affairs*, 1965, pp. 293–305.
'Parliamentary Party Discipline in Opposition: The PLP 1951–64', *Parliamentary Affairs*, 1968, pp. 124–36.
'The Conscience Clause of the Parliamentary Labour Party', *Parliamentary Affairs*, 1966, pp. 224–32.
H. B. Berrington, 'The Conservative Party: Revolts and Pressures, 1955–61', *Political Quarterly*, 1961, pp. 363–73.
J. M. Burns, 'The Parliamentary Labour Party in Great Britain', *American Political Science Review*, 1950, pp. 855–71.
J. B. Christoph, 'Capital Punishment and British Party Responsibility', *Political Science Quarterly*, 1962, pp. 19–35.

J. A. Cross, 'Withdrawal of the Conservative Party Whip', *Parliamentary Affairs*, 1968, pp. 166–75.

R. H. S. Crossman, 'Reflections on Party Loyalty', *New Statesman*, 2 April 1955, pp. 200–1.

R. E. Dowse, 'The Parliamentary Labour Party in Opposition', *Parliamentary Affairs*, 1960, pp. 520–9.

and T. Smith, 'Party Discipline in the House of Commons—A Comment', *Parliamentary Affairs*, 1963, pp. 159–64.

L. Epstein, 'Cohesion of British Parliamentary Parties', *American Political Science Review*, 1956, pp. 360–78.

'New MPs and the Politics of the PLP', *Political Studies*, 1962, pp. 121–9.

D. G. Hitchner, 'The Labour Government and the House of Commons', *Western Political Quarterly*, 1952, pp. 417–44.

R. Jenkins, 'Party Discipline in the House of Commons', *Listener*, 26 January 1956, pp. 127–8.

J. J. Lynskey, 'The Role of British Backbenchers in the Modification of Government Policy', *Western Political Quarterly*, 1970, pp. 333–47.

R. Miliband, 'Party Democracy and Parliamentary Government', *Political Studies*, 1958, pp. 170–4.

J. S. Rasmussen, 'Party Discipline in War-Time: The Downfall of the Chamberlain Government', *Journal of Politics*, 1970, pp. 379–406.

'The Relations of the Profumo Rebels with Their Local Parties', *Institute of Government Research, Comparative Government Studies I*, Tucson, Arizona, 1966.

'Government and Intra-Party Opposition: Dissent within the Conservative Parliamentary Party in the 1930's', *Political Studies*, 1971, pp. 172–183.

J. E. Schwarz and G. Lambert, 'Career Objectives, Group Feeling and Legislative Party Cohesion: The British Conservatives, 1959–68', *Journal of Politics*, 1971, pp. 399–421.

[The following definitions may be helpful to readers of the article by Hugh Berrington opposite: *Party votes*—votes cast by a party in a division in which more than nine-tenths of the party members taking part voted on the same side of the question. Divisions where more than nine-tenths of both main parties voted on the *same* side are excluded. *Non-party votes*—votes in which one-tenth or more of the party members taking part voted differently from the rest of their party.—Ed. note.]

Party discipline and cohesion in Parliament
Partisanship and dissidence in the nineteenth-century House of Commons*
by Hugh Berrington

It has become almost axiomatic amongst historians and commentators to decry the erosion of backbench independence. The emergence of a disciplined and automatic majority has, it is said, enabled the executive to ride roughshod over the protests of the Opposition, to impose its own policies on Parliament without effective challenge, and to ignore personal liberties and individual rights. For Richard Crossman, the independence of the private member made the Commons 'the most important check on the executive'. 'Party loyalty', he went on, 'has become the prime political virtue required of an M.P. and the test of that loyalty is his willingness to support the official leadership when he knows it to be wrong.'[1] Nevertheless, scrutiny of the issues which provoked backbench disaffection in the nineteenth century suggests that the romantic picture of crusading knights fighting for the rights of the legislature against executive tyranny is a crude if unwitting distortion. Most of the intra-party disputes took the form of sectional conflict—the continuing struggle within the Liberal Party, of radical and moderate; most of the revolts took the form of extremist rebellions against the dominant centre—not of 'moderate' challenges to an extreme and partisan executive. Moreover, the effect of centre-oriented revolts, both in the earlier and the later periods, was in most divisions to *strengthen* the government of the day and to weaken the opposition party. In all but two of the ten sessions which were studied the Opposition cast more crossbench non-party votes than the party in government.[2] Governments had occasion to hope for support from opposition dissidents more often than to fear defection from their own side. Of course, governments might occasionally suffer defeat at the hands of an alliance, often fortuitous, of some of their own supporters and the Opposition, or alternatively, from a more mixed coalition including the Irish. The more frequent result however, was to strengthen morally and often numerically the position of the government on the particular question.

Thus the consequences of backbench independence have been grossly exaggerated by some commentators. Governments were sometimes defeated on the floor of the House; set against the bald figures of non-party votes, the number of defeats is surprisingly small.[3] What of course gave strength to governments was that the attack so

* Reprinted by permission from *Parliamentary Affairs*, 1968, pp. 338–75, and comprising the concluding sections of the article, with footnotes abridged and appendices deleted.

often came from their own most extreme supporters. They could call in the Opposition to redress the balance. In the ten years from 1851 to 1860, when the House was at its most fragmented and which included nearly three years of minority government, a total of only forty-seven amendments to government legislation were carried against the government Whips.[4]

The surface fluidity of politics during the middle part of the nineteenth century concealed a basic stability—a stability which rested on a widespread consensus.

Backbench independence of the party Whip contributed little, at least in the latter part of the nineteenth century, to parliamentary control of the executive. The numerous revolts on the estimates provided an example, not of effective parliamentary review or of a salutary and systematic scrutiny of expenditure, but of attempts at arbitrary retrenchment and capricious economies. Assaults on estimates for new frescoes in the Science and Art Museum, or on appropriations for minor works in consular buildings were not the work of a legislature organized to examine, and to make significant criticisms, of Supply. Labouchere's guerrilla raids on the spending departments were not a substitute for a rational and coherent appraisal of the estimates.

Moreover, few of the crossbench revolts arose over 'redress of grievance' debates—classically, the kind of issue where the legislature had a special function to scrutinize and to control the executive. The record, even when extended to include extremist and bi-partisan revolts, would not be impressive. A Unionist revolt over the treatment of engineers at Coopers Hill College; demands for the recognition of the inventor of the postal order, for an annual allowance to the daughters of another inventor Sir William Palliser,* and hostility to a civil servant who had associated himself with Dr Barnardo—this selection hardly affords a resounding tribute to the independent backbencher.

In particular, we may note the large part played by territorial interests in the crossbench deviations from party rule. The agricultural interest and the Londoners amongst the Liberals in 1890; the dairy lobby in 1899 and the graziers in 1903—these examples show that the material claims of the constituency, were often more urgent than the promptings of conscience.

The growth of party conformity: a re-assessment

The most widely accepted explanation of the rise of disciplined parties is to be found in the pages of Ostrogorski; the extension of the

* See *House of Commons Division List No. 90*, 1890.

franchise, and the redistribution of constituencies, destroyed the friendly and personal relationship which had hitherto existed between candidate and voter. The Caucus, which developed to organize the new, large and ill-educated electorate, demanded total and unthinking submission from the member, a demand made vicariously, on behalf of the party leaders, who were bound to the Caucus by tacit understandings of mutual obligation.

> The election over, the Members returned, once more it is the party orthodoxy, according to the daily market quotation certified by the Caucus, which is set up as the criterion of the parliamentary conduct of the Member. . . . Unable to use his discretion freely, and prevented from seeking his political line of conduct in his own knowledge and conscience, the Member ceases to be a representative, and becomes a delegate, a subordinate.[5]

> Now under the Caucus, and thanks to it, in both parties refractory Members are called upon by their respective Associations to fall in behind the leader and they must comply if they want to be re-elected. Thus in the intimate relations between the parliamentary chief and his followers, there has been imported from outside a regular intimidation agency, which makes the Members, for the nonce, simple puppets on the parliamentary stage.[6]

Ostrogorski's analysis has been uncritically accepted by many later commentators, but a re-examination is now due. One implicit assumption, to be found in both Ostrogorski and Crossman, is the identification of *moderation* with *independence*. The Caucus drove out the moderates, on either side, whose occasional deviation from their party had given the House a corporate identity and a degree of independence from the executive. Moderation was replaced by a mechanical partisanship, and independence by undeviating conformity.

Yet it is wrong to equate the two. On the Liberal side, the independent was much more likely to be located on the extreme wing of the party than in the centre. This was true both before and after the split of 1886, both before and after the emergence of the Caucus. Certainly, the Liberal right wing in 1883, and probably in 1881, gave little trouble to the government Whips. It was the radicals who, in division after division, voted against the government.

In the early eighties, it was the Liberal leadership, and their more obedient supporters, who stood for 'moderation', and the perennial independents who constituted the extremist section of the party. *In 1883, the leadership of the two parties was on the same side in 46 per cent of the 'Whip' divisions.* It was not the independents, but the official Liberals, who supplied the moderating element in the Parlia-

115

ment of 1880–5. Government in the early eighties was almost as much 'government by the centre' as it was 'party government'. There was no call for fair-minded and moderate backbenchers to temper partisan tyranny. The Cabinet itself reflected the undogmatic mood of the House. Even its Irish policy was a compromise, its land measures satisfying the radical wing of the Liberal Party, and its resort to coercion satisfying the Conservative Opposition and the Whig section of its supporters. The Cabinet still contained, in the chief ministries, representatives of Whig aristocracy; however uneasy they might be, they served to restrain the government from radical adventures.

Government in the early eighties bears some resemblance to the situation twenty years before when the Palmerston government, dependent on Whig and *radical* support for office, relied on Whig and *Conservative* support for the passage (or to prevent the passage) of legislation. In the sixties there was a definite if secret understanding between Derby and Palmerston;[7] in the eighties, Front Bench co-operation took a less well-defined, but none the less significant form. There were repeated complaints, from the radicals in 1883, and some even in 1890, of a conspiracy between the leadership of the two parties.[8]

Sometimes this tacit agreement between the two Front Benches became formalized. Thus, in 1882, when the government incurred trouble from radical backbenchers who were hostile to the attack on Egypt, the Liberal Whips appealed to the Conservatives for support. 'Our Party,' wrote Walter Long, 'was divided from various internal causes and it was a fact known to all that we were not in a position to turn the Government out. The only course open to us was to support them against the more extreme Members of their own party. To do this we divided ourselves into "watches" and undertook to support the Government when they were in difficulties.'[9]

There were several reasons for the dominance of the centre in 1883. The moderate Whig elements, men of inherited beliefs and traditional rivalries, still comprised an influential section of the Liberal Party. The electoral regime restricted the growth of the radical wing. In the counties where the franchise was still based upon a relatively high property qualification, and in the small rural boroughs where personal influence still counted for much, the conservative elements of the Liberal Party held sway. The policy of the Gladstone government had to be framed so as not to disturb the loyalty of the right-wing Liberals. Moreover, we see in 1883 the familiar tendency for party leaders and followers to diverge, under the responsibility of office. Their backbench followers, untroubled by administrative needs, or the pressure of harsh political fact, could still declaim the slogans they had voiced in opposition. For men in office, principles declared a few years before had to be bent and pared to fit the exigencies of government. Denunciations of jingoism had had to be inhibited when the needs of the situation, as perceived by the government, forced them to intervene abroad. Calls for economy seemed less urgent, when confronted by the needs of the departments.

Finally, we must note the crucial significance of parliamentary procedure. The closure reforms of 1882, and the earlier changes in procedure, still allowed immense opportunities for obstruction, or even for the legitimate prolongation of debate.[10] Governments could not be sure of the amount of time that would be available for their business, or precisely at what time or even on what day their business would be reached. This was one ostensible reason for framing the chief measures of the year, the Corrupt Practices Bill and the Agricultural Holdings Bills, so as to soothe Conservative sensitivity. The government could have avoided the criticisms of its radical followers by introducing legislation of a more drastic kind. But, apart from the risks posed by the possibilities of Whig secession, bills of such a kind might not have passed through the House in the time available. The deficiencies of parliamentary procedure obliged governments to bring in relatively non-contentious bills and reinforced their own leanings towards moderation. It was the procedural changes, and the time-table reforms of 1902, which enabled governments to introduce highly controversial legislation, and so satisfy the appetites of their more extreme supporters.[11] It was not so much that partisan governments used the techniques of party discipline to capture control of the timetable of the House. It was rather that governmental control of the timetable facilitated the growth of party unity.

On the Liberal side, the Caucus, so far from being a 'regular intimidation agency' acting on behalf of the parliamentary leaders, was more likely to applaud those Members who defied the Whips and stood firmly for their radical principles. The Liberal Caucus, at least in the early stages, made for more, not less, indiscipline.

In a more general sense, the spread of democracy served to reduce, rather than to increase, the unity of the Liberal Party. As Ostrogorski himself notes, the growing differentiation in society,[12] a differentiation given more accurate political expression through the Acts of 1867 and 1884–5, had its effect upon the composition of the parties. Welsh tenant-farmers, Scottish crofters, Metropolitan collectivists, mining Lib. Labs., found their way to Parliament in substantial numbers. Parliamentary reform did not merely radicalize the Liberal Party, it also fractionalized it. The initial effects of the reforms were to enhance, not to diminish, the problems of the Liberal Whips. The undoubted rise in party voting in the last quarter of the nineteenth century cannot be ascribed simply to the growth of the Caucus, or the advent of mass democracy.

Nor too was the trend towards greater party unity as smooth and consistent as Lowell claimed. Between 1860 and 1871, the unity of the parties increased considerably but the fall in the number of extremist rebellions was bigger, relatively, than the drop in crossbench rebellions, suggesting that the majorities in the two parties had moved farther apart from each other—in short that there had been increasing polarization. The partisan policies of the first Gladstone government, embodied in a programme of far-reaching reforms, had, not surprisingly, separated the leadership of the two parties. By the early eighties the Liberal leadership had exhausted its élan, and the consensus between Whig and Radical had been severely strained. Between 1871 and 1883, the proportion of non-party votes changed little, but there was a change in the kind of dissidence; the number of extremist votes rose, especially on the Liberal side, whilst crossbench votes fell in both parties. The majorities of the two parties were coming closer together. Unable to satisfy radical appetites, Gladstone had to confront radical rebellion. The old Front Bench consensus re-appeared.

Thus it was not until the re-alignment of parties over Irish Home Rule, and the important procedural changes of the late eighties, that the movement towards greater party unity was resumed. These years saw the almost total disappearance of both crossbench and extremist revolts on the Conservative side; in the Liberal Party, centre-oriented deviations decreased still further from the low level of the eighties, and extremist deviation fell more slowly, and somewhat jerkily.

Concentration and competitiveness

Robert Dahl, writing in *Political Oppositions in Western Democracies*,[13] suggests six important ways in which oppositions can differ from one another. Two of his concepts, concentration or organizational cohesion, and competitiveness, are of special relevance to the changes which took place in the nineteenth-century House.

Concentration depends on the extent to which opposition displays organizational cohesion. In the modern British two-party system, public and visible opposition is largely, though not wholly, concentrated in *the Opposition*—the second largest party in the House of Commons; in contrast, in a country with a multi-party system, opposition is likely to be dispersed amongst several parties.

The *competitiveness* of opposition depends on the degree to which parties simultaneously belong to a winning coalition. If they never do so the parties can be said to be in a relation of perfect competitiveness. In so far as two or more parties do belong to a winning coalition, their relationship is not competitive, but *co-operative*. Competitiveness of opposition is, of course, connected with the degree of concentration.

It was not until 1894 that the two British parties could be said to be in a strictly competitive relationship. Previously, the leadership of the two parties had often formed part of a winning coalition. In 1883, this occurred in 46 per cent of the 'Whip' divisions. By 1890, this had fallen to 16 per cent, by 1894 to 13 per cent, and by 1903 to 8 per cent. In the non-competitive divisions the dominant pattern in 1883 was of an alliance of the Liberal and Conservative Front Benches against the radicals; to a lesser extent, the two Front Benches would be found in alliance against the diehard Right, or against a combination of backbenchers drawn from both parties. Between 1890 and 1899 the area of competitiveness increased; but amongst the non-competitive divisions the pattern was overwhelmingly of a Front Bench alliance against the radicals. The diehard Right simply went to sleep, and alliances between backbenchers of the two parties hardly ever took place.

In 1903, the area of competitiveness expanded again, but in this session the bi-partisan backbench alliance was the most conspicuous feature of the non-competitive divisions.

Growing concentration of opposition can also be discerned.[14] Table 1 shows the degree to which, session by session, the majorities of the two parties were on different sides in the divisions lobbies.

Table 1 Concentration and dispersion of opposition

Year	*Party vote cast by both parties*	*Non-party vote cast by one or both parties*	*Totals*
	%	%	%
1836	34	33	67
1850	18	42	60
1860	5	46	51
1871	38	38	76
1881	49	16	65
1883	35	20	55
1890	65	28	93
1894	84	5	89
1899	75	20	95
1903	86	6	92

Whip divisions in which majorities of the two parties were on different sides

Between 1860 and 1871 there was a sharp increase in the number of divisions in which majorities of the two parties voted on different sides; in the early eighties the proportion fell substantially, and in 1883 nearly reached the previous low level of 1860. The session of 1890 witnessed a marked increase; but it must be recalled that there were numerous divisions in which, though a majority of Liberals voting voted against a majority of Conservatives, the Liberal leaders either abstained or were to be found in the Conservative lobby. The same consideration holds good for 1899.

The distinctive feature of British opposition does not merely lie in its concentration within a particular party majority; it also lies in its concentration behind a particular team of leaders. As we have seen, these were by no means identical, especially in the later sessions. Table 2, therefore, shows the number of divisions in which the party leaders (or failing the presence of the party leaders, the majority of the party members voting) were to be found on different sides.

Table 2   Concentration and dispersion of opposition

	Whip divisions in which the leaders of the two parties (or in default of leaders voting majorities) were on different sides					
Year	Col. 1 Party votes cast by both parties	Col. 2 Non-party votes cast by one or both parties (other than Doubtful)	Col. 3 Total	Col. 4 Doubtful non-party votes	Col. 5 Grand total	Col. 6 No. of divisions
	%	%	%	%	%	
1883	35	12	47	7	54	191*
1890	65	7	72	12	84	208
1894	84	2	86	1	87	214
1899	74	6	80	4	84	312*
1903	86	4	90	2	92	225

* Three divisions were excluded from 1883 and 6 from 1899. In the three divisions in 1883 the Conservatives were evenly divided and no leader voted. In 1899, a Front Bencher voted with the Government in 5 divisions; an overwhelming majority of Liberals voted against the Government and all 5 divisions were party votes. In the remaining division the Liberals divided evenly, no leader voting.

Col. 3 shows the most significant figures, since it excludes those divisions in which non-party votes were cast on the opposition side and in which no opposition leader voted. The proportion of divisions in which the party leaders were on different sides rose dramatically between 1883 and 1890, and rose again, substantially, in 1894; interestingly enough, the percentage of these divisions fell only a little in 1899, despite widespread lamentations of a breakdown in the party system. Then in 1903 the figure reaches a new peak. Col. 1 shows the increase in the proportion of divisions where the leaders were on different sides and in which party votes were cast. Again, there was a marked change between 1883 and 1890, a less strong rise from 1890 to 1894, a modest drop in 1899, followed by a new high level in 1903. One reservation must be expressed about these figures. In some divisions, the Liberal Opposition cast a party, and often a unanimous, vote, despite the absence of all the party's leaders. Thus, the growing homogeneity of the Opposition reflects not merely a positive rallying of backbenchers around recognized leaders in the daily business of the House; to some extent it may reflect the growth of voluntary abstention by the leaders—an unwillingness, so to speak, to interfere with their backbenchers' fun. Whereas in 1890, Opposition leaders might have publicly dissented from their backbench followers, and gone into the government lobby, this rarely occurred in 1903. Back-benchers would challenge the government, on Supply, perhaps, or on the committee or report stages of Bills, without either the help or the disapproval of their leaders. It is interesting to note here that despite the procedural changes for Supply, passed in 1896, Supply debates remained very much a backbencher's occasion. The Opposition leaders rarely spoke in them and often failed to vote. Nevertheless, even this abstention of the leaders (and more generally of the party's right wing) represents a growing concentration of opposition.

Government and opposition

It is above all in the relationship between government and opposition that the mid-nineteenth-century Parliament differs so profoundly from the Parliament of our own day. Until the last decade of the nineteenth century, the relationship was asymmetrical. The obligation to initiate and to lead, which rested on government, was not par024paral-leled, to the same degree, by the duty of the official Opposition to criticize and to check. The government, as the body responsible for day-to-day administration, could not abdicate its duty to give a lead to the House on the issues which came before it. Often in declaring its position and putting on the Whips the government were acting, not as the leadership of a party, but as the heads of the executive departments. Party support was transformed into support for executive decisions often lying far outside the scope of normal party controversy, decisions which were tangential to the philosophies and interests of the two parties; to this extent, the government's backbench following was changed from a political party into an administrative party. Party connections made possible, not the enactment of a party programme, but the smooth implementation of executive policy. 'For the party the Cabinet were the necessary and irreplaceable men; for the Cabinet party was a lever to gain support for policies essentially administrative.'[15] This view of governmental initiative was, as we have seen, often shared by the Opposition, especially by its leaders. The government was, in one respect, simply an agency for introducing agreed policies, which should not on such matters, therefore, be opposed. 'It is a pity', said Mr W. A. M'Arthur, Liberal Member for Mid-Cornwall, speaking in support of the Western Australia Constitution Bill, 'that a question of Government and Opposition should be introduced at all into colonial questions, for all ought to be equally interested in the progress of the colonies.'[16] Such opposition as was voiced tended to come from the men on the extremes of either party—but especially from the radicals.

The government, therefore, was obliged to offer some cues to the House—cues which would normally mobilize most, if not all, of its own supporters and perhaps the leaders of the opposition party. But the Opposition in turn did not offer the same cues to its supporters. Since it had no responsibility for governing, it had no obligation to declare its opinions on the minutiae of legislation. It is not surprising that the Conservative Party should have divided so often under the regime of Stafford Northcote. Often, the leadership had no view, no line to enforce. The same was true of the Liberal Opposition in 1890. There was nearly always a government line, because the government fused two separate roles—that of party leadership and that of administrative leadership. The Opposition Front Bench had only one role to perform. The growth of party conformity in Parliament to a considerable degree represents a change in the nature of the Opposition. The government's official duty to propose was matched, in course of time, by the Opposition's official duty to criticize.

'Party government' and 'government by the Centre'

But what forces account for the rapid if somewhat uneven and unsymmetrical growth in party conformity in the last two decades of the century?

In the first place, it might be argued, the apparent disappearance of backbench dissidence is an artefact of simple technical changes in parliamentary procedure. The figures deal with voting on the floor of the House of Commons; procedural changes, such as the increasing reference of Bills to Standing Committees, and a growing tendency for the full House to confine itself to the weightier issues of government, might account for the diminution in non-party votes. The relatively minor questions, it might be said, that parties divided over in the early eighties, had been delegated to committees, or were now being ignored altogether.

It is true that, using Lowell's measures of party voting, there was much more dissidence within the parties on the Standing Committees than on the floor of the House. Such a finding is hardly surprising; the committees were likely to include those Members with an initial interest in the subject matter of the Bill under discussion, and hence a greater tendency to follow their own judgments. Moreover, Bills which were controversial in a party political sense were not likely to be referred to a Standing Committee. It is not easy to determine whether the business dealt with on the floor of the House in 1903 was more substantial than the matters so taken twenty years before. But if we take the formal stages of legislation as our criterion, it is clear that divisions on committee and report stages (counting only those where the government Whip was invoked) represented as big a share of the divisions in 1903 as in 1883. Divisions over estimates accounted for a substantially higher proportion of the divisions in 1903 than in 1883.

Table 3 *Divisions arising out of committee and report stages and the Estimates in House of Commons (divisions where government whip not applied are excluded)*

	Committee and report	Estimates
1883	49%	21%
1903	52%	28%

Procedural motions arising in connection with a clause, amendment or Supply vote have been included under the appropriate stage of legislation. Thus 'Committee and report' includes divisions on procedural motions arising out of the relevant debates. Divisions arising out of the amendment to the motion 'That the Speaker leave the Chair' going on into Supply have been excluded.

Moreover, the number of government Bills dealt with by the Standing Committees does not show any consistent increase during the sessions studied. Four were referred in 1883; three in 1894; six in 1899; and eight in 1903. It hardly seems plausible therefore to attribute the growing unity of the parliamentary parties to the increased importance of the issues coming before the full House.

It is also clear that the payment of M.P.s and the introduction of a class of members dependent on their parliamentary salary for a livelihood, which has long been regarded by nostalgic Whigs as subversive of the independence of the legislature, played little, if any part, in the diminution of parliamentary independence. The near monolithic solidarity of the Conservatives in the nineties, and of the Liberals during 1894, long preceded the payment of members from official funds. A private income cannot confer independence upon those who neither can, nor care to, display it, nor does it protect men from the temptations of office, or the allurements of 'honours'.

Then there is the view that it was the emergence of the Labour Party which transformed Parliament from being a body with a life and will of its own, to a machine which registered the decisions of government. 'It was not until the rise of working class parties,' writes Mr Crossman, 'based on trades unions and disciplined according to their canons of working class solidarity that the "iron law of increasing oligarchy" completed the transformation of the system. . . . The emergence of Labour as the alternative government had an important effect on its opponents. The Conservative Party was compelled in certain respects to copy it. Gradually it was transformed . . . into a modern carefully disciplined mass party.'[17] Leaving aside Mr Crossman's extraordinary assertion that the Labour Party's avowed aim was social revolution, his interpretation can be dismissed by a glance at the timing of these changes. The Conservative Party was more united, judging by the proportion of non-party votes, in 1890 than the Labour Party was, according to Beer's samples of divisions, in either 1906 or 1908. This unity was actually stronger in 1894 and 1899 than it had been in 1890. Moreover, even in the period 1924–8, the Conservatives cast almost as many party votes as Labour. The evidence indicates that the unity of British parties was forged, not in the furnace of the class war, but in the heat of the age-old struggles of nationality and religion.

Table 4   Party votes in the House of Commons

Year	All divisions Conservative	Labour
	%	%
1890	88	
1894	92	
1899	91	
1906 (sample)	80	80
1908 (sample)	79	87
1924–28 (average)	97 (96·6)	97 (97·3)

The figures for 1906 and 1908 are taken from S. H. Beer's *Modern British Politics* (London, 1965), pp. 122–3. The figures for 1924–8 were calculated by Russell Jones in his thesis, 'Party Voting in the English House of Commons', and were made available to me in a private communication from Professor Beer.

A further explanation lays stress on the growing complexity and technicality of legislation. Men who are unable to make up their minds, on the evidence before them, not unnaturally accept the advice of their leaders. No strain is imposed on their consciences, because on most questions their consciences have nothing to say, whether or not they attend the debate. In recent times this view has been advanced by Nigel Nicolson[18] but it was voiced in the 1890s by W. E. H. Lecky who himself served as a Unionist M.P. 'Crowds of measures,' wrote Lecky, 'of a highly complex and technical character are brought before him [the M.P.] at very short notice. A member of Parliament will soon find that he must select a class of subjects which he can himself master, while on many others he must vote blindly with his party.'[19] Again in 1912 Dr Robert Farquharson, who had for many years represented Aberdeenshire as a Liberal, expressed similar sentiments.

But then you must puzzle your brains over incomprehensible bills and tedious blue-books . . . but confused by contradictory statements and plausible arguments and subtle word-spinning, you get more and more mentally fogged, and at last you give up the attempt at full comprehension in despair, and simply follow your leaders with sheeplike docility at the advice of the Whips.[20]

Complaints that the votes were swayed by members who had not heard a word of the debate, and came in when the division was called, were expressed in the eighties and the nineties.[21] Certainly, the issues which occupied most of the time of the House in 1883 were not remote from the average member's experiences and prejudices. Few M.P.s could have found the Corrupt Practices Bill, and the amendments offered to it, too abstruse for personal judgment; the Agricultural Holdings Bills engaged both the material interests of a large section of the House, and the inherited animosities of the urban radicals. It is not easy to determine, however, whether a change in the nature of the issues after 1883 explains the pronounced fall in backbench dissidence. In any case, the argument assumes a dual process. Increasing technicality meant members could no longer advert to their own judgment or experience; the resulting vacuum was filled by party. We still have to explain why the vacuum was filled by party allegiance, and not by sectional affiliation, or pressure-group membership.

A definitive answer to this whole problem must await research on a number of related questions. We know extraordinarily little about the transformation of the House of Commons between the passing of the Second Reform Act and the outbreak of the First World War. Little

125

has been written about the changing role of 'the Opposition' in the House of Commons. No one has yet traced for example the way in which the organized opposition assumed the initiative in the criticism and scrutiny of executive actions. No one has yet delineated the interplay between procedural changes, and changes in the activities of the organized parties. Limitations on the initiative of the backbencher as embodied in say the closure or the guillotine, and later the kangaroo must have been reflected in greater party cohesion in the division lobbies.

Clearly there can be no single, simple answer to this problem. The growth of party conformity was part of a series of related tendencies —the reform of procedure, the growth in the functions of government, the drastic changes in the suffrage and the distribution of seats.

The major cause of the increasing strength of party ties lay in a basic change in the relationship between three elements in the nineteenth-century House—the government, the majority party and the opposition. Until 1886, the relationship between the government and its party followers, and the government and the opposition, were ambivalent. Governments depended on the support of their party to stay in office; to pass legislation or repel criticism, they shifted alternately from the support of the opposition to the support of their own party. 'Party Liberalism—the popular slogans for which the executive had reluctantly to act as impresario—it did not believe. . .' 'The Cabinet,' wrote John Vincent, 'were not so much opposed to Reform, National Education, the Ballot, Church Rate Abolition, and all the other panaceas of party politics, as unable to see such matters as bearing on Imperial government till they became irresistible.'[22] The increase in the radical contingent in the Liberal Party, which followed the Reform Act of 1867, made more acute the cleavage between the party interest and the administrative interest. The crisis of 1886 resolved this dilemma.

The great split in the parties over Irish Home Rule accelerated the effects of widespread popular enfranchisement. It no longer became possible for ministers to rely on the support of the opposition leaders to carry through government legislation. Ireland became a great wedge, splitting the tacit Front Bench coalition asunder. 'We are in a state of bloodless civil war,' said Salisbury to his Cabinet colleague W. H. Smith.[23] Party leaders were compelled to find a new basis for legislative support—and they found this in their backbench followers.

These followers, too, wanted from their side of the bargain, some influence on policy. The Unionist attack on the Liberal government of 1892-5 introduced a new element into British political life—a systematic, united and prolonged attack over the whole range of government policy. The Liberal government could neither seek support from the Opposition nor risk alienating its followers. The events of 1886 forged a new identity between the leaders and the led.

Since the early part of the nineteenth century, British government has been subject to a continuing tension between the claims of national leadership and administrative feasibility on the one hand, and party on the other. A minister always occupies a dual role; as a party leader he shares, and must be responsive to, the special demands of his party; but as a minister, confronted by the need for workable solutions to immediate problems, surrounded and advised by men who do not share his special party stance, he finds himself drawn to decisions which owe little to his party creed. In the mid-nineteenth century this tendency to take a national or administrative view of problems was increased by the consensus amongst the politically dominant classes. Thus, governments of both parties repeatedly found themselves pursuing crossbench policies—those that represented the highest common denominator of agreement—amongst the politically influential groups. The centre orientation of these policies was reflected in the high level of agreement between the party leaders in the House of Commons.

The events of 1886 shattered this unity; manifestly, Mr Gladstone's Irish policy broke the ruling class consensus. Governments found themselves unable to rely on opposition support for their decisions; inevitably they were obliged to find this support amongst their backbench followers. The radical, or the Tory diehard, became a loyal conformist in the division lobbies because his leaders were now pressing his demands for legislative change, or voicing his feelings in defence of established institutions.

Yet the change has been one of form, rather than substance. The problem remains; how can a government, at one and the same time, be true to its own party and to the realities of the situation as it sees them? Nevertheless this tension between the claims of party, and the national good, as Ministers tend to see it, was probably less acute in the period between the Home Rule split of 1886, and the First World War, than in the fifty years before and the fifty years since this period. Many of the characteristic radical demands were *symbolic*; disestablishment of the Welsh Church, reform of the House of Lords, the abolition of plural voting, did not run counter to awkward realities. Such measures were always administratively realistic; they raised no difficult problems of economic feasibility although in some fields, particularly those of defence and foreign policy, radicalism did come into serious friction with the claims of the 'national interest'. It was the ruling-class consensus, as much as the inexorable pressures of 'the possible', which prevented the fulfilment of radical demands of a symbolic kind before 1886. In the collectivist politics which

127

emerged after 1918, it was the horrid face of economic reality, as well as fear of alienating moderate support at the polls, which enhanced the inherent tension between partisanship and government office.

Disraeli once claimed to have educated his party; the Liberal Party could claim to have educated its leaders. The radical (as distinct from the collectivist) policies of the Liberal governments after 1906 were the delayed result of the radicalization of the party which took place after the Whig secession of 1886. Liberal M.P.s ceased to vote against their leaders, because their leaders identified themselves with their causes. Conservative M.P.s showed even greater fidelity because party loyalty was the only barrier to radical political change.

Conventional interpretations of nineteenth-century parliaments lay stress on the moderation of the backbenchers. Leaders were inhibited from pursuing partisan policies by the existence of a numerous class of centre-minded M.P.s, able and willing to vote, on occasion, with the opposition party. 'What he (Bagehot) liked most about Parliament,' wrote Richard Crossman, 'was the existence of a solid centre, composed of the majority of solid, sensible, independent M.P.s, collectively able to make and unmake ministers, to defy when necessary their own whips, and above all, to frustrate the growth of "constituency government" outside.'[24] What Mr Crossman forgets is that Bagehot went on to emphasize the moderation, not only of members, but of party leaders.

Of all modes of enforcing moderation on a party the best is to contrive that the members of that party shall be intrinsically moderate, careful and almost shrinking men; and the next best to contrive that the leaders of the party, who have protested most in its behalf, shall be placed in the closest contact with the real world. Our English system contains both contrivances; it makes party government permanent and possible in the sole way in which it can be so, by making it mild.[25]

It was the party leaders, perhaps more so than the backbenchers, who were the cornerstone of 'moderation' in the nineteenth-century House; and the apparent decline of 'independence' amongst private members represents more the transformation of the party leaders into the collaborators of their backbench followers than it does the regimentation of the backbencher in support of Front Bench measures.

Notes

1 R. H. Crossman, in Introduction to W. Bagehot, *The English Constitution*, London, 1963, p. 43.

2 Crossbench votes, in this context, are defined by reference to the behaviour of the majority of opposition members voting, for the years 1836–81, and by reference to the behaviour of opposition leaders for the period 1883–1903.

3 In his introduction to Bagehot's *The English Constitution*, Crossman states that divisions in which nine-tenths of government supporters obeyed the Whip formed only 16 per cent of the total in 1850 and sank to 6 per cent in 1860. He is wrong, his error being caused by a misunderstanding of the term 'True Party Division'. Moreover, he altogether overlooked the importance of the direction of dissidence, as well as its volume. Taking Lowell's figures at their face value it might have been expected that governments would have suffered many more defeats than they actually did.

4 A. L. Lowell, *The Government of England*, New York, 1920, Vol. I, Chapter 17.

5 M. I. Ostrogorski, *Democracy and the Organisation of Political Parties*, Vol. I, p. 606.

6 *Op. cit.*, p. 609.

7 G. E. Moneypenny and W. Buckle, *Life of Benjamin Disraeli, Earl of Beaconsfield*, Vol. II, 1860–81, pp. 27–8 and 112.

8 *Parl. Debs*, 1890, Vol. 346, c. 275 and 41; 1883, Vol. 281, c. 1739.

9 Lord Long of Wraxall, *Memories*, London, 1923, p. 83.

10 J. Redlich, *The Procedure of the House of Commons* (trans. by A. E. Steinthal), London, 1908, Vol. I, pp. 175ff., pp. 194ff.

11 *Ibid.*

12 Ostrogorski, *op. cit.*, p. 602.

13 R. A. Dahl, ed., *Political Oppositions in Western Democracies*, New Haven, 1966, Chapter 11.

14 It is true that if all three nineteenth-century parties are considered the Irish Nationalists tempered the concentration of opposition. As we are interested, however, in the evolution of the British parties it seems appropriate to exclude the Irish.

15 John Vincent, *The Formation of the Liberal Party, 1857–68*, London, 1966, p. 13.

16 *Parl. Debs*, 1890, Vol. 346, c. 406.

17 Crossman, *op. cit.*, pp. 40–2.

18 N. Nicolson, *People and Parliament*, London, 1958, p. 71.

19 W. E. H. Lecky, *The Map of Life*, London, 1899, p. 122.

20 R. Farquharson, *The House of Commons from Within*, London, 1912, p. 86.

21 See *Parl. Debs*, 1890, Vol. 342, c. 1085; 1890, Vol. 345, c. 620; 1883, Vol. 283, c. 14.

22 Vincent, *loc. cit.*

23 Sir H. Maxwell, *Life and Times of W. H. Smith*, Vol. II, p. 240.

24 Crossman, *op. cit.*, p. 46.

25 W. Bagehot, *The English Constitution*, pp. 160–1. See also Bagehot's article, 'Not a Middle Party but a Middle Government', *The Economist*, 17 January 1871.

The changing Tories*
by Anthony King

Amidst the Tory turmoil of the spring of 1968 perhaps the most significant incident has tended to be overlooked: the refusal of twenty-five Tory M.P.s to support the opposition's reasoned amendment to the Race Relations Bill—an amendment which condemned racial discrimination, accepted the need for measures to deal with it, and rejected the government's Bill only on 'on balance'. The twenty-five rebelled even though the sacking of Powell seemed to indicate that the party's leaders were not motivated by racism. The rebellion raises two questions. First, is there now, in some meaningful sense, a 'left wing' in the Conservative Party? Second, are Tories who dissent from official policy becoming readier than they were in the past to demonstrate their disagreement publicly?

The twenty-five who abstained last week, apart from their act of insubordination, differ strikingly as a group from the general run of Conservative M.P.s. They are younger on the whole than their colleagues: whereas 54 per cent of all Conservative M.P.s are under fifty, of the abstainers 72 per cent are still forty-nine or younger. The abstainers are also better educated, 84 per cent having been to university compared with 67 per cent amongst the party in general. Far from representing some new grammar school generation, no less than eighteen of the twenty-five attended Oxford or Cambridge and 88 per cent public schools—considerably higher proportions than for the rest of the party.

Moreover, most of the rebels sit for a particular kind of constituency: suburban or rural, prosperous, in the main far from the areas most affected by immigration. Of the parliamentary party as a whole, 55 per cent represent seats in Greater London, East Anglia, and the south and west of England. Among the abstainers the figure is much higher: 76 per cent. The names of the rebels' constituencies tell the story: Surbiton, Guildford, Dorking, Bromley, Chelmsford, Maldon, Wanstead and Woodford, Westbury, Tavistock, Norfolk Central, Norfolk South. Only two abstainers came from the midlands, two from the north-west.

But these facts, however striking, would be unimportant were there not reason to believe that the rebels share views on policy matters extending somewhat beyond the immediate issue of racial discrimination. Evidence on this sort of point is hard to gather. Ideally, one would interview at some length a carefully chosen sample of Tory M.P.s. Alternatively, the pattern of Conservative signatures on

* This article was first published in *New Society*, 2 May 1968, the weekly review of the social sciences, 128 Long Acre, London WC2.

early day motions could be elicited; the analysis of such motions by S. E. Finer and his colleagues, *Backbench Opinion in the House of Commons 1955-9*, although out of date by now, remains much the most searching study ever published of parliamentary opinions.

There is, however, another source of evidence available, although a crude one: the divisions in the House of Commons on which Conservatives have been divided, some abstaining or voting against the leadership, others going their own way on free votes. If division lists and reports of abstentions are studied, it emerges that seventeen of the twenty-five have taken a 'left' position before. (Two of the twenty-five have been in the House only since by-elections late last year.)

The Tory left-wing rebels

	Capital punishment	Oil sanctions	Homosexual law	Immigration Act	Race relations
	Dec. 1964	Dec. 1965	Feb. 1966	Feb. 1968	April 1968
Sir Tufton Beamish	x	*	*	*	–
Paul Channon	*	–	*	x	*
Nigel Fisher	–	*	*	*	*
Ian Gilmour	*	–	*	*	*
Brian Harrison	*	–	–	*	*
Terence Higgins	*	*	–	*	–
John Hunt	x	*	*	*	*
Patrick Jenkin	*	*	*	–	–
Michael Jopling	*	*	–	–	*
Norman Miscampbell	*	*	*	x	*
Norman St John-Stevas	*	*	*	*	*
Sir George Sinclair	x	*	–	*	*
Dame Joan Vickers	*	–	–	*	*
Dennis Walters	*	–	*	–	*

* Voted or deliberately abstained in 'liberal' direction;
x Voted or deliberately abstained in 'illiberal' direction;
– Did not vote, cause of abstention or reason for pairing unknown.
Sources: Hansard, *The Times*.

The table sets out the record of a number of M.P.s on five issues since 1964. The five comprise most of the important occasions since the Conservatives left office when they have openly split in the House. Three of the votes were whipped; two were free votes. The M.P.s are those who abstained last week and also took a liberal stand on at least two other occasions. Three M.P.s who did not abstain on the

Race Relations Bill—Beamish, Higgins and Jenkin—are included because of their record otherwise. One of the three, Patrick Jenkin, is said to have considered rebelling despite being on the Opposition Front Bench.

The table not only indicates which Tory members have been consistently liberal; it also suggests that there is a substantial overlap between views on race and Rhodesia, on the one hand, and views on matters of conscience like capital punishment, on the other. The overlap does not amount to complete identity. Many who supported the abolition of capital punishment have taken a tough line on immigration and race; some liberals on racial questions opposed abolition. But that overlap is there all the time.

The pattern in the table is suggestive. Are we to infer from it that there now exists a Tory left wing? The answer is, almost certainly, no. In the first place, as Sam Brittan argues at length the terms 'right' and 'left' are too impoverished of meaning to be useful in making any but the crudest classifications. Was it right-wing or left-wing to advocate devaluation? If one maintains that tolls should be introduced to help pay for motorways, is one moving to left or right? The questions are as unhelpful as they are unanswerable.

More to the point, even if neat Right and Left labels could be attached to the opposing points of view on all major issues, few Conservatives would be found taking consistently Right or Left positions. The table somewhat obscures this point, because it deals with two types of issue—the Commonwealth and race, and reforms of conscience—on which attitudes do converge. Finer and his colleagues found a decade ago that right-wing views on Suez were linked, for instance, to right-wing views on penal reform.

But there, for the most part, the convergence ends. Many of the liberals on race supported Humphry Berkeley's Sexual Offences Bill, but so did Enoch Powell, Patrick Wall, Derek Walker-Smith, and Ronald Bell. Sir Harry Legge-Bourke, who abstained last week and also voted in favour of Rhodesian oil sanctions, was for long a vocal opponent of Britain's entry into Europe. More important, many of the M.P.s who emerge from the table as 'left-wingers' are left-wing in any generally recognized sense only on these kinds of issues. A number—notably Terence Higgins and Patrick Jenkin—hold views on economic and social policy which would commonly be regarded as well to the Right.

This criss-crossing pattern of cleavage inhibits the development of Tory factions analogous to those in the Labour Party. Allies on one issue either become enemies on the next, or else simply do not feel strongly enough on the next issue to want necessarily to work together.

No continuing habits of collaboration develop. Partly for this reason, groups of Conservative M.P.s do not label themselves and are not labelled by others. In a new situation there are no stable groupings which can be counted on to behave in predictable ways. As a former Tory M.P. put it a generation ago: 'In general we find it difficult to arrange our colleagues in neat categories ... We do not think in these terms.' The contrast with Labour is vivid. However, there is reason to think that—despite the absence of Conservative factions—the *style* of controversy amongst the Tories will come more and more to resemble Labour's.

The degree of Conservative unity in the past can be exaggerated. The Tories' Suez split, although something of an aberration, lasted long and cut deep. More recently, disputes have developed around the Common Market, resale price maintenance, Rhodesia and, not least, the leadership itself. Nevertheless, the Conservatives have traditionally tried hard to confine their differences within doors—to avoid the embarrassing public speech, the calculated leak to the press, the open split on the floor of the House. The Tory forum used typically the whispered conversation in the corridor, the private party meeting, even the private dinner party.

The explanation for this mannerly style of controversy lay partly in the absence of stable factions and partly in the fact that the Conservatives were not, by any reasonable measure, as deeply divided in the 1950s and early sixties as the Labour Party. But it also lay to a considerable degree in the social structure of conservatism in the House of Commons. As Jean Blondel, Samuel Beer and others have pointed out, the origins of most Tory M.P.s in the respectable middle and upper-middle classes meant that the Conservative ethos was suffused with the values of club and public school.

Equally important, the party's hierarchical values were supported by the existence of a palpable hierarchy. Not only were Conservative M.P.s of higher social status than Conservative workers and voter, but the party leadership was considerably more upper class than the rank and file of M.P.s. For example, in 1955 Sir Anthony Eden's cabinet consisted 55 per cent of old Etonians compared with 23 per cent in the party as a whole. Under Harold Macmillan the gap between leaders and followers showed, if anything, a tendency to widen.

In the last three years this gap has suddenly narrowed. It is not that Conservative M.P.s increasingly come from humble or, at any rate, lower-middle-class origins; on the contrary, the proportion of ex-public schoolboys on the Tory benches is now higher than under Macmillan (81 per cent to 72). Rather, it is that the leadership has ceased to be dominated so completely by the upper classes. Former Conservative ministers like Charles Hill and Reginald Bevins have told in their memoirs how isolated they felt as self-made, still relatively poor, newcomers amongst the men of wealth and secure social station predominant in the Eden, Macmillan and Home cabinets. They would feel isolated no longer—or at least not to anything like the same degree.

The main change has, of course, been the election of Heath. The fact that he was elected and did not emerge in the traditional way is in itself significant; the old leadership elements had already been deprived of one of their chief prerogatives. But more significant are the changes in Conservative style that have followed. The Conservative Party today is probably more egalitarian and less deferential in its internal relationships than at any time since the war.

The twenty-five who abstained are of the same generation as Heath; the status of their educational background is at least as high; they represent remarkably similar constituencies. Indeed, in many cases their social origins (seven of the twenty-five went to Eton) mark them out as Heath's superiors. It would be absurd to suggest that the social parity between the rebels and Heath's Front Bench in any sense caused last week's revolt. But in subtle ways the new egalitarianism within the party is facilitating greater outspokenness and a greater unwillingness simply to accept leads from above. Hierarchical values are disappearing with the hierarchy.

And there is another factor in play. Ever since Labour became a major political force, the Labour Party, like the Conservatives, has contained a substantial middle-class element. But, whereas most middle-class Tory M.P.s were businessmen, farmers and retired service officers, a high proportion of middle-class Socialists were teachers and journalists. In other words, Labour in the House of Commons had an 'intelligentsia', a component of men and women skilled in the manipulation of words and ideas, whereas the Tories did not. Hence in part the traditional Conservative suspicion of 'cleverness'.

But in the last few years the Conservatives have been acquiring an intelligentsia of their own. Their ideas may differ from those of their Labour opposite numbers, but their style and habits do not. Referring again to the twenty-five, one notices that Edward Boyle is a writer and publisher as well as an old Etonian; that Ian Gilmour's background is in journalism; that Michael Heseltine is a publisher; that David Howell was once Director of the Conservative Political Centre and has written widely on economic and political subjects; that the reputation of Norman St John-Stevas is based largely on his writings. The list could be extended. It seems highly probable that the intrusion of this element, too, will cause future Tory controversies to be better publicized and more fully articulated than in the past.

One imagines that these changes will develop slowly and, at least for the next few years, will not reach far. The habits of generations die hard. Perhaps more tantalizing is the question: will controversies amongst Tories come to be invested with the personal rancour that distinguishes Labour's struggles? In the past, the Conservatives have managed to combine deep political differences with remarkable personal amity. One wonders whether this tradition can survive current controversies, especially if race relations remains among them for long.

References

S. Beer, *Modern British Politics*, London, 1965.
J. Blondel, *Voters, Parties and Leaders*, Harmondsworth, 1963.
S. Brittan, *Left or Right: The Bogus Dilemma*, London, 1968.

Party organization and party liaison in Parliament: the organization of the Parliamentary Labour Party

Section reprinted from 'Parliamentary Report-Session 1967–8', in *Report of 67th Annual Conference of the Labour Party, Blackpool, 1968*, pp. 57–9, published by the Labour Party, Transport House, Smith Square, London, 1968.

Organization of the Parliamentary Labour Party

The Officers

The Rt Hon. Douglas Houghton was re-elected Chairman. On 2 November, 1967, it was announced that Mr W. W. Hamilton, Mr Edward Milne and Mrs Joyce Butler had been elected Vice-Chairmen.

The Liaison Committee

The Liaison Committee consisted of the Chairman, the Vice-Chairmen, the Leader of the House (Rt Hon. Fred Peart), the Deputy Leader of the House and Chief Whip (Rt Hon. John Silkin), the Rt Hon. Lord Campion representing the Labour Peers and the Secretary of the Parliamentary Labour Party (Mr Frank Barlow). The General Secretary of the Party (now Sir Leonard Williams) and later the Acting Secretary (Miss Sara Barker) have attended meetings of the Committee, thus enabling the Parliamentary Party to keep close contact with the National Executive of the Party.

Subject Groups and Chairman, etc.
Area Groups and Chairman

Group	Chairman	Vice-chairman
Agriculture, Fisheries and Food Group	C. Kenyon	B. Hazell
Arts, Cultural Activities, Leisure and Sports Group	Rt Hon. G. Strauss	John Parker A. Blenkinsop
Aviation Group	John Rankin	R. Howarth
Commonwealth and Colonies	T. Driberg	S. S. Allen
Communications Group	H. Jenkins	M. English G. Wallace
Defence and Services	Sir Geoffrey de Freitas	R. Edwards

Group	Chairman	Vice-chairman
Economic Affairs and Finance	J. Barnett	J. Dickens
Education	R. Mitchell	K. McNamara
Films Group	H. Jenkins	C. Johnson
		Lord Strabolgi
Foreign Affairs	Rt Hon. P. Noel-Baker	F. Allaun
Forestry	J. Parker	A. Manuel
Health Services	L. A. Pavitt	Dr S. Summerskill
Home Office	V. Yates	Paul Rose
Housing and Local Government	A. Blenkinsop	J. Silverman
Overseas Development	F. Judd	F. Hooley
Power and Steel Group	H. Neal	E. Wainwright
Public Works and Buildings	C. Johnson	
Science, Technology and Atomic Energy	E. Moonman	S. Orme
Social Security	H. Brown	
Transport	A. Manuel	Rt Hon. G. R. Strauss
Legal and Judicial	W. Wells	
Common Market and European Affairs Group	S. Silkin, Q.C.	W. Molloy
Consumer Protection	W. T. Williams, Q.C.	A. Gardner
Parliamentary Reform	D. Coe	M. English
Shipping and Ship-building	Rt Hon. E. Shinwell	S. Mahon

A new group, called Prices and Productivity Group, has been set up. Mr Ron Brown is its chairman.

East Anglia	G. Wallace	
East Midlands	H. Neal	Sir Barnett Janner
Home Counties	Albert Murray	R. C. Mitchell
Lancashire and Cheshire	Frank Allaun	Mrs Braddock
London and Middlesex	Joyce Butler	C. Johnson
Northern Group	J. Tinn	E. Milne
Scottish Group	P. Doig	G. Lawson
Welsh Group	J. Idwal Jones	D. Coleman
West Midlands	J. Horner	Mrs Renée Short

Group	Chairman	Vice-chairman
South Western	W. A. Wilkins	A. Palmer
Yorkshire Group	D. Griffiths	A. Roberts

Code of Conduct

At Party Meetings on 28 February 1968, and 21 March 1968, the Parliamentary Party adopted the following Code of Conduct:

1. Conduct
It is the duty of Members to conduct themselves at all times in a manner consistent with membership of the Parliamentary Labour Party, and in particular:
(a) to act in harmony with the policies of the Parliamentary Labour Party;
(b) to be in regular attendance at the House and to maintain a good division record, and
(c) to refrain from personal attacks upon colleagues, orally or in writing.

2. Co-ordination and Collective Action
(a) Area Groups for the study of regional problems, and Subject Groups for the study of particular aspects of Party policy may be set up by the Parliamentary Party. No such Group or any other organized Group is permissible unless approved in writing by the Chief Whip.
(b) Before tabling any Early Day Motion, Private Member's Motion, or Prayer, or amendments thereto, a Member shall first consult the Chief Whip. For the purpose of securing concerted action in the House, Members shall consult the Chief Whip before tabling any Motion, Amendment or Prayer. The tabling of any such Motion, Amendment or Prayer shall be delayed for one sitting day should the Chief Whip so request.

3. Voting in the House
While the Party recognizes the right of Members to abstain from voting in the House on matters of deeply held personal conviction, this does not entitle Members to vote contrary to a decision of a Party Meeting, or to abstain from voting on a Vote of Confidence in a Labour Government.

4. Discipline
The Chief Whip may take or recommend disciplinary actions in

138

respect of any breach of paragraphs 1–3 above by any Member, as provided for below:

(*a*) *Reprimand*

A reprimand may be given by the Chief Whip in writing, and reported to the Liaison Committee.

(*b*) *Suspension from the privileges of membership of the Parliamentary Labour Party* (referred to as 'suspension')

On the recommendation of the Chief Whip the Liaison Committee may seek approval of a Party Meeting for the suspension of a Member for a period to be specified in the Motion.

A suspended Member may not attend any general meeting of the Parliamentary Party or its Area or Subject Group Meetings.

He will however be expected to comply with the Party Whip and to conform with whatever pairing arrangements apply to other Members of the Party from time to time.

The period of suspension may be extended by a Party Meeting if the Chief Whip and the Liaison Committee are of the opinion that the conduct of the suspended Member during the period of suspension has given rise to further dissatisfaction:

Provided that the Liaison Committee may include in any Motion for the suspension of a Member authority to the Chief Whip to extend the period of suspension for one further period, not exceeding the period specified in the Motion, after consultation with the Liaison Committee.

The Chief Whip may at his discretion, after consultation with the Liaison Committee, end the period of suspension earlier than the specified date.

The National Executive Committee of the Labour Party shall be notified of suspension.

(*c*) *Withdrawal of the Whip*

Withdrawal of the Whip (i.e., expulsion from the Parliamentary Labour Party) may be decided upon by the Party Meeting at which prior notice of motion has been given by the Liaison Committee.

Withdrawal of the Whip shall be reported to the National Executive Committee.

(*d*) *Member's right to be heard*

Any Member against whom disciplinary action is proposed under paragraphs (*b*) (suspension) and (*c*) (withdrawal of the Whip) shall be given at least three days' notice, and shall have the right to be heard at the Party Meeting before the Motion is put to the vote.

5. Minutes of meetings of the Parliamentary Party shall be available for inspection by any Member on application to the Secretary.

On 26 May 1968, the Party approved the Motion:
'That for the purposes of the Constitution of the Labour Party, the Code of Conduct shall be regarded for all purposes as the Standing Orders of the Parliamentary Labour Party.'

6 Parties in local government

Introduction

Political parties have not had quite the monopoly in local government which has characterized their role in the political system at the national level. Although many candidates in the local elections immediately after the Municipal Corporations Act of 1835 were quick to adopt labels (in elections in Colchester there were 'Conservative Churchmen', 'Radical Dissenters' and even 'Radical Churchmen') the truly independent candidate has managed to survive.

Overall, two-thirds of local councillors are members of political organizations, though the proportion varies considerably from 95 per cent of county borough councils to about half this proportion in the rural districts. Not all of these were actually introduced to council work by the political parties, some 12 per cent joined after or about the same time as they joined the council.[1] However, the parties clearly do perform the bulk of the recruiting function in local government.

On the whole party politics plays a rather smaller part in local government than is often thought, and certainly three-quarters of all councillors surveyed by the Government Social Survey in 1966 said that they did not think party politics affected the work of their council very much. It must be remembered that many of the decisions taken are routine measures concerning the day-to-day running of libraries, markets, sewage, caravan sites, etc.

Why, then, are the parties as active in local government as they are? In part, the answer is, as Ivor Gowan points out, a natural extension of the movement at the national level—and also there are clearly some local issues which raise matters of principle over which the parties differ.

However, we can go further than this. Not only do parties help to recruit local councillors, but the performance of this function together with the associated electoral activity helps the parties in their contest for national power. Regular local activity helps to reinforce party loyalty, and in a limited way brings to the attention of the voter that the party is concerned for his welfare and can help him in some of his everyday problems (e.g. many councillors hold problem 'clinics', similar to those held by M.P.s, in which housing and other personal problems are taken up).

Rudimentary as party organization often is at local elections, were there none at all, the organization of forces for a general election would be correspondingly more difficult. Local elections give parties the opportunity to go through the motions of electioneering and to 'show the flag' to their constituents.

Of course, for the Nationalists, local government has had a different significance. It is through success in local elections that the two parties hoped to establish their claim as credible parties in their respective regions. Both the S.N.P. and Plaid Cymru suffer from the effects of the electoral system in much the same way as do the Liberals. The vote of these parties is spread relatively evenly, e.g. in May 1967 the S.N.P. took 23 per cent of the votes in Glasgow without winning any of the thirty-seven wards.[2] However, tactics adopted locally (what one might call the 'gadfly' approach to local government, in which S.N.P. councillors show little voting discipline[3]) are not such as to produce a coherent party image likely to further the Parliamentary aspirations of the party. On the whole Plaid Cymru lags behind the S.N.P. in terms of success in local elections; the party is possibly correct when it feels that many people are put off by the bomb scares which are the occasional manifestation of Welsh extremism.

Notes

1 See the survey of local councillors conducted by the Government Social Survey for the Committee on the Management of Local Government, 1967.
2 *Economist*, 6 May 1967.
3 See Jane Morton, 'Scot. Nats. in Office', *New Society*, 10 October 1968.

Further reading

Much of the writing on local politics has been in the case-study form; where a work is primarily the study of one council or area this is indicated in parentheses.

F. W. Bealey et al., *Constituency Politics*, London, 1965. (A study of Newcastle-under-Lyme.)
H. Benham, *Two Cheers for the Town Hall*, London, 1964. (Chapter 19 discusses parties and politics in Colchester.)
A. H. Birch, *Small-Town Politics*, London, 1959. (A study of Glossop.)
G. Block, *Party Politics in Local Government*, London, 1962.
J. G. Bulpitt, *Party Politics in English Local Government*, London, 1967. (Attempts a typology of local party politics and presents four case-studies as illustrations.)

G. W. Jones, *Borough Politics*, London, 1969. (A study of Wolverhampton Town Council. See especially Chapters 8–10 and the bibliography.)

J. M. Lee, *Social Leaders and Public Persons*, London, 1963. (A case-study of the relationship between social change and the nature of politics in Cheshire.)

D. S. Morris, 'Scottish Nationalist Councillors', unpublished M.Sc. thesis. Dept. of Politics, University of Strathclyde, 1968.

A. M. Rees and T. Smith, *Town Councillors*, London, 1964. (A study of Barking Town Council.)

M. Stacey, *Tradition and Change*, London, 1960. (Chapter 3 describes politics in Banbury.)

H. V. Wiseman, *Local Government at Work*, London, 1967. (Politics in the Leeds City Council. See especially Chapter 4, and the useful, if short, bibliography.)

Articles

T. Brennan *et al.*, 'Party Politics and Local Government in Western South Wales', *Political Quarterly*, 1954, pp. 76–83.

E. Dell, 'Why Whip the Council?', *Socialist Commentary*, February 1960.

J. E. MacColl, 'The Party System in English Local Government', *Public Administration*, 1949, pp. 69–75.

H. Maddick and E. P. Pritchard, 'Conventions of Local Authorities in the West Midlands', *Public Administration*, Part I, County Borough Councils, 1958, pp. 145–55; Part 2, District Councils, 1959, pp. 135–43.

L. J. Sharpe, 'The Politics of Local Government in Greater London', *Public Administration*, 1960, pp. 157–72.

W. Thornhill, 'Agreements between Local Parties in Local Government Matters', *Political Studies*, 1957, pp. 83–8.

J. Warren, 'The Party System in Local Government', in S. D. Bailey, ed., *The British Party System*, London, 1952.

The role and power of political parties in local government*
by Ivor Gowan

Any systematic party organization outside Parliament dates from the immediate aftermath of the 1867 Reform Act which added many millions of urban voters to the electoral roll. Joseph Chamberlain, on the Liberal side, and Lord Randolph Churchill, on the Conservative, both realized the implications of this Act and began forming local Associations in the interests of their own parties. The idea quickly spread. A national organization and the nucleus of a professional staff supplemented the work of the local Associations and in due course the pressure of the local Associations spread from the organization of elections to the making of policy. The political parties were at their strongest in the large provincial cities, especially Birmingham and Liverpool. It is not surprising therefore to find that municipal elections also tended to be fought on party lines in the 1870s, especially in those boroughs where Liberals and Conservatives felt their organization was capable of gaining control for them.

The entry of the Labour Party upon the scene was later. The aims of this party were primarily concerned with improving the fortunes of the working classes and, at a later stage, with the introduction of some form of Socialism into Great Britain. For many years there had been much argument between those who wished to 'permeate' the existing parties—a favourite idea of the Fabians—and those who wished to set up their own party organization. In 1900 the Labour Representation Committee was formed—the forerunner of the Labour Party—and this step largely settled the matter in favour of those who favoured a new political party. This comparatively late start meant that up to the First World War Labour lagged behind the already established parties in its influence and achieved only a limited success in its aim of returning its own Members of Parliament.

With the extension of the franchise to women after the First World War the stage was set for the more recent developments in British party politics which will be within the experience of most readers. The schism and feuds of the Asquith and Lloyd George governments, combined with great economic and social changes, placed the Liberals in a disadvantageous position with Labour for the allegiance of the working men and women. As a result, since 1925, the Conservative and Labour parties have in their turn provided Government and Opposition, with the Liberals for the most part holding a handful of

* First published as two articles in the *Municipal Journal*, 22, 29 September 1961. Reprinted in abridged form with the permission of the author and the editor.

seats in the House of Commons despite the fact that their electoral strength in the country remains considerable.

In the last thirty years, it should be noted, the major political parties have developed far beyond election machines. They have both given special attention to research and the publication and dissemination of new ideas on matters of national importance, particularly on social and economic affairs and on defence. They have built up separate organizations specially devoted to the interests of particular groups such as women, trade unionists, young people and university students. They have studied the techniques and applied the lessons of public persuasion and public relations. In total their impact on a great section of our national life is considerable.

This background has been important in the understanding of the development of parties in local government. It is of course immediately apparent that, in a sense, the development of party organization in local affairs is one aspect only of the wider national growth, and that obvious parallels occur at every stage. But as we change our terms of reference it also becomes clear that we are not only concerned with one aspect of the national party organization. There is also a qualitative difference, based on the special circumstances in which local authorities operate.

Let me turn at this point to some of these differences. Firstly it appears that whereas party allegiance and party organization are accepted nationally as indispensable in the efficient conduct of politics, this is not so in local government. Over quite a considerable section of the community and in quite a variety of councils there is no general agreement on the need for party organization. Further, even when parties are formed they bear different titles in many cases from the national party. Labour, it is true, contests national and local elections under the same name. But in many cases its opponents call themselves Progressives, Moderates, Independents or Ratepayers rather than Conservatives. Yet despite the apparent antipathy for uniformity, some of the devices and conventions of party machinery have been accepted increasingly. Certainly in many of the major authorities—the county boroughs and some of the county councils— party attitudes and party machinery have taken root as an inevitable and on the whole welcome addition to the instruments of effective and democratic local government.

A second point of difference is that of scale. Despite the wide range in population between the largest and the smallest councils, local authorities on the whole are small. This has advantages. Candidates for the council are known to the voters for their personal qualities and standing. Election campaigns are not expensive. An air of informality often surrounds the administration of the council's services. On this account the influence of the independent councillor can still count for a great deal. Not surprisingly, the more formal type of party machinery is found most frequently in the larger county councils and county boroughs, where conditions generally closely resemble those of large-scale organization.

A third point of interest concerns the suitable milieu and conditions for the operation of political parties. It will be generally agreed that the most favourable opportunities for the clash of parties concern matters of major policy. Defence, nationalization, the welfare state, are all issues on which genuinely opposing attitudes can be developed, and on which party debates can be based. Parliament, whose main concern is legislation, easily became moulded to the forms and conventions of party. Local government, however, is concerned not with legislation but with executive action. It is true, of course, that alternative courses of executive action can be combined with differences on policy, as for example on a decision whether to build comprehensive or grammar schools, or on whether to subsidize the rents of council houses. Issues of this character generally provide the meat of debate in party disputes in the council chamber. But, let us be frank. Over the great mass of issues that come before the councils, party attitudes are unreal and artificial. A decision to implement a 'traffic-warden scheme', to build an art gallery or to decrease the number of dustbin collections can indeed be important and controversial. But they are palpably not issues of principle.

My fourth and last point is fundamental. Political parties took their origin from, and make their biggest contribution to, national affairs. The work of all councils is mainly local. Is it possible for the two opposites to become reconciled? The answer naturally reflects the extent to which local authorities are now concerned with national policies in such fields as education, planning and the social services. On issues such as these it is quite possible for parties to argue matters of principle and for their differing philosophies to be carried into local government. At the same time on a multitude of local decisions reflecting the pressures of a district, ward or a parish, party loyalties are bound to wear pretty thin.

It seems on reflection, therefore, that neither the historical background nor the analysis of party principles takes us very far in understanding the place of parties in local government. For while it is clear that the organization of national parties coincided with the growth of local parties in our larger towns, the subsequent development of party influence in national and local affairs has been widely different.

Nationally the sway of parties is complete; in town and county hall it remains partial and uneven. Most local authorities, it is true, now rely to a large extent on party organization in some way or another, but the measure of resistance to it is still quite strong in many places. The most fruitful approach will now be to examine those aspects of the machinery of local government that have lent themselves most easily to party organization.

Party politics took root in the larger industrial towns before permeating the smaller urban areas and the countryside. They were also a feature of the north of England and the Midlands before they spread to the south of the country. Redlich and Hirst had this to say on the subject: 'By 1890, it would indeed be difficult to find any great English town, outside the metropolis, with a municipal council elected on other than party lines.'

Mr Clare, town clerk of Liverpool towards the end of the last century, is quoted as saying that the Liberals and the Conservatives used the elections to put before the electorate the current problems of the authority and the policies that they would pursue in dealing with them. He went on:

> These burning questions are questions of policy which create differences of opinion, such as whether a lease of tramways should be renewed, or whether some municipal service should be undertaken. The party in power takes one view and the other party naturally opposes them.

The London County Council had been organized on party lines from the very beginning of its life. In the first elections held in 1889, the Progressives (Liberals) gained two-thirds of the seats, the remaining third going to the Moderates (Conservatives).

Labour's first impact on local government elections was made through the agency of the Independent Labour Party which gained notable successes in London's metropolitan boroughs in the decade before 1914. After the party's constitutional changes in 1918, the Labour Party itself began to finance and sponsor its own candidates in many boroughs and some counties throughout the country and made much progress, particularly at the expense of the Liberals. In the 1919 elections Labour gained 412 seats and for the first time gained control of a large county borough, Bradford. At the same time the party won control of twelve metropolitan boroughs.

Within the last forty years, of course, the Labour Party's strength in local government has grown commensurately with its progress in national politics. Its greatest successes were gained in the years immediately following the end of the Second World War. Little now divides the parties. In the 1961 local government elections, Labour gained 43·3 per cent of the votes cast in contested elections

147

compared with 44·7 per cent won by the Conservatives and their allies.

It would be wrong therefore to ascribe to the Labour Party the praise or blame for the introduction of party politics into local government, although this view is widely held. On the other hand the Labour Party undoubtedly extended the areas in which politically organized councils were to be found.

In one other respect Labour made a considerable innovation. For the first time, a close link was forged between the local party Associations and the national party organization. For the Labour Party this link was a matter of principle. In its view local government, as well as Parliament and the central government, had a part to play in the implementation of Socialist policies. In consequence the party as a whole formulated policies which it expected Labour-controlled councils to follow. Moreover, in the local authority elections the efforts of the local parties were supplemented and reinforced by the larger resources of the national party.

The Labour Party Conference went on to formulate model standing orders for the organization of party groups on local councils and specialists were appointed to the staff at party headquarters to give guidance and help to councillors in the formulation of their policies.

The Conservative Party does not possess the same kind of uniform organization throughout the country. In some areas, particularly in some of the agricultural counties of southern England, the Conservative Party does not sponsor official candidates but supports those standing under a variety of names. The decision is left entirely to the local Association.

Nor were the Conservatives speedy in setting up a national organization for local government affairs. Only in 1946, after heavy losses in the local elections, did the party decide that where the gap between them and their opponents was fairly narrow they were at a serious disadvantage against highly organized and disciplined opposition. Accordingly many more officially sponsored candidates were backed by the resources of the party. At the same time a local government department was added to the Central Office organization and a National Advisory Committee on local government was set up. By these methods more expert advice was made available to the local Associations, while more enthusiasm and drive were brought into the party's local government activities. Since 1946 too the Conservatives have held an annual local government conference.

In many respects, therefore, it seems that both major parties have a good deal in common in the way they have integrated local government affairs into their organizations. The model standing orders for the local groups are peculiar to the Labour Party, while the annual conferences are a special feature of the Conservatives. Neither Central Office interferes frequently or directly with the conduct of local groups. The services of the headquarters organization are mainly advisory. Only in the general philosophy of the parties is there a difference of emphasis. The Labour Party tends to regard local government as part of its overall policies and plan. Conservatives tend rather to stress the independence of their local Associations and to deprecate any encroachments upon this.

The conduct of elections is naturally an important part of the activities of any political party. This aspect of local government politics falls entirely to the local parties and Associations which are active both in the selection of candidates and in the conduct of the election campaign itself. Both major parties are currently concerned with the dearth of suitable candidates for the local council and by the lack of enthusiasm from the public in giving support to those who have been selected.

The reasons for this apathy are outside the scope of this article, but its effects are significant. The effective running of the local party organizations tends to be in the hands of a small group of people from whose own number, for the most part, local councillors tend to be chosen. As a result councillors may well be an unrepresentative cross-section of the community. This tendency, in its turn, detracts from the prestige of the local authorities themselves.

Turning from the elections to the impact of the parties upon the conduct of local government affairs, interest passes from the local Associations to the party groups on the councils. Each group normally consists of all the members of the same party who have been returned to the council. They are by no means universal, as some councils still function on strictly non-party lines, but most will nowadays have a Conservative and Labour group while some will have a Liberal group as well. The somewhat odd phenomenon of an Independent group is also found on some councils.

The principal aim of each group is naturally the effective deployment of its membership in the council and committees. If the party in question has won the previous election and is therefore in control of the council its main purpose will naturally centre on the task of making that control effective and of steering the party policy through the council machine. If the group is in a minority it will seek to concentrate on opposing the majority party and on giving expression to its own views at the appropriate stages of council business.

Membership of any party organization naturally tends to limit the complete freedom of the individual councillor, and I regard it as axiomatic that membership of a group will imply the acceptance of a certain amount of discipline by the councillors concerned. But the extent of the discipline is a matter on which opinions will differ. Let me give the Labour and Conservative views on the matter.

The Labour view is taken from a memorandum adopted by the National Executive Committee in 1938:

> Group meetings should be held regularly, and attendance at the meetings should be regarded as a duty to the party. Regular meetings are important, so that all members can have a voice in considering the policy and action of the group; for otherwise it may be difficult to secure party co-operation on the council. Any differences of individual opinion must be thrashed out within the group and not in public for it is a serious source of political weakness and embarrassment to have public conflict between Labour representatives, and nothing can be more fatal to electoral success.
>
> Members of the group are expected to abide by group decisions and not to speak or vote in opposition in the council, unless the group has decided to leave the matter in question to a free vote.

The Conservative attitude is taken from the central office publication, *Local Government and the Party Organization, 1950*:

> It is advisable, in order to ensure co-operation, that group or party meetings should be held prior to the council meetings. This enables members to be fully informed on matters arising, particularly on those of a committee upon which a member does not sit. It is often possible to determine upon an agreed line of action, but this does not mean that a member who does not agree with the majority must be pilloried for opposing. Scope must be allowed to individual members to exercise a full measure of thought and action.

Comparing these two statements, one sees that the need for party discipline is more clearly defined in the Labour view, while the safeguards for the freedom of the individual councillor is more specifically stated by the Conservatives. The Labour formula is impregnated with the principle of sanctity of a majority decision that is characteristic of all aspects of the Socialist movement. Conservatives tend to rely not so much on the specific rule as on the underlying tendency to conform which is characteristic of much of their political activity.

In the end it would appear that group discipline springs more from personalities than from direct rules—and in these matters there is not so much difference between the parties.

In considering the practices and conventions of the parties in local authorities, it must not be assumed that what is described as a common practice is necessarily applicable to all councils that are run on political lines, or that it can apply in any way to those places where there is a non-political approach to council business.

But there has developed, particularly in the last fifteen years, a range of practices that may almost be called 'standard' at least for the large and medium-size authorities. It is on these that I wish to concentrate. The resultant picture can hardly be true in its entirety for any council, and the individual circumstances of others may make it seem specially distorted in some cases.

Let me return to the party groups. Each group will normally elect an executive or 'policy committee' and a number of officers, always a chairman and secretary, and in the bigger authorities, one or more Whips. The round of council committee engagements, so pressing in itself on the time of the councillor, will leave little time for frequent or diverse party group activities.

In most authorities the principal activity is the meeting of the full group, which takes place usually after the cycle of monthly or quarterly committee meetings and before the full meeting of the council. This meeting of the group has a two-fold purpose. Firstly, it is a convenient method of conveying a good deal of information. Councillors will already be aware of what has been going on in the committees of which they are members. They will not have similar knowledge of what is happening in other committees. It is therefore the usual practice, at the group meeting, to put everybody in the picture of the whole range of council activities.

The second function of the group meeting is the taking of decisions, and it is not surprising that the attention of commentators on the subject has turned to this aspect. The full council, shortly after the group meeting, is going to be faced with a series of recommendations from its numerous committees and most of them will be accepted with little dissension. But some will touch on matters which are of importance to the party as a whole. It is on these occasions that a committee decision may be displeasing to the party group as a whole.

The discussion at the group meeting then will be vital. If the party has been able at an earlier stage to get its way in committee, it will be the task of the members of that committee to persuade the group to follow their lead. If they succeed that is the end of the matter. If they fail, and the group takes a different decision on the line to be taken at the council meeting, an embarrassing situation can arise. On some occasions the canons of party discipline may imply that members should vote differently in council from the way in which they originally voted in committee.

The Labour Party usually takes a strict line here. Members rebelling by casting a vote contrary to a group decision are apt to incur sanctions, sometimes even to be expelled from the party itself. Conservatives rarely go quite so far, though in some authorities the effect of the group decisions on subsequent party action are much the same as with their opponents.

At this point we might have appeared to come to the very nub of the question. On matters of policy, there is no doubt that the approbation of the majority party group is the indispensable prerequisite for a successful move in the council. Here a decision will be made which will subsequently secure the ratification of the council. The contents of the decision may be complex. Much pressure and a lot of advice—especially that of the officials—will have shaped it, but the seal of approval comes at the party meeting. It is on this point that both the supporters and the critics of party groups can direct their fire. On the one side the process can ensure logic, consistency and a policy that is identifiable by officials and the public and on which the opposition can make its attacks. On the other hand, decisions are taken in secret. No one, outside the group, can evaluate the motives or the arguments that have prevailed. On occasion expert guidance may appear to have been less important than prejudice, dogma or even intrigue. Such are the dangers to which the system is exposed.

To what extent does the competence of the party group conflict with the activities of the individual councillor? In theory, it might appear that there was little overlap because the privileges open to the member under the standing orders of councils are in no way curtailed. Indeed the group mechanism itself, it should be stressed, is recognized only by convention and does not impinge upon the conduct of council business.

Nevertheless, the model standing orders for Labour groups do, in fact, seek to limit the actions of individual councillors:

Individual members of the Labour group shall not submit or move any resolutions or amendments at meetings of the council unless such resolutions or motions or amendments have first been submitted to, and received the approval of, the policy committee and/ or the group meeting, or, in case of urgency, have received the approval of the leader of the group or his deputy.

Individual members of the Labour group may without consultation ask questions at meetings of the council, provided the tendency of such questions is not likely to be in conflict with the policy of the Labour group, in which case an officer of the group should be consulted.[1]

Fortunately general practice among Labour groups does not follow the letter of these standing orders. Taken literally, they might appear to impose a restraint upon elected members far greater than the discipline of the House of Commons places on M.P.s and one that is scarcely justified by council business.

Turning from matters of policy decisions to the procedure of local authorities, the most consistent application of the party machinery is in the selection of members of the council for offices of one kind or another. The majority party, of course, wields the ultimate control here, and can get its way.

But, as in all democratic assemblies, there is generally a realization that a majority is temporary and that undue curtailment of the rights of the minority may not only lead to obstruction in the conduct of affairs, but may also boomerang against the offenders after the next election. It is noticeable that there is generally a more urbane spirit and more accommodation between the parties when the political balance is delicate than when one party's majority seems unassailable over long periods of time.

The precise way in which the parties co-operate in these matters varies widely. At the one extreme, there is no more than a general understanding that each side will respect the other's rights; in other cases, there is a formal agreement covering almost every possible contingency. Such agreements, although ultimately unenforceable, mostly become accepted as rules of conduct, as essential in their way as the more formal standing orders in council procedure.

Four important points are usually settled in these party agreements. Firstly, the parties generally establish a convention concerning the selection of the mayor or chairman of the council. Except in some of the counties and rural districts where the same chairman, from the majority side, tends to stay in office over a lengthy period, the agreement will specify for what proportion of time the mayor or chairman shall be drawn from each party.

Secondly, there is usually an understanding about the election of aldermen, the most frequent formula being that there shall be an allocation of aldermanic seats in proportion of the party strength of the elected councillors.

Thirdly, the machinery of consultation between the groups defines the number of places to which each party shall be entitled on the council's committees. It is becoming increasingly rare for this matter to be settled on other than a proportional basis, by which each party is allocated the number of committee seats which corresponds with its relative strength on the council as a whole. Some cases still occur, unfortunately, where a majority party gives a negligible number of seats to its opponents on some key committees.

Finally, there is the question of committee chairmanships and vice-chairmanships. Broadly speaking, there are two approaches on this

153

matter. In a great number of councils there is the convention that the majority party shall provide the chairman of all but the least important committees on the ground that an effective chairman needs the political support of a majority of the members of a committee. In other councils, the parties each take the proportion of chairmanships corresponding to their membership on the council, although, even when this occurs, it is unlikely that the majority will relinquish such important posts as the chairmanship of the finance or education committees.

I have left until the end the most important post in the party hierarchy—the leader of the council. This is the post always associated with Lord Morrison of Lambeth when he led the Labour Party in the London County Council in the 1930s, at the time when the public called him 'the Prime Minister of London'. The leader of the council is, of course, the dominant figure of the majority party. In some councils he is given a special place in the council chamber directly opposite the leader of the minority party. He guides and controls his party's contribution to the business and debates of the council and without superseding the functions of committee chairman in matters relating to their special field, he makes major pronouncements on council policy.

There is some danger that, surrounded by weak colleagues, and with an ineffective opposition, the leader can become the 'boss', and that the party system is then prone to degenerate into 'one-man' government. Such cases are fortunately rare and can be avoided altogether by limiting the term of office of the leader to a fixed number of years.

To sum up let me quote from the late Mr J. H. Warren's conclusion. After a balanced exposition of the pros and cons of the party system in local government, he says:

> The public should not conclude from reports of 'heated party debates' in the council chamber that this represents what happens in every stage and phase of council work. It is not. The atmosphere of the committee is usually not a party one, nor is it in general one of recrimination or heated debate, but of good-tempered discussion.[2]

Provided that party loyalties do not drive every other consideration into the background, the system continues to make a valuable contribution to local government affairs.

Notes

1 Model Standing Orders for Labour groups on local authorities outside the administrative county of London. 7(a) and (b).
2 J. H. Warren, *Municipal Administration*, p. 208.

7 Parties, elections and the public

Introduction

The major function of party organization, and often the major rationale for the existence of political parties, is to fight, though not necessarily to win, elections at both the national and local levels. Attitudes towards elections on the part of party leaders and activists may often vary considerably. There are also important differences within parties, as well as between, on how best to fight elections, and on the relative importance of the role of organization, finance, candidates and party image in achieving electoral success. For minor parties, elections provide the opportunity to engage in political debate at a time when the attention of the average voter to politics and party competition is greater than usual. For the major parties, elections are serious affairs providing crucial tests of their ability to capture the support of large segments of the electorate, and to obtain or retain control of the rule-making bodies. The responses of political parties as expressed in election campaigns to the challenge of elections are many and varied, though for those parties and their constituency organizations for whom such campaigns involve serious competition for political power there are some important similarities.

Election campaigns

Ideally, a constituency party should be almost as active between elections as at elections. Social occasions raise money for the party, and keep voluntary workers in touch with one another; meetings, perhaps with speakers from outside the constituency, provide political education and reinforcement of political ideas.

Voluntary workers prepare canvassing cards from the electoral register, distribute literature and generally set up the organization required to run the campaign. Precisely how canvassers are organized varies from constituency to constituency and from party to party; sometimes they work in teams, sometimes individually. The Conservatives, for example, are urged by Central Office[1] to form canvassing corps in each ward or polling district, under the direction of a

District Warden. In large areas these are grouped under the care of a Group Warden. If some areas are under-provided with canvassers, a flying squad is to be organized from among the younger and more active canvassers. The group, containing four canvassers and a squad leader, undertakes work under the direct orders of constituency headquarters. However, as R. T. Holt and J. E. Turner show, it does not always pay to be too rigid concerning campaign organization.

Canvassing, in the fullest sense of the word (including some attempt to spread the gospel and to make conversions), is increasingly being replaced by a survey type of approach in which the main objects are to discover exactly where party supporters are, to distribute literature, and also remind voters of the election and of the party's presence in the constituency.[2] Canvassing cards are carefully marked with the party affiliation (or marked 'doubtful'), and with other relevant information such as whether transport will be needed on polling day. Supporters requiring postal votes are noted, and every effort is made to get them to register. On the whole the Conservatives are the most successful party in this respect and little thought is required to realize how crucial such votes can be. In the 1966 General Election, as R. L. Leonard points out, 'the postal vote exceeded the majority in twenty-four seats, won by the Conservatives. It seems probable that in about half of these constituencies this factor alone accounted for the Conservative victory.'[3]

During the campaign, posters, handbills, stickers and so on are distributed; meetings are organized, perhaps with the candidate attending several in one evening, dashing breathlessly from one to another.[4]

On election day, committee rooms are organized by reliable members of ward committees who act as clerks-in-charge, and co-ordinated by the ward chairmen. Each committee room has the relevant sections of the marked electoral register, and is responsible for marking off electors who have voted, according to the information supplied by tellers stationed outside the polling booths. Teams of canvassers call on pledged supporters urging them to vote. The Conservatives, with their higher proportion of full-time workers, tend to be fairly active all day, while other parties tend to cram most of their activity into the last four or five hours of polling. During this time every effort is made to contact all known supporters. Finally, the agent and other helpers attend the count to represent the interests of the candidate.

This is the basic pattern of general electioneering which most parties follow, to a greater or lesser degree. Obviously variations occur, and in particular gimmicks or various distinctive tactics are used in order to 'put one over on the opposition'. For example, eve-of-poll literature may be distributed, motorcades through the constituency may be organized, considerable efforts may be made to attract local press attention and so on.[5]

Though it is reasonable to assume that the Conservatives possess a general superiority in registering postal voters, this does not necessarily extend to the campaign as a whole. In their study of an election campaign in Barons Court, Holt and Turner show that, apart from the postal vote, the Conservatives were out-organized in the 1966 Election. They argue that in contrast to that of the Conservatives, the Labour organization in Barons Court was decentralized, more flexible, and could offer the right kinds of incentives to party activists.

Local elections

Not all elections are regarded in the same light by the parties. For the smaller parties, anxious to establish themselves, local elections often assume an importance in the work of the party greater than that for the major parties. Local elections are often entered with great enthusiasm and considerable organization, and in many cases, where effective organization is a crucial factor, council seats are won owing to the apathy or disarray of the major parties. The emphasis placed by the Liberals at their 1970 Conference upon involvement in the community suggests that in some areas the major parties may be forced to pay greater attention to local party organization if they are to resist such a challenge. Conservative and Labour organization, in areas which are traditional strongholds for either party, tends at times to become lax, and in some instances virtually disappears. In really safe areas, the sitting councillor may not bother to campaign at all, in other areas the party faithful may perform a few of the tasks associated with electioneering, more as an annual ritual affirming their loyalty to the party than as an act of organization aimed at securing the election of the party's nominee. For example, it is not uncommon for a party to canvass only that part of the ward known to contain most of its supporters ('canvass' here meaning at least the distribution of literature, at most inviting electors to vote for the party) and for no records to be made. On election day tellers may be stationed at some of the polling stations. Committee rooms may or may not be set up; where they are, they may serve social rather than political functions. Owing to the lack of properly marked electoral registers little use can be made of the tellers' reports. Quite frequently only the candidate and/or his agent is in evidence during the day, though they may be joined by a dozen or so people, some with cars, in the early evening. The last few hours of polling is then spent frantically knocking-up as many electors as possible, regardless of party, avoiding those streets known to be bastions of the opposing party.

Of course, no party aims at this kind of approach to elections, and most parties offer plenty of advice on how to conduct electoral campaigns,[6] yet the above sketch is often closer to the reality of local election activity.

Public images of parties

The impressions of the political parties held by voters are of considerable importance in understanding the relationship between parties, elections and the public. As Graham Wallas pointed out,[7] merely mentioning a political party by name may induce mental associations and conjure up emotional reactions. It is the generalized attitudes and beliefs about the parties which shape the behaviour of the electorate.[8] A number of attempts have been made to identify such party images and some of these are listed in the bibliography.

Perhaps the most obvious aspect of party images is that based on class divisions. Clearly the images of the parties change depending upon to whom one is talking, but many electors see the Conservative Party as being the party for the rich or for big business, though associated with this is the notion of 'free enterprise'. The Labour Party is seen as the party for 'the working class' and for 'the underdog', and is also associated with the welfare state. Labour is also thought to be more interesting, more modern, and more youthful than other parties.[9]

One should not regard such findings as fixed in any way. Images will change as the parties change and as their behaviour and policies are interpreted by the electorate. Occasional empirical studies, though sometimes able to study the phenomena in relative depth, can show only 'snapshots' at particular moments. Often these snapshots are not entirely comparable. On the other hand, survey organizations, such as Gallup Poll, are able to provide a more continuous monitoring, even though they do not have the resources to study images in depth. The main academic discussions of images are indicated in the bibliography while subsequently we reproduce some Gallup Poll data on the public images of the three main parties.

Notes

1 'The Voluntary Worker and the Party Organisation', *Organisation Series*, No. 9, Conservative and Unionist Central Office, 1961.
2 D. Butler and D. Stokes, *Political Change in Britain*, London, 1969, p. 326.

3 R. L. Leonard, *Elections in Britain*, London, 1968, p. 167.
4 See D. Marquand, 'At the Hustings', *Encounter*, August 1965, pp. 84–7.
5 For some discussion of the tactics and attempts of third parties to attract attention and support, see J. D. Lees, 'Aspects of Third Party Campaigning', *Parliamentary Affairs*, 1965–6, pp. 83–90.
6 See for example the Conservative Central Office Organization Series, the Labour Party pamphlet 'Party Organisation', and the guide for members of the Liberal Party, 'Effective Organising'.
7 G. Wallas, *Human Nature in Politics*, London, 1908.
8 Butler and Stokes, *op. cit.*, p. 359.
9 Further details may be found in the books listed in the bibliography; see especially Abrams and Rose, Butler and Stokes, Milne and Mackenzie, Trenaman and McQuail.

Further reading

Elections and analyses

On the functions of elections, see R. Rose and H. Mossawir, 'Voting and Elections: A Functional Analysis', *Political Studies*, 1967, pp. 173–201. For historical and general discussions of elections, see H. Hanham, *Elections and Party Management* and R. L. Leonard, *Elections in Britain*, London, 1968 (contains a good account of the technicalities surrounding elections), also P. G. J. Pulzer, *Political Representation and Elections in Britain*, London, 1968.

There are many sources for the results and analyses of elections, including the press and various almanacs. The following represent the sources most commonly used:

D. Butler and J. Freeman, *British Political Facts, 1900–67*, London, 1968.
F. W. S. Craig, ed., *British Parliamentary Election Results, 1918–49*, Glasgow, 1969.
H. Durant *et al.*, 'Election '66', *Daily Telegraph*, London, 1966.
B. R. Mitchell and K. Boehm, *British Parliamentary Election Results, 1950–64*, Cambridge, 1966.
The Times, 'House of Commons'. This gives results, analyses, biographies and photographs of members. Issued after each election.

For election reports including some accounts of constituency election campaigns, with some analysis, see the Nuffield series of election studies:
R. B. McCallum and A. Redman, *The British General Election of 1945*, Oxford, 1947.
H. G. Nicholas, *The British General Election of 1950*, London, 1951.
D. E. Butler, *The British General Election of 1951*, London, 1952.
D. E. Butler, *The British General Election of 1955*, London, 1955.
D. E. Butler and R. Rose, *The British General Election of 1959*, London, 1960.
D. E. Butler and A. King, *The British General Election of 1964*, London, 1965.

D. E. Butler and A. King, *The British General Election of 1966*, London, 1966.

D. Butler and M. Pinto-Duschinsky, *The British General Election of 1970*, London, 1971.

On the influence of public opinion polls on parties and elections, see R. Hodder-Williams, *Public Opinion Polls and British Politics*, London, 1970. For an interesting collection of party manifestos, see F. W. S. Craig, ed., *British General Election Manifestos 1918–66*, Glasgow, 1970. On the electoral effects of minor parties, see F. W. S. Craig, ed., *The Minor Parties at Parliamentary Elections since 1918* (forthcoming), and *British Parliamentary Election Statistics 1918–68*, Glasgow, 1968. See also the following:

H. B. Berrington, 'The General Election of 1964', *Journal of the Royal Statistical Society*, Series A (General), Vol. 128, Part 1, 1965, pp. 17–66.

'The 1966 Election: An Analysis of the Results', *Swinton Journal*, Autumn 1966.

P. A. Bromhead, 'The General Election of 1966', *Parliamentary Affairs*, 1966, pp. 332–45.

D. E. Butler *et al.*, 'The Strength of the Liberals under Different Electoral Systems', *Parliamentary Affairs*, 1968–9, pp. 10–15.

J. P. Cornford, 'Aggregate Election Data and British Party Alignments 1885–1910', in E. Allardt and S. Rokkan, eds, *Mass Politics*, New York, 1970.

M. G. Kendall and A. Stuart, 'The Law of the Cubic Proportion in Election Results', *British Journal of Sociology*, 1950, pp. 183–96.

Constituency electioneering

P. Barker, 'Constituency Report: The Fight for Halifax', *New Society*, 15 October 1964.

R. Gregory, 'Local Elections and the "Rule of Anticipated Reactions"', *Political Studies*, 1969, pp. 31–47.

P. Jenkins, 'Labour's Election Machine', *New Society*, 28 May 1964.

G. Kaufman, 'Jeremy Thorpe's Devon', *New Statesman*, 27 August 1965.

D. Kavanagh, *Constituency Electioneering in Britain*, London, 1970.

D. Marquand, 'At the Hustings', *Encounter*, August 1965, pp. 84–7.

Aspects of organization

'The District Committee Room—the key to success', *Conservative Central Office Organization Series*, 1969.

'Electoral Registration', *Conservative Central Office Series*, 1968.

G. O. Comfort, *Professional Politicians, a Study of the British Party Agents*, Washington, 1958.

R. Rose, 'The Professionals of Politics', *New Society*, 8 August 1963, pp. 10–12.

J. Thompson, 'Square Deal for Agents', *Crossbow*, 1960, pp. 37–40.

Voting patterns

It is not possible, nor is it central to our theme, to review the general findings of voting studies. However, readers wishing to study this aspect of political behaviour should consult the following:

M. Abrams and R. Rose, *Must Labour Lose?*, London, 1960.
A. J. Allen, *The English Voter*, London, 1964.
F. W. Bealey *et al.*, *Constituency Politics*, London, 1965.
M. Benney *et al.*, *How People Vote*, London, 1956.
J. Blondel, *Voters, Parties and Leaders*, London, 1969.
J. G. Blumler and D. McQuail, *Television in Politics*, London, 1968.
J. Bonham, *The Middle Class Vote*, London, 1954.
I. Budge and D. Urwin, *Scottish Political Behaviour*, London, 1966.
D. Butler and D. Stokes, *Political Change in Britain*, London, 1969.
J. H. Goldthorpe *et al.*, *The Affluent Worker*, Cambridge, 1968.
R. T. McKenzie and A. Silver, *Angels in Marble*, London, 1968.
R. S. Milne and H. C. Mackenzie, *Straight Fight*, London, 1954.
　Marginal Seat, London, 1958.
E. A. Nordlinger, *The Working-Class Tories*, London, 1967.
W. G. Runciman, *Relative Deprivation and Social Justice*, London, 1966.
L. J. Sharpe, *A Metropolis Votes*, Greater London Papers No. 8, 1962.
　Voting in Cities, London, 1967.
J. Trenaman and D. McQuail, *Television and the Political Image*, London, 1961.

Articles

R. J. Benewick *et al.*, 'The Floating Voter and the Liberal View of Representation', *Political Studies*, 1969, pp. 177–95.
M. Benney and P. Geiss, 'Social Class and Politics in Greenwich', *British Journal of Sociology*, Vol. 1, 1950, pp. 310–27.
A. H. Birch and P. Campbell, 'Voting Behaviour in a Lancashire Constituency', *British Journal of Sociology*, Vol. 1, 1950, pp. 197–208.
P. Campbell *et al.*, 'Voting Behaviour in Droylesden in October 1951', *The Manchester School*, Vol. 20, No. 1, 1952, pp. 57–66.
J. P. Cornford and J. A. Brand, 'Scottish Voting Behaviour', in J. N. Wolfe, ed., *Government and Nationalism in Scotland*, Edinburgh, 1969, pp. 17–40.

Campaign effectiveness and party incentives: the case of Barons Court

'The Labour organisation, being often more amateurish and incompetent, takes longer to get its machinery into operation.' (D. E. Butler, *The British General Election of 1951*, p. 148.)

'At every level the Conservative party organisation was larger, better equipped, and more efficient than its rivals.' (D. E. Butler and Antony King, *The British General Election of 1964*, p. 215.)

These two statements, admittedly from the same stable, reflect a view often stated that the organization of the Labour Party in the constituencies is inferior to that of the Conservatives. It is therefore interesting when deviant examples exist and are analysed. Such an example is described by R. T. Holt and J. E. Turner in their study of the campaign in the Barons Court constituency at the 1964 General Election. (Reprinted with permission of The Macmillan Company from *Political Parties in Action. The Battle of Barons Court*, by R. Holt and J. Turner. © The Free Press, a Division of The Macmillan Company, 1968.)

Both the Conservative and Labour parties committed considerable resources to canvassing the intentions of voters. Holt and Turner analyse a sample of the canvass returns of the two parties and conclude 1) that the Labour Party canvass was more thorough than that of the Conservatives (they contacted 5,000 more voters than the Tories and had fewer workers), 2) that the canvass of both parties was remarkably accurate (about 83 per cent of voters who were identified as supporters of one or the other party were probably actual supporters of those parties), 3) that the Labour Party was better at redeeming election pledges in strong Tory districts than the Conservatives were in strong Labour areas, though the Conservatives did better in marginal areas, 4) that whereas nearly 78 per cent of the registered voters who were pledged to either party went to the polls, the comparable figure for unpledged registered voters was only just over 46 per cent, thus seemingly justifying the effort put into canvassing.

The difference in performance between the parties (a 76 per cent canvass for the Labour Party compared with a 63 per cent canvass of the electorate by the Conservatives) can be attributed to the management of the canvass, and in particular to the fact that the organization of the Labour Party was both decentralized and flexible. The authors discuss the canvass as a device for gathering certain types of needed information as follows:

In running an effective campaign, both aggregated and disaggregated information are necessary if the results of the canvass are to be of maximum utility. But these two types of information become the basis for different kinds of decisions which have to be made at different levels of organization. At the polling-district echelon, for example, disaggregated information is the most important. On election day, the polling-district committee room must have available the name, address, polling place, and registration number of every voter who has promised to support the party. At this level of organization, none of the basic decisions which have to be made depend upon aggregate information (such as the *total number* of pledges).

By contrast, the central headquarters makes little use of disaggregated information in its basic operations; it follows the progress of the canvassing primarily through the analysis of gross figures. If an examination of cumulative reports reveals that the canvass is lagging in a particular ward, the party leaders can direct more manpower into that area. Apart from those occasions when an individual voter desires to meet with the candidate, or when voters requiring transportation have to be identified so that their requests can be handled from the center, none of the staff at the main headquarters needs such specific information as the names and addresses of individual pledges.

Thus, under ordinary circumstances there are no significant informational advantages to be gained through a system of centralized canvassing. On the other hand, a centralized operation does involve heavy costs. While their late start probably impaired the Tory effort to realize their canvassing objectives, the fact that they did less canvassing with more manpower can to some extent be attributed to the time waste incurred in processing the canvassers through central headquarters.

It must be emphasized, however, that in those cases where it is beneficial for the people at the center to have disaggregate information available to them, the Conservative machine showed up to excellent advantage. The most notable example of this was in the processing of the postal vote. The Tory system of 'priority' postal votes and centralized registration of the postal voters required that disaggregated information be channeled to the main headquarters, and for this reason the party could derive advantage from centralizing the entire operation.

If the centralized management of canvassing activities was one reason why the Tory canvass was less efficient than Labour's, why did the Conservatives decide to adopt this system? It was certainly not because the agent favoured the centralized pattern; indeed, she preferred exactly the opposite. But, just as Mr Clarke could not have employed centralized methods even if he had wanted to, Mrs Bowman had little option but to reject decentralization. The reason for this was because of the weakness of several ward organizations. The Conservative agent simply could not run the risk of turning the important job of canvassing over to some of the outlying units. Had she been the agent in Barons Court for eighteen or twenty months prior to the election, she would have had more time to build up these ward organizations to a position of strength so that they would have been able to undertake more of the campaign tasks. (The wards were in a healthier condition by 1966, and the canvassing activities were more decentralized.) (pp. 242–4)

Although the Conservative agent had more full-time workers at her disposal, she tended to be restricted in the extent to which she could assign them to jobs as needed:

> Mrs Bowman's problems of achieving sufficient flexibility in personnel assignments and of maintaining surveillance over the units of the organization were directly related to the fact that most of the full-time Tory workers came from outside the constituency. Some of these people were personally committed to Mrs Bowman, who had recruited them for a specific executive task, which in many instances they had carried out in previous campaigns. Other workers had been sent out from the Central Office, and here again Mrs Bowman usually moved them into a specific assignment. From whatever outside source they came, however, a certain period of time was needed to 'break them in' and to enable them to become acquainted with the members of the local association with whom they would be working closely. These outside people could hardly be expected to have detailed knowledge about Barons Court as a constituency or about the idiosyncrasies of the local party organization. Quite apart from the fact that the agent felt an obligation to keep these outside workers in the posts for which some of them had specifically volunteered, she was concerned about the time that would be lost if she reassigned them—a reshuffling that would require them to go through another 'break-in period'.
>
> Shifting personnel about during a three-week campaign can only be effective if the persons concerned can begin to function effectively in their new jobs right away; but the outsiders who came to Barons Court were not equipped to shift gears that quickly. The Barons Court Tories were unable to find enough local people who could devote sufficient time to the campaign. Veterans of previous elections, the outside people had made a time commitment to the Conservative Party and not necessarily to Barons Court. In other

words, they had a larger option than would ordinarily be the case; if they could not do in Barons Court what they wanted to do, they were free to go into some other marginal constituency where their desires would be met. Mrs Bowman knew what each of these key workers could do well, and she recruited each individual for a special purpose. Thus, each worker had an advance understanding with the agent as to what his responsibilities were to be. For this reason the agent was understandably hesitant about making any shifts in assignments; she did not want to impose duties upon any worker that she knew the individual might object to.

Even if they were willing and able to be reassigned, the people from outside the local party could not be assigned to surveillance tasks. In a voluntary organization, where interpersonal relationships are delicate, as well as important, effective surveillance can be carried out only by persons who are well known and respected in the organization and who have good rapport with the activities in charge of the outlying committee rooms. (pp. 249–50)

The question arises, why did the Conservatives have to rely so heavily on outsiders, while the Labour Party was able to recruit workers from its own members? And further, why are so many workers prepared to devote so much time to campaigning? In answer to these questions, Holt and Turner suggest that a system of incentives operates in both organizations. The system, in the long run, affects the size and quality of the pool of talent from which activists are drawn.

Since the Conservatives received much more help from outside the constituency than Labour did, and since this seems to the authors to be a general pattern in the London area, it is hypothesized that the Conservatives operate a more effective incentive system *above* the constituency level. For example more Tory than Labour activists probably aspire to parliamentary careers, and Conservative agents are not slow to recognize this.

Perceptive Tory agents in the London area recognize that a volunteer who has visions of getting into the House can be of good use in a campaign, especially if he is at the stage of trying to get on the candidate list at the Central Office, or has just recently been placed on the list. In speaking about this matter, one London agent pointed to a young gentlemen who was dashing through the door on his way to carry out a campaign assignment: 'That young man wants to get on the candidate list, and I can flog him half to death! I doubt that he has much of a chance of being selected by a constituency party. But I can't worry about that now. I need a reliable person who will be available most of the time to do important chores, and he is always at my beck and call!'

In the case of the Conservatives, many parliamentary aspirants seem to perceive that active participation in a campaign is likely to improve their chances of getting on the list and of eventually being selected as a candidate. On the other side of the coin, some Tory agents recognize these people as a fruitful source of executive manpower for their campaign battles, and they are eager to recruit them. But does the Conservative Party actually manipulate the access to candidacy as a way to reward activists for their hard work in political campaigns?

The answer to this question appears to be both yes and no. When an individual applies to the Central Office for placement on the candidate list, the vice-chairman of the party organization and his colleagues who make this decision scrutinize the prospect's record of political activity. If he is young, does not come from distinguished Conservative lineage, and has not done much political work, he may be told to get more political experience by attaching himself to a local association and by working in some election campaigns, and to apply again a few years hence. But if the applicant is middle-aged, is well established in business, comes from a long line of officeholding Tories but has had little political experience, he may be placed on the approved list.

The Central Office attempts to maintain a record of the political activity of parliamentary aspirants who are being considered for placement on the candidate list, as well as those who are already on the list but who are anxious to be presented to a constituency so that they can have a crack at selection. The Central Office agent is the individual responsible for reporting on the political performance of these candidature-seekers. After a campaign in a regular election or in a by-election, he may contact the agent in the constituency where an individual has been working, requesting an evaluation of him as a prospective candidate. The Tory candidate in the constituency may also be contacted for this appraisal, though this is rare. While the aspirant may request the agent or the candidate to write a letter to the Central Office in his behalf—or they may volunteer to do so—the Central Office tends to give less weight to these recommendations than to the inquiries it initiates.

This assessment of campaign performance by the Central Office generates the impression among many aspirants that a young man who works diligently and effectively for the party and who meets other specifications may be 'rewarded' by being placed on the candidate list. 'Reward' is, of course, a tricky 'careerist' term, and very few aspirants and not many more agents would deign to use it, though some of the latter would recognize its appropriateness when it was suggested to them. Among the people with parliamentary ambitions there were reports—some of them apparently apocryphal —of the otherwise promising young man who did not take his organizational and campaign work seriously and who was not placed on the candidate list. These serve to indicate how some aspirants perceive the consequences of their political activity.

Whether exceptional service during election campaigns helps a parliamentary hopeful who is already on the list to win a candidacy is another matter. That the Central Office has enough influence over the selection process to be able to reward an aspirant for superior party work is clear enough. When a constituency party is looking for a candidate, the Central Office, when asked for advice, may respond in different ways. It typically sends a list of all potential candidates who are looking for a constituency of the type making the request. However, a high official in the Conservative organization informed us that if the Central Office has a few men whom it particularly wants to place, it may recommend from three to five people and supply background information on each of them. Since recommendation by the Central Office is generally recognized as improving one's chances of being selected, the recommendation itself could be used as a 'reward'. In some cases, however, the Central Office can go much farther than this. When asked whether one member of the recommended group might be singled out for particular support, a highly placed Tory official, who for obvious reasons must remain anonymous, replied in words to this effect: 'Never in writing. But if there is a man we would especially like to see chosen, I will have a personal chat with the chairman of the selection committee (who is usually the chairman of the association), and indicate our choice. Normally this is enough to get the right man through the selection committee. Sometimes, however, one of the other aspirants—usually a local man—may have the chairman of the committee in his pocket. Then I might take the chairman of that association aside and remind him that association chairmen whose work is appreciated by Central Office are sometimes placed on the Honours List. Rarely does this fail to accomplish our objective.' But such a technique cannot be used in some constituencies, and, in any case, is employed only in exceptional circumstances.

Thus it is apparent that the Conservative Central Office could use its recommendations to selection committees as a reward for faithful campaign service to the party. (pp. 255–8)

In contrast to this many Labour activists regard an opportunity to run for the local council as highly desirable, while most Tory activists tend to regard it as an onerous duty.

The evidence suggests that, in the London area, service on local councils is more attractive to members of the working class who are active in politics than to members of the middle class. On the surface, this may seem like a strange twist in British local government and politics. The typical textbook usually calls attention to the sense of responsibility for local government and civic affairs that characterizes local Tory dignitaries. While this situation may still prevail in the rural areas and in some safe Conservative districts in urban centers, it does not appear to be true of the marginal constituencies in London.

It may be that the Tories find other outlets for their energies, and derive satisfaction and acclaim for other kinds of community service. Perhaps, too, the political climate in the marginal constituencies makes it difficult for the Conservatives to render the type of service in local government that they were able to perform in the past.

Although Barons Court is a marginal *parliamentary* constituency, it was in 1964 located in two boroughs where Labour commanded a strong majority. Indeed, the councils in Hammersmith and Fulham were dominated by the Socialists for many years. The important point is this: in a district that has moved from the Conservative column into the marginal category in parliamentary elections, Labour is likely to have won control of the Labour council already or will have made significant inroads into it. In other words, barring an adverse national swing or the emergence of a local issue, the Labour Party tends to run stronger in local than in parliamentary contests. This means that the Labour Party, for local government purposes, has certain safe wards under its control and has a stronger hold over other wards that are not so firmly in the Labour camp when it comes to electing a member of parliament.

Under these circumstances, candidacies for local council seats grow less attractive to the activists in the Conservative Party. The organization is able to offer fewer safe wards to its enthusiasts, who are forced to spend their time on harder campaigns in marginal wards. And even if they win, they often find their organization in a hopeless minority position on the council. Thus, not only do they lose control over policy, but they no longer have access to the important committee assignments and committee chairmanships which are appealing to individuals who seriously engage in local politics. (pp. 267-9)

As with service on local councils, the Tories were not much inclined to regard the holding of party office as a 'reward'. On the other hand, if a constituency Labour Party is issue-orientated, members can maximize their influence by attaining party office. One way of attaining office is to work hard for the party organization. Thus such work can be seen as leading to the reward of membership of, say, the General Management Committee, and therefore to participation in policy-making.

Of more interest to the Conservative activists is the Honours List. This, while not being in the forefront of their minds, is seen by workers as a reward for faithful party service (a fact apparently recognized by Edward Heath on becoming Prime Minister in 1970):

For officials in the Central Office and those in the Parliamentary Party who have an interest in organizational problems, the Honours List is clearly conceived as one device for rewarding the faithful, the hardworking, and the electorally successful officials who are responsible for their constituency organizations. One high party official, who has a great deal to do with national organization, perceived a clear relationship between the Honours List and the recruitment of the necessary volunteers to man the important party posts. In fact, he exhibited some concern about the party being out of power and being deprived access to the Honours List; he indicated that thought was being given to the establishment of some alternative. This official was the one who most clearly recognized that commitment to the party and its principles was not enough to hold an organization together. Some system of rewards had to be available, and these rewards had to be valued by the local people whom the party desired to have undertake the volunteer positions of responsibility.

While the Honours List *is* involved in the reward system of the Conservative Party, let us be clear about how we think it operates. We are *not* trying to imply that a young man joins the Conservative Party, works in his ward and at the association level, and then finally accepts the responsibilities and tasks of the chairmanship *because* he has had his eye on an O.B.E. from the beginning. This is obviously not the case. It seems more likely that an individual may join the party for any number of reasons, and 'apolitical' social motivations may be as important as the political. However, after growing involved in party work and holding office for whatever reason, the person who displays a talent for organization may be considered for the chairmanship. By this time, many of the rewards that were available to him for previous activity have begun to lose their efficacy. It is at this point in his career that the Honours

List may begin to look attractive, especially if he is engaged in professional or business employment, where honorific symbols after the surname are often expected.

It should be noted that the Honours List has very limited application as a 'reward' in a single constituency. Since the awards are relatively few and there is a large number of good Conservative parties which must be given recognition, the most that can be expected (for political reasons) is for one party activist from a marginal constituency to be placed on the list only about every seven to ten years. . . .

Some well-informed agents will go so far as to say that the main political use of Honours is not as a reward but as a technique for 'buying off' a long-tenured but ineffectual chairman in an effort to infuse the organization with new blood. In other words, Honours may occasionally be granted 'on condition that' the recipient resign his post. Obviously, most association officers who have given years of devoted service to the party would be greatly insulted if anyone implied that they worked hard largely because they desired to get on the Honours List. They would be even more insulted if they felt that Honours were given as a bribe to get rid of the ineffectual rather than as a reward for real achievement. We underline the fact that in our discussion of the Honours system we have made neither of these claims. Our evidence that the Honours List provides an efficacious reward for a limited number of party stalwarts comes primarily from comments volunteered by rank-and-file Tories who perceive it as such and justify its use, and from responses by high Conservative officials who recognize the reward potential of the list and have made use of it in this way.

While the middle-class Labour activist may not covet an O.B.E., he is not completely immune from the desire to have some symbolic inscription after his name. For some people, an appointment as a justice of the peace may bring a certain satisfaction. Justices of the Peace occupy an ancient and honored place in English history, but their present significance may perhaps be judged less by history than by the cynical pundits who designate the position as a 'poor man's baronetcy'. One occasionally encounters Labour activists who would like to become J.P.s, especially professional and business people who are able to make adjustments in their work schedules so that they can serve several times a week in their official capacity. When the Labour Party is in power at the local level, an appointment as a justice of the peace is one way in which the local party organization can help to provide recognition for an individual who has given outstanding service to his party and to the community. We found no activists in the Conservative Party who indicated any desire to become a J.P. The Labour people, when interested, seem to prefer initials that are something more than honorific, while Tories seem inclined to the view that the more honorific the symbol, the better. In either case, however, the two parties have managed to build parts of an incentive system around what at least some of their members desire. (pp. 277–9)

Finally, the Conservative Party manages to link the social life of its members with their political organization much more effectively than the Labour Party. Astute Conservative leaders can bestow positions of social leadership upon those who are active in the Association.

It should be noted that Holt and Turner do not argue that only these rewards are relevant in determining party activity and that there is no ideological commitment on the part of activists. What they do argue is that such commitment to party aims does not help in distinguishing between the two parties in terms of levels of activity.

Thus, of the rewards available to the Conservatives, the effective ones operate above the constituency level. The only really local reward which appeals to Conservatives, social leadership, was not available to the Barons Court Conservatives because there was little social life within the Association. On the other hand, the Labour Party in Barons Court was relatively rich in rewards sought by its volunteers.

Parties and party images

It is unfortunate that so important an aspect of political parties as their public images should not be continuously measured and charted. Even the Gallup Poll, which does provide a considerable body of data over time on various political questions, has not monitored images consistently. Academic studies are, for the most part, 'one-off' studies, and since they often approach the problem differently from one another they are rarely strictly comparable. Recent studies have, however, begun to examine the change of images over time (see particularly Butler and Stokes, *op. cit.*, Chapter 16).

Basically, three approaches have been adopted in monitoring images. Firstly, and most commonly, electors have been asked questions of the form: 'Which of the following descriptions fit the Conservative Party?' Secondly, electors have been asked: 'Which is the best party for . . .?' Thirdly, and most recently, a semantic differential method has been used, in which respondents have been asked to rate the parties on scales constructed from bi-polar adjectives (e.g. weak . . . powerful). This last approach is used by Butler and Stokes, and further details and references can be found in their book.

Although they have not monitored party images continuously, the Gallup Poll did ask the same question at the time of the 1959, 1964 and 1966 Elections, and the results are reproduced in this section. This approach may be examined in conjunction with that of Butler and Stokes, who cover a roughly similar period (1963–6).

The question asked by Gallup was: 'Which party do you think can best handle the problem of . . . or isn't there much to choose between them on this issue?' The figures in the tables are the percentages of the sample opting for each of the categories. The three columns represent, from left to right, the results in 1959, 1964, and 1966 respectively. These figures are reproduced, with kind permission, from the Gallup Political Index Nos 54 and 72.

It should be noted that these figures refer to the electorate as a whole. While supporters of all parties may be expected to exhibit a degree of agreement on certain images and therefore credit those images to the same party, on many other issues supporters would be likely to take a more partisan approach. The Gallup figures presented here are, of course, simply aggregates, making no distinctions between the views of supporters of different parties. For a discussion of party images as seen by party supporters see Abrams and Rose, *op. cit.*, Chapter 1, and Bealey *et al.*, *op. cit.*, Chapter 10.

The difference between the well-to-do and ordinary people	1959	1964	1966
Conservative	24	23	22
Labour	27	28	29
Liberal	5	6	4
Nothing to choose	20	18	18
Don't know	24	25	27

Personal freedom from restrictions and controls	1959	1964	1966
Conservative	41	34	31
Labour	23	25	26
Liberal	6	6	4
Nothing to choose	13	14	17
Don't know	17	21	22

Having the best ministers and leaders			
Conservative	42	37	28
Labour	24	33	35
Liberal	2	4	3
Nothing to choose	16	11	14
Don't know	16	15	20

Britain's reputation abroad			
Conservative	45	41	36
Labour	21	23	27
Liberal	3	4	3
Nothing to choose	16	15	14
Don't know	15	17	20

Foreign affairs			
Conservative	43	40	33
Labour	21	23	26
Liberal	3	4	2
Nothing to choose	14	12	14
Don't know	19	21	25

Armaments and national defence			
Conservative	35	37	27
Labour	21	26	26
Liberal	2	4	2
Nothing to choose	20	11	18
Don't know	22	22	27

H-bomb			
Conservative	32	37	22
Labour	25	21	22
Liberal	3	3	3
Nothing to choose	20	12	21
Don't know	20	27	32

Maintaining value of the £ sterling			
Conservative	49	36	34
Labour	17	25	28
Liberal	1	3	3
Nothing to choose	12	13	14
Don't know	21	23	21

Prices and cost of living			
Conservative	41	34	32
Labour	38	36	35
Liberal	4	5	3
Nothing to choose	9	11	15
Don't know	8	14	15

Increasing production, country's prosperity			
Conservative	44	39	30
Labour	26	32	36
Liberal	3	4	4
Nothing to choose	12	9	11
Don't know	15	16	19

Increasing export trade

	1959	1964	1966
Conservative	43	37	33
Labour	23	29	32
Liberal	3	4	3
Nothing to choose	14	11	12
Don't know	17	19	20

Income tax and other taxes

	1959	1964	1966
Conservative	40	36	30
Labour	32	32	31
Liberal	3	5	4
Nothing to choose	13	13	17
Don't know	12	14	18

Full employment, short-time working

	1959	1964	1966
Conservative	36	35	29
Labour	39	39	41
Liberal	2	4	3
Nothing to choose	14	11	13
Don't know	9	11	14

Strikes and trade disputes

	1959	1964	1966
Conservative	28	27	22
Labour	40	42	39
Liberal	3	5	2
Nothing to choose	15	9	16
Don't know	14	17	21

Nationalization and private enterprise

	1959	1964	1966
Conservative	37	36	29
Labour	33	32	35
Liberal	4	4	3
Nothing to choose	7	8	10
Don't know	19	20	23

Housing and rents

	1959	1964	1966
Conservative	32	31	27
Labour	43	41	38
Liberal	3	4	3
Nothing to choose	12	9	15
Don't know	10	15	17

National Health Service

	1959	1964	1966
Conservative	28	32	25
Labour	44	40	45
Liberal	4	5	4
Nothing to choose	16	11	13
Don't know	8	12	13

Pensions and welfare of old people

	1959	1964	1966
Conservative	26	29	24
Labour	48	43	46
Liberal	5	6	5
Nothing to choose	12	10	12
Don't know	9	12	13

Hanging and capital punishment

	1959	1964	1966
Conservative	24	21	26
Labour	18	18	21
Liberal	3	3	2
Nothing to choose	21	26	24
Don't know	24	32	27

Immigration of coloured people

	1959	1964	1966
Conservative		30	26
Labour		20	26
Liberal	*	3	3
Nothing to choose		19	20
Don't know		28	25

* Not available.

175

8 Parties, policy-making and innovation

Introduction

In order for a political party to attract regular financial organizational and electoral support it is valuable, though not essential, to have a consistent and distinctive policy programme. Cultural traditions and constitutional realities in Britain make political parties aware of the need to be programmatic in nature if they are to attract support, though programmes may be simple and dominated by a single issue, or complex, and even confused. Most parties, whether Scottish National, Ulster Unionist, Conservative or Labour, appeal in terms of specific principles and policies, whether they be Home Rule for Scotland, the maintenance of the ties between Ulster and Britain, free enterprise, or public ownership of the means of production, but in national election campaigns when the major issue, as perceived by the majority of electors, seems to be 'which party will form the next government', they are obliged to make policy statements on a wide range of domestic and foreign issues.

The need to present policy statements in order to obtain support for party candidates and capture political office may also incidentally help to make the political system work, but such formal activity may be less necessary for parties in other systems such as the U.S.A.[1] The value of party policy-making to the political system as a whole is not restricted merely to those parties comprising the official Government and Opposition in Parliament. In a democratic system parties are expected to act as major instruments of communication, innovation and adaptation, but in part because of the preoccupations of the major parties with winning control of government in Britain and maintaining its existing structure, such functions may also be performed by other parties. The Conservative and Labour parties possess important sources for policy innovation such as the Bow Group or the Fabian Society, but much of the motivation for innovation within these parties is promoted by the desire to maintain or regain control of the existing government.[2] They can and do respond to established group pressures, but minor parties can act as valuable policy innovators reflecting new group or regional attitudes which

176

are neglected by the major parties irrespective of their electoral value. For example, it would be difficult to make out a rational case in terms of electoral advantage for the Liberal Party in its advocacy of British entry into the European Common Market in the early and mid-1960s, while survey evidence indicates that S.N.P. demands for complete self-government for Scotland are shared by a minority of its supporters who nevertheless approve of the efforts of the party to raise the issue of greater Scottish control of Scottish affairs.[3] One consequence, however, of raising new policy issues is that the major parties are likely to take them over as their own if they appear to gain a positive electoral response.

An important point raised here is the extent to which party policies are made by the party leadership, and the existence of important differences between the policy attitudes of party leaders, party activists and the mass supporters of the party.[4] Evidence suggests that such differences often occur, and major parties often avoid taking extreme positions on particular policies in case this might weaken mass or other support. In this chapter such factors are considered in relation to the function of policy innovation in two particular areas: (1) the role and influence of national party conferences in party policy-making and governmental decision-making, (2) the role of political parties as vehicles of institutional or system reform. The analysis is not intended to be comprehensive or necessarily representative, but demonstrates how such party activity can contribute to the redefining of existing policies and the ventilation and possible adoption of new policies.

It is useful also to make some general points about the nature of policy-making in the two major parties. Both parties are programmatic (the Conservatives perhaps less so than Labour) and have mass membership support. The Conservatives, unlike Labour, have generally not subscribed to the view that the mass membership or even party activists should make party policy, though it should not be inferred from this that they have never tried to make or influence policy, or have never succeeded. The function of the mass membership has not, however, been to commit elected Conservative office-holders to policies which they may not wholly support. In contrast, largely because of its extra-parliamentary origins, elected office-holders of the Labour Party are considered, formally at least, to be servants of the Labour movement. This has caused considerable conflict within the Labour Party, and problems for the leadership, especially when in office, and has resulted in several notable Annual Conference conflicts.[5] Hence the failure of Hugh Gaitskell to eliminate the constitutional commitment to public ownership (the famous Clause IV struggle), and the acceptance by the 1960 Conference of a

177

defence policy unacceptable to the P.L.P., who avoided serious difficulties by getting their views accepted at the 1961 Conference. These instances occurred while the party was out of office, but they emphasize the difficult position of the P.L.P. and the N.E.C. should differences arise when the party is in office, with the rank and file asserting that conference decisions bind the P.L.P., and the party leadership refusing to implement such resolutions as policies, without specifically rejecting the autonomy of the annual conference. Such conflict provides a severe test of rank-and-file loyalty if, for example, the party leadership, as the government, presents and seeks to implement policies which have not and would not be approved by conference.

All this assumes that the major parties develop policies in a systematic way, and can put them into practice once elected. Despite the size and resources of the research sections of national party headquarters available to help in the formulation of policies, their policy programmes often seem little more than vote-catching devices. The policy motivations of minor parties may also be influenced by electoral considerations, but it is still plausible to claim for such parties a role as policy innovaters. S.N.P. advocacy of Home Rule for Scotland is hardly a policy calculated to preserve the party in the long-term, since implementation of this goal would probably mean the end of the S.N.P. as a cohesive political force. It is important, therefore, to distinguish between policy innovations by minor parties whose incidental effects would be to improve their electoral position (changes in the electoral system such as the introduction of proportional representation or the alternative vote system) and those whose electoral effects would be negligible and possibly even disadvantageous.

The role of a minor party M.P. is also influenced by factors of party policy and its exposition, and the nationalist M.P.s provide interesting case-studies in the use of the parliamentary forum to press for constitutional change.[6] Study of the policy-making and policy innovation aspects of party activity illustrates the complex amalgam of different and often differing groups and factions which comprise a political party.

Notes

1 See L. D. Epstein, *Political Parties in Western Democracies*, pp. 261–272.
2 For analytic discussion of the function of parties, especially the major party out of power and minor parties, as policy innovators, see T. Lowi,

'Towards Functionalism in Political Science: The Case of Innovation in Party Systems', *American Political Science Review*, 1963, pp. 570–83.
3 See J. P. Cornford and J. A. Brand, 'Scottish Voting Behaviour', in J. N. Wolfe, ed., *Government and Nationalism in Scotland*, Edinburgh, 1969, pp. 17–40.
4 This complex question is explored in R. Rose, 'The Political Ideas of English Party Activists'.
5 See in particular L. D. Epstein, 'Who Makes Party Policy: British Labour 1960–61'.
6 On this point, see J. E. Schwarz, 'The Scottish National Party: Non-violent Separation and Theories of Violence', *World Politics*, 1970, pp. 496–517.

Further reading

The Conservative and Labour Party headquarters publish annual reports of party conferences, with verbatim accounts of debates and other material reported to the conferences. The Conservative, Labour and Liberal parties have within them organizations publishing pamphlets on policy matters by individuals or groups, intended to open up discussion within and outside the party. The Bow Group (which also has a quarterly magazine, *Crossbow*), the Fabian Society and the New Orbits group are examples of these in each party. Magazines which are independent of particular parties but are intended as organs to stimulate discussion by party activists on matters of party policy and strategy include *Socialist Commentary* (see the supplement to the October 1967 issue by three Labour M.P.s entitled *Change Gear! Towards a Socialist Strategy*), and *New Outlook*, a liberal journal. *Liberal News* is also published as a fortnightly newspaper of information and debate for Liberal activists.

Conservative Central Office subsidizes Swinton Conservative College as a centre for meetings of party officials and activists, and the *Swinton Journal* prints articles on policy matters. The Conservative Political Centre publishes a range of pamphlets on policy matters, and the Labour Party research department publishes an *Economic Brief* ten times a year on aspects of economic policy.

For discussion of the process of policy formulation in the Liberal Party, see J. S. Rasmussen, *The Liberal Party*, Chapter 6.

Articles

J. Biffen, 'Party Conference and Party Policy', *Political Quarterly*, 1961, pp. 257–66.
A. P. Brier, 'Analysis of Liberal Activists', *New Society*, 4 November 1965, p. 22.
I. Bulmer-Thomas, 'How Conservative Policy is Formed', *Political Quarterly*, 1953, pp. 190–203.
R. E. Dowse and J. Stanyer, 'The Party Activists', *New Society*, 15 October 1964, p. 6.

L. D. Epstein, 'Partisan Foreign Policy: Britain in the Suez Crisis', *World Politics*, 1960, pp. 201–24.

'Who Makes Party Policy: British Labour, 1960–61', *Midwest Journal of Political Science*, 1962, pp. 165–82.

W. Fienburgh, 'Put Policy on the Agenda', *Fabian Journal*, 1952, pp. 25–33.

D. Hennessy, 'The Communication of Conservative Policy 1957–59', *Political Quarterly*, 1961, pp. 238–56.

K. Hindell and P. Williams, 'Scarborough and Blackpool: An Analysis of Some Votes at the Labour Party Conferences of 1960 and 1961', *Political Quarterly*, 1962, pp. 306–20.

M. P. Kochman, 'Liberal Party Activists and Extremism', *Political Studies*, June 1968, pp. 253–7.

G. Loewenberg, 'The Transformation of British Labour Party Policy Since 1945', *Journal of Politics*, 1959, pp. 234–57.

R. T. McKenzie, 'Policy Decisions in Opposition: A Rejoinder', *Political Studies*, 1957, pp. 176–82.

H. G. Nicholas, 'The Formulation of Party Policy', *Parliamentary Affairs*, 1951, pp. 142–53.

F. S. Northedge, 'British Foreign Policy and the Party System', *American Political Science Review*, 1960, pp. 635–46.

'The Parties and Foreign Policy', *Political Studies*, 1960, pp. 183–6.

J. S. Rasmussen, 'Party Responsibility in Britain and the United States', *Journal of American Studies*, 1967, pp. 233–56.

R. Rose, 'The Political Ideas of English Party Activists', *American Political Science Review*, 1962, pp. 360–71.

'The Bow Group's Role in British Politics', *Western Political Quarterly*, 1961, pp. 865–78.

'Parties, Factions and Tendencies in Britain', *Political Studies*, 1964, pp. 33–46.

S. Rose, 'Policy Decisions in Opposition', *Political Studies*, 1956, pp. 128–38.

'The Labour Party and German Rearmament: A View from Transport House', *Political Studies*, 1966, pp. 133–44.

G. F. Rutau, 'The Labour Party in Ulster', *Review of Politics*, 1967, pp. 526–35.

Lord Windelsham, 'The Communication of Conservative Policy 1963–64', *Political Quarterly*, 1965, pp. 164–80.

National party conferences, party policy and government

The national party conference is an important arena of compromise and conflict for a political party, and can serve a variety of functions. It serves a valuable social function in bringing together rank-and-file activists from all parts of the country, and helps to strengthen their support and loyalty to the party, and is also a source of formal and informal personal communication between the different sections and levels of the party. However, it can also be dysfunctional in that conference debate may expose latent or manifest conflicts within a party and so affect party unity. Party leaders are therefore anxious to avoid open conflict in debate and voting, especially with the increasing mass media coverage of the party conferences of those parties with parliamentary representation, and try to control the pattern of conference resolutions and debate whenever possible. Resolutions are chosen which will allow full and open debate but which are not likely to lead to serious disagreement. Attempts are also made to debate matters of topical importance and allow opinion to be ventilated on a range of policy statements.

The role of the national party conference in policy-making, however, differs over time for any single party and between parties. In particular, when a party is in control of government the annual conference can be a scene of massive unity or an irritating, even embarrassing experience for the leadership. The Labour Party, in particular, when in government, has often encountered disquiet from a conference which is dominated by trade-union delegates, as the example which follows illustrates. The example also testifies to the particular dilemmas and difficulties involved in asserting the principle of democratic decision-making, but at the same time registering disquiet without undermining the authority of the party leadership in the eyes of the wider public, and without seeking to usurp the right of the party in government to make policy decisions as a government and not seem beholden to its rank-and-file activists. Annual party conferences certainly debate party policies, but they play a limited role in the actual making of policies. Party manifestoes which may form the basis of election campaigns are usually drawn up by groups within the party leadership and presented to annual conferences for approval rather than emerging from the formal debates and votes of such conferences.

At the 1968 Labour Party Conference there was much evidence of rank-and-file disquiet, both from constituency and trade-union delegates, at some of the legislation passed by the Labour government and the evidence of public discontent shown in a series of serious local election and parliamentary by-election defeats. The conference

181

rejected several recommendations of the N.E.C., beginning with an extremely divisive debate over the prices-and-incomes policy of the government. Opposition came in particular from the unions who carried a resolution calling for the repeal of legislation restricting wage and salary movements and the rejection of any further legislation which might curtail basic union rights. The speeches which follow from a debate on the final morning of the conference illustrate the dilemma facing the unions, of not wishing to disown a Labour government yet wanting to affirm their serious reservations about certain legislation. The final statement by the then Prime Minister was equally difficult, involving the need to recognize and accept the warnings given yet refusing as head of the government to be dictated to by the unions or by the conference as a whole. At the 1970 Labour Party Conference, as Leader of the Opposition, he was unable to prevent passage of a motion declaring that conference decisions should be binding on M.P.s both in Opposition and government.

Report of 67th Annual Conference of the Labour Party, Blackpool 1968 (pp. 293–300). Four minor speeches are deleted.

Mr H. Scanlon (Amalgamated Union of Engineering and Foundry Workers) moved Composite Resolution No. 20.

This Conference declares its support for the Labour Government in carrying out its election programme of 1966, and recognises the difficulties both at home and abroad with which the Government has been confronted during its term of office and, subject to the reservations involved in the policy decisions of the T.U.C., pledges support to the Government. [Resolution carried.]

He said: Madam Chairman and Conference, to paraphrase Willie Simpson on Mark Twain, our moving of this resolution may amaze our friends and certainly will be misrepresented by our enemies. But the resolution will be moved and the resolution says what it means and means what it says. It is positive in its approach, calling for the fulfilment of the 1966 programme, rather than condemning what has been achieved.

It highlights what, by democratic decisions, this Labour Party and the T.U.C. consider the greatest barrier to the achievement of that programme, namely the manner in which the wages policy has been operated; and we make no apologies for returning to this theme. Is not the greatest difference between the rank and the file and the Government simply this: the Government consider the Prices and Incomes Act an essential weapon in fulfilling that programme; the

182

membership are convinced, as never before, that this is the most disastrous way of preventing the fulfilment of that programme?

And we say to the Government and to the Executive, it is not a question of either preventing wage increases by statutory measures or, as George Brown suggests, that the higher paid workers, or the so-called higher paid workers, shall subsidise the lower paid. It is a simple, straightforward socialist belief of ensuring that less of the national gross product goes in rent, interest and profit and more goes in wages and salaries. (*Applause.*)

Let us now remind ourselves of our programme. We undertook to build more houses, schools, roads, hospitals and to improve our educational standards by raising the school leaving age; to raise pensions and health service standards; to raise living standards, a necessary part of which was to plan for full employment by fiscal measures and by direction of industry into depressed and grey areas.

Of course, we know these things must be paid for. The world does not owe us a living. We knew that in 1964. We know it infinitely better in 1968. The key to the fulfilment of this programme is, as Michael Foot said, an expansionist economy—to insist upon a high investment, high productivity, high wage economy as originally envisaged in the national plan.

Yes, and the trade union movement is prepared to play its full part in this programme. We know that a prosperous and efficient industry is more likely to mean high wages and living standards for our members than a poor and inefficient industry.

In spite of all that has been said about labour problems, in spite of all the adverse criticism in the Press and elsewhere, the British motor-car industry is still one of the most efficient in Europe, and we say that having visited Italy, Germany and France to see their counterparts. The same can be said of the oil refining and chemical industries, and it is not just a coincidence that relatively high rates of pay prevail in such industries.

It is the less efficient industries with a calibre of management that Donovan described as incredibly low that present the problems to us.

Our achievements to date were so well stated by the Prime Minister in his statement it would be churlish to try and add to it. We support, and will work for the return of, a Labour Government, not in any negative way that a Tory Government would be so much worse—that is a blinding flash of the obvious. What we say is, Powellism, with its free enterprise law of the jungle and blatant racialism, is equally obnoxious but slightly less nauseating than the more gentle Tory line of so-called superior educated and wealthy manipulators of finance knowing what is better for the lower orders.

Neither have we to be reminded of what will happen to the trade unions if Tories are returned to power. All the clever talk about free trade unions, about free collective bargaining, cannot hide their intention of making agreements and procedures legally enforceable, and this against the advice of the Royal Commission.

They know better than anybody that if workers, under severe provocation, break a contract, the present law is adequate to deal with it. But they equally know that if they can introduce a law which attacks and confiscates trade union funds by the imposition of punitive and crippling fines, they render the trade unions impotent in their future battles with unscrupulous employers. (*Applause.*)

We support a Labour Government because we believe it can, and must, fulfil its election pledges. We know that the trade unions gave birth to this Labour Party because industrial gains were being negatived by political action of the employing class. We have, since its birth, been able to conduct a dialogue, and, although at times our views may differ, we know that through the medium of our decisions at the T.U.C. and at these Annual Conferences, we are able to convince and influence successive Labour Governments as to the correctness of our cause.

We must, however, refer to the growing practice of pretending that Conference decisions do not matter. (*Applause.*)

Democracy is not an abstraction, to be used only when decisions coincide with the views of our leaders, whether those leaders be politicians or trade unionists. The great debate does not mean that we, through our constituency parties and our branches, our regional conferences and this great Conference, debate and discuss all the issues that are before us only to have them ignored if those decisions do not suit.

Conference decisions are not always a reflection of what the general electorate may desire, but they are a far greater reflection of what is universally felt than the personal opinion of any trade union leader or politician. (*Applause.*) In the past sincere and genuine criticism has been equated with disloyalty and has resulted in too much internal bitterness and recrimination, both politically and industrially.

Therefore, we say that this resolution does two things: it sounds a warning to the Government that our support means also the fullest use of our critical faculties rather than our unconditional acceptance of everything that is done. It also says to the rest of the country that despite our reservations this Labour Government has the capacity to build the type of society we would wish to see, and is worthy of our continued support. Let those of us who are critical of aspects of Government policy—and rightly critical—be a little more forceful in criticism of Conservatism and all it stands for (*Applause*) for we know

184

what will happen if this Labour Government is not returned at the next election. The lesson of those 13 years does not need to be restated at this Conference.

We look forward to the completion of the 1966 election programme and pledge our full support for its implementation. We equally look forward to the Government heeding our reservations, so we can come forward with unqualified support next year and we look to that Conference as a springboard for a great socialist victory at the next general election. (*Applause*.)

Mr P. Cheney (Merton and Morden C.L.P.) moved the following amendment to the Composite Resolution:

Line 5: Delete 'subject to the reservations involved in the policy decisions of the T.U.C.' [Amendment lost.]

First of all, let us congratulate Hugh Scanlon in what, by his own definition, was an intellectual speech. We are putting forward this amendment because, in our view, the motion is based upon a distortion of the relationship between decisions of the Trades Union Congress and those of this Labour Party Conference. The Labour Party has its own decision-making process—that is, this Conference, which is quite separate and apart from that of the T.U.C. To make one determine the other is, in our view, wrong as well as undemocratic.

As the representative of Merton C.L.P., of course, I respect decisions made at the Trades Union Congress, but those decisions are for the T.U.C. to make and act upon themselves. I believe it is our duty, in this Labour Party Conference, to make our decisions and to act upon them in our own way.

If Conference were to accept this composite without our amendment we would be saying that the Constituency Labour Parties should be bound by decisions made at the T.U.C. at which they are not represented.

It is an unfortunate but well-known fact that some Trade Union Congress unions are not even affiliated to the Labour Party. (*Applause*.) The delegates to the T.U.C. are made up of a wide political spectrum: Tories, Communists, Chinese Communists, Trotskyites and even some Labour Party supporters. Why then should decisions made by that Congress be made mandatory upon this Conference? Surely no one should expect our Conference to accept the reservations expressed by the T.U.C.

This would be even more true had the original wording of the resolution stood by which support for Government policy was qualified, subject to policy decisions for the A.E.F. Such arrogance!

Perhaps the best argument for amending this motion is the pressure that has been brought upon me by the A.E.F. to withdraw the amendment. I was reminded more than once that my constituency has a financial arrangement with some trade unions. In my view, this type of pressure is intolerable. Even in the days of Carron's Law it was not sought to control the Constituency Labour Parties in this way. Apparently, under Scanlon's Law the movers of the composite have even greater territorial ambitions. (*Applause.*)

There is a suspicion that Hugh Scanlon is using this platform and this Conference to solve problems that have gone far beyond his capacity to control. (*Applause.*) I might remind him that this Conference is not an extension of the A.E.F. National Committee. (*Applause.*)

Unless, Madam Chairman, I can be given an assurance that by accepting the unamended composite local and regional Labour Parties are not to be subject to the diktat of George Woodcock or even the A.E.F., then I must ask Conference to decide by its own vote whether or not we are the masters or the servants in our own house. (*Applause.*)

The Chairman: Comrades, I am reminded that we have a very heavy agenda and a short morning. I must now call on our Prime Minister, Mr Harold Wilson, to reply.

Rt. Hon. Harold Wilson, M.P. (Prime Minister): Madam Chairman, comrades, I will be brief. The National Executive Committee, and the Labour Government equally, are quite happy to recommend, with appropriate reservations, to Conference the acceptance of Composite Resolution No. 20 moved by Hugh Scanlon on behalf of the A.E.F. and expressing the support of this Conference for the Labour Government. We support the amendment.

This resolution, I think, embodies the mood of this Conference.

We are, and must remain, a Party of protest against everything in British society that needs changing and must be changed. But a Party whose protest is not negative. As every debate this week has emphasised, a Party which accepts the responsibility of Government.

What we have seen this week is the emergence of this Labour Party as a Government Party. We have laid down the conditions under which Labour can be accepted as the continuing Government Party. Just as next week, let us express the charitable hope, in this hall the Conservatives will be able to establish the conditions which will fit them to be what they are manifestly not worthy of being today, a responsible instrument of continuing Opposition. (*Applause.*)

At this Conference we have debated, and reached decisions on, the most urgent problems Britain is facing at home and in our overseas relationships.

In the National Executive Committee's document we have accepted the need for two-way participation and laid down procedures for ensuring it. But this participation has been, and is, a continuing process: a process we seek to intensify and develop.

The speeches this week have been a contribution to the policies which your Government will be carrying through. Every resolution carried against the platform this week—and you have not been un-productive in this regard—we accept as a warning to the Government. A warning, not an instruction. No-one has ever seriously claimed that a Government which must be responsible to Parliament can be instructed. This was repeatedly said from this platform under the last Labour Government and never seriously challenged.

But I think we all feel the debates and the resolutions have not all been on subjects which have hit the headlines. For me, one stands out in particular. In the debate on handicapped children, I think we were all moved by the speech by the delegate representing the National League of the Blind and Disabled. (*Applause.*) I am proud to be able to tell you that that delegate is a Labour county councillor represent-ing Kirkby in my own constituency.

Now, this Conference has demonstrated that Labour's strength is changing Britain, and this is as true of all the issues that were debated on Monday as of all the other issues that have been debated through-out the week.

A strong movement and strong Government. I repeat that your Government will stand by the policies which must be carried through to secure economic strength and to secure all that depends on the achievement of economic strength.

On Tuesday I spelled out the evidence of developing industrial strength which must be the basis of our economic recovery. It is from that strength that our developing political strength will be re-newed.

Only a few months ago our enemies tried to break our nerve, to write us off. Today, our most hostile critics have to accept that they have failed. (*Applause.*)

I spoke on Tuesday of the conditions on which we must insist for economic recovery. Given this, there is nothing now which can halt the inexorable success of the Labour movement except the Labour movement itself.

If political success depends upon economic success, let me remind this Conference that economic success equally depends on sustaining the rapid increase in production and productivity which you and which everyone represented here has made possible by their efforts over this past year. Production, productivity, exports, everything we have achieved at so great a cost, can be imperilled by ill-considered industrial action, whose effect can only be to put the employment of so many of our people at risk. (*Applause.*) Day by day we read of hard

187

won export orders frustrated by sectional and self-regarding action which no one here would defend.

This movement—and I speak now for the whole Labour movement which is represented here—will not readily forgive any action which endangers our common purpose.

So as we go from here to carry the fight back into the country, let us proclaim this theme of unity, comradeship and loyalty which has animated all our debates this week. I have called this movement, every delegate here and all whom we as delegates represent, to proclaim their support for their Government—a Government whose courage has given us the strength to change Britain, a Government which has earned the right to ask the country to support us in bringing about that change.

This week we have spoken for Britain. It is now to Britain that we must go out and speak. (*Prolonged applause.*)

The Chairman: Thank you, Harold, we have got your message.

Nationalists in Parliament: Strategies for constitutional change

The growth of Scottish and Welsh nationalist movements as political forces in the latter part of the 1960s produced new and distinctive patterns of party activity. Both the S.N.P. and Plaid Cymru, while opposed to the structure of the existing political system, decided to work within it to achieve change and operate in a party system where their main task was to persuade the government party to accede to many of their demands. Their elected representatives in Parliament adopted a uniform and often complementary tactic, relying in particular on asking questions and making speeches designed to 'expose' injustices suffered by their countries, and hoping that evidence of increasing electoral support would force the government to move in some way towards their basic goals.

The S.N.P. demands for complete self-government are linked with the presentation of an alternative economic policy to be pursued by an independent Scottish government. Plaid Cymru seeks self-government for Wales but not complete separation. The S.N.P. pledges to send M.P.s to Westminster to vote and work 'in the interests of the people of Scotland' and 'in support of legislation which is in accord with the S.N.P. policy', and on securing a majority of Scottish seats in the House of Commons would demand the creation of a Scottish legislature, or would join with any other Scottish M.P.s who care to join them, in forming a Scottish government, loyal to the crown. (*SNP and You: Aims and Policies of the Scottish National Party*, 3rd ed., S.N.P. 1968, pp. 2–3, 7.) The distinctive nature of the S.N.P. platform is recognized by H. J. Hanham who asserts: 'Anyone who reads the SNP 1946 policy statement (which is still official SNP policy) will recognise that he is reading an unusual document. For it deliberately sets out to offer something quite different from the offerings of the other parties.' (H. J. Hanham, *Scottish Nationalism*, London, 1969, p. 175. An Appendix contains the full statement of aims and policies, see pp. 213–30.) This attempt at policy innovation and distinctiveness is reflected at the constituency level where the party is strong, and detailed policy statements concerning specific constituency problems are set out (see *Blueprint for Argyll*, Argyll Constituency Association, S.N.P., 1968). It is also reflected in the activities of the 1320 Club which published policy studies such as *In Defens: A Pilot Outline of Scotland's Defence Requirements*, 1968, and in the articles of the monthly newspaper, the *Highland Nationalist*.

Along with assertions of policies of self-government, there are attempts to extract limited concessions from the government. Plaid

Cymru claim that continued political pressure produced a B.B.C. Welsh Home Service, a Welsh Day in Parliament, a Welsh Grand Committee, a Secretary of State for Wales and a planning authority for Wales. Both parties also claimed credit for having extracted from the Labour government in 1968 the appointment of a Commission to enquire into the constitution and government of the United Kingdom. Other parties, including the Liberals and the Communists, have also taken a keen interest in Home Rule policies, and the Liberals have put forward bills to provide separate Parliaments for Scotland and Wales. However, the party distinguishes its position from the S.N.P. and demands Scottish self-government and control of home affairs, but not complete separation, and it has been an important force in raising the broader issue of constitutional change and the devolution of governmental authority. The S.N.P. and the Scottish Liberal Party have moved from positions of antagonism to formal and informal attempts to discuss their respective policies and discussion of possible electoral pacts or agreements, but there is less evidence of such activity between Plaid Cymru and the Welsh Liberal Party. The total effect of the activities of all these parties in raising questions of the location of governmental authority has been considerable, and forced the major parties to provide their own recommendations on such matters.

An example of the type of parliamentary efforts to raise substantial policy questions by nationalist M.P.s is shown by the speech of Gwynfor Evans, then a Plaid Cymru M.P., taken at random from a parliamentary debate on Welsh affairs in 1969.

Parliamentary Debates (Hansard), Fifth Series, Vol. 782 (22 April 1969), columns 361–8.

> **Mr Gwynfor Evans** (Carmarthen): During the past year we have had eight or nine hours in which to discuss Welsh affairs on the Floor of the House. It looks as though during the current year the number of hours allowed for this purpose will be even fewer. It is incredible that our country, which has so many problems to face, should be allowed only one day a year—and that a short day—to discuss its problems in this Chamber.
>
> **Mr Alec Jones** (Rhondda, West): The hon. Gentleman must realise that many of the major problems of Wales are discussed on the Floor of the House day in and day out and that there is ample opportunity for those who seek to use the opportunities created in this House for the purpose to express in this Chamber the opinions and desires of our people.
>
> **Mr Evans:** Unfortunately, it is not the problems of Wales that are discussed. They are part of bigger problems which are discussed,

and to which the hon. Gentleman has referred. We do not get anything like the time allowed to countries comparable in size to Wales to discuss our affairs. And even when we discuss Welsh affairs, as we are doing today, we can arrive at no decision. It is merely a matter of the Government listening to what we say. We can make no decisions because there is no legislation before us. Before 1945 we did not have even one day on which to discuss Welsh affairs, so the present situation is an improvement on that.

There are so many problems to face and to solve that I can do no more than refer to some of the more urgent ones. Communications have been referred to, and I make no apology for referring to them again, because road, rail, sea, and air communications are the key to industrial and economic development. One of the main reasons why we have not seen in Wales the kind of economic development that we should have liked to see, and one reason why economic development has failed to match the needs and opportunities of our time, is that we in Wales are at a disadvantage compared with neighbouring regions of England when it comes to matters such as roads and railways.

That is one major reason why last year—and this is one of the facts to which the Minister did not refer in his opening speech—we had 45,000 fewer jobs for men in Wales than there were four years previously. That is one reason why unemployment remains chronically high at about the 40,000 mark, despite the heavy emigration. That is one reason why the activity rate in Wales has fallen to 47·4 per cent compared with 57·4 per cent in England. A fact which I elicited from a Department is that if we had a rate equal to that in England, which in itself is not very impressive, 200,000 more people would be at work in Wales. It is not merely that the rate has fallen absolutely. In comparison with England the gap is widening. There is a bigger gap each year between the Welsh rate and the English rate. Even in comparison with England the Welsh situation is unsatisfactory, and it is deteriorating. For Ministers to say, as they do time and again, that this is due to the large number of self-employed persons in Wales, and to the number of people employed in agriculture, is puerile.

The showpieces filling the Government's window—and we have heard about these again tonight—are the advance factories. We have heard a lot about millions of square feet of factory space being provided. When I asked a Question about this a few weeks ago I was told that the Board of Trade factories built and tenanted since 1964 employed 600 men and 400 women. At Crynant in the Neath area the Cefncoed colliery, which used to employ 800 men, closed the other day. There is now an advance factory in that area

191

—it was shown on television the other night—which employs only two persons.

Mr Donald Coleman (Neath): Is the hon. Gentleman aware that by indulging in that kind of talk he is undermining the efforts of the man who is running this factory? Is he aware that that man is confident that he can succeed with this factory? The kind of talk that we get from the hon. Gentleman shows that he is doing everything possible to undermine the future of the Dulais Valley.

Mr Evans: I can understand the hon. Gentleman getting annoyed, because this factory is in his constituency. I am putting this forward as a corrective to the golden glow that we had from the Minister. Listening to the right hon. Gentleman one would have thought that everything in the garden was lovely. I am putting forward facts which help us to see the situation in perspective. One of the main reasons for the situation is the lack of development of communications.

Admittedly, there was a tremendous leeway to be made up in road construction. That is the responsibility not only of the present Government but of the English Government, of whatever colour. That leeway required that we should spend at least twice as much as we are now spending on roads in Wales. If we had a Welsh Government, even on our present income we should be able to do just that and we should, indeed, have been doing it for years. Instead, according to the White Paper, the amount is being reduced.

Not only have we failed to make up leeway. The priorities for communications are wrong because the Government have no strategy for economic development in Wales. The Westminster Governments have spent more on the Severn Bridge than the total annual expenditure on roads in Wales. Indeed, the total estimated expenditure for next year is still less than the sum that was spent on the Severn Bridge.

We have heard of some of the results of building the Severn Bridge. Industries have been moving from Wales—from Cardiff, in particular—over the bridge to Bristol. The Town Clerk of Cardiff has said that the City is losing not only to Bristol, but mainly to Bristol, industries and commercial headquarters worth £200,000 annually to Cardiff in rates.

Another example is the Cardiff-Merthyr road, which is to be the first section of the Cardiff-Caernarvon road, the north-south road running throughout Wales. I am glad that a start is being made at last but, at the present rate of progress, the highway will not reach Caernarvon until about the year 2,100 A.D. and the Cardiff-Merthyr section will not be finished until about 1995. In the South-West itself, we see the same sorry story of grossly inadequate highways. The congestion on the roads there is the factor which most inhibits development of the area. Hope deferred in the Carmarthen area makes the heart there grow sick.

I turn to the subject of ports on the Severn sea—a better phrase than 'Bristol Channel'. Bristol's prosperity was based on the slave trade, when ships were small. Now that ships are very much bigger, it hopes to maintain and develop its prosperity by means of the Portbury scheme. It can be said that this scheme is a dead duck, for the simple but sufficient reason that there is not enough water in that part of the Severn sea—the part beyond Cardiff—to carry big ships. It would mean prohibitive costs for dredging in order to take up to Bristol the huge ships now being built.

This is also a factor in Severn-side development. It is ridiculous to think that we can develop a conurbation on a vast scale there, for I do not think that any Government would be foolish enough ever to invest the vast sums of money necessary to make that kind of development possible.

Mr William Edwards: Does the hon. Member fail to understand that Bristol has sufficient capital resources of its own to develop the port in the way it wishes? It is a Government decision which is preventing Bristol from using its own capital resources to develop the port, even though the natural resources may not be of the best.

Mr Evans: I am afraid that Providence has provided that the facts of nature are all against it. Far more sensible would it be to develop the Swansea Bay area. That area will certainly have a great future when we get Welsh Government. It has all the natural advantages, including the tremendous advantage of depth of water near the coast at Swansea. Up to a few hundred yards off the coast there are 30 fathoms of water. The possibility is there of development of a Europort with an ideal site. Perhaps the hon. Member for Merioneth (Mr William Edwards) would like to see such development in Blaenau Ffestiniog, but Swansea has more advantages.

One notes that the temper and anti-social outlook of British Railways in Wales is revealed by the scandalous destruction of valuable station buildings. When private persons deliberately destroy valuable property they get gaoled, but the British Railways Board, which destroys property to the tune of hundreds of thousands of £s, get C.B.E.s and knighthoods. There is a grave danger of the Board destroying one of the most important lines left open in Wales, a line which runs through central Wales.

I am glad that the right hon. Member for Leeds, North-East (Sir K. Joseph), when he was Minister for Welsh Affairs, gave great

193

assistance in combating a similar proposal made by the Railways Board to close the line. It is partly due to his assistance that the line was kept open. I hope that the present Secretary of State will give similar assistance now that the line is again threatened. If the Government allowed the Board to do this they would deserve to be cast into outer darkness by the people of the large area which the railway serves.

We need modernisation of railways and electrification of the lines, but that is something which we are not to have. This connects with the intention of the Government completely to re-organise the whole electricity industry. The Government should be warned that if they do not recognise Wales as an entity in this matter and establish a board for the whole of Wales which would be responsible for the generation and distribution of electricity in the whole of Wales, they will face even more serious trouble than they face now.

We also need a water board with adequate powers, not merely a water resources board about which we have heard tonight. We need a board which could develop, control and sell water resources, as is done not only on the Continent of Europe, but in the United States.

Mr Hooson: I have followed the hon. Member's argument with interest, but I should like to know whether he can give an example of any country which actually sells water as opposed to obtaining capital for development of a dam.

Mr Evans: I gave the example of Switzerland where water is sold from one canton to another. This happens also between different States in the United States of America. There is no difficulty about it. Water, being one of our great natural resources, could be developed in this way for the benefit of Wales. Just as we do not get the kind of Council for Wales that Welsh people demand, and do not get an elected council but merely an advisory council, so we do not have a Countryside Commission to look after our National Parks. We do have the separate boards which are not needed by Wales. A so-called Rural Development Board is to be imposed on a part of Wales although no one except Ministry officials wants it. The purpose was bluntly stated by the Ministry spokesman in the recent hearing at Aberystwyth when he said that it is to accelerate the formation of commercial holdings. That is a great Socialist objective, but it is not something that the farmers enjoy and approve. It involves getting rid of the small farm, the family farm, by amalgamation. I am delighted that Carmarthenshire is to escape the Board's attentions, even though the Report of the Inquiry at Aberystwyth says that—in its early stages of operation—note that apparently it is only then that this will happen—the Board will need to be wise, patient and forbearing in its public relations.

Mrs Winifred Ewing (Hamilton): Would the hon. Gentleman explain to me why, when so many bodies wish to have an elected council in Wales, we do not have one? Would he care to say how many bodies wished to have an elected council?

Mr Evans: I understand that all the political parties in Wales wished that. I understand that there was strong opposition from certain Scottish interests, and that it was mainly because of Scottish opposition that——

Mr Hector Monro (Dumfries): Absolute rubbish.

Mr Evans: One knows that Cabinet secrets are not revealed——

Mrs Ewing: The united Front Bench speaks again.

Mr Evans: In relation to Wales and Scotland, there is complete collusion between the two sides. Their policies towards Wales are very similar.

I return to the question of the Rural Development Board. One sees that only in its early stages of operation is it required to exercise wisdom, patience and forbearance. Evidently, the need will cease after a few years of operation. That is just what the farmers of the area have feared all along.

We shall have a farcical situation if the Government insist on thrusting this engine of their bad policies on an unwilling people. The Tories have made clear several times that when they come to power in a year or two one of their first actions will be to abolish the Board. In those circumstances, what could be sillier than going ahead with the plan?

The Government's penchant for far bigger units, amalgamation, and centralisation is seen not only in things like farms and hospitals but also in local government reorganisation, where they propose——

The Minister of Agriculture, Fisheries and Food (Mr Cledwyn Hughes): The hon. Gentleman is indulging in the grossest exaggeration, but he would be prepared to admit that the existence of the Rural Development Board means that about £500,000 a year will be invested in the area to improve roads and other amenities. Is he against that as well?

Mr Evans: I do not think that it means that at all. The figure of £500,000 is mentioned, but there is no guarantee that even a few pounds of it will be used. Most of that money can be obtained in other ways from grants which are already available.

I was about to speak about the knocking together of local authorities. It is the Government's plan, as we know from their White Paper, to knock together the Welsh county councils and to

195

abolish the small urban councils which have done splendid work in Wales. They should drop these reactionary proposals just as they have dropped the Parliament (No. 2) Bill.

Another futile proposal which should have been dropped is the Constitutional Commission. When the Government announced it six months ago, the Press was almost unanimous in saying that it was just a time-wasting gimmick. It has been said that a week is a long time in politics, but six months have passed since the Commission was announced, and it has not yet even met. It is too late to play at politics like this.

The Welsh people have been infected by freedom beyond hope of recovery. Hundreds of thousands of Welshmen are now hopeless cases dedicated to national freedom. Even long-standing Conservative Unionists of both the Tory and Labour Unionist Parties have lost their immunity from infection. Wales is lost to England, because she is finding herself.

Mr J. Idwal Jones (Wrexham): What does the hon. Gentleman mean by 'Labour Unionists', in the light of his denial that he is a national separatist?

Mr Evans: I had already sat down, but I am glad to be able to say, if the hon. Gentleman did not already know it, that the Labour Party is a Unionist party. It does not believe in a separate Government for Wales. What does it believe in, therefore? It believes in political and constitutional unionism between England and Wales, just as the Tory party has hitherto believed.

Additional sources

Black Paper on Wales, Plaid Cymru, Cardiff, 1967.

E. H. Davies, 'Welsh Nationalism', *Political Quarterly*, 1968, pp. 322–32.

W. P. Grant and R. J. C. Preece, 'Welsh and Scottish Nationalism', *Parliamentary Affairs*, 1968, pp. 255–63.

J. G. Kellas, 'Scottish Nationalism' in D. Butler and M. Pinto-Duschinsky, *The British General Election of 1970*, Appendix V, pp. 446–62.

J. P. Mackintosh, 'Scottish Nationalism', *Political Quarterly*, 1968, pp. 389–402.

I. McLean, 'The Rise and Fall of the Scottish National Party', *Political Studies*, 1970, pp. 357–72.

K. O. Morgan, *Wales in British Politics*, Cardiff, 1963.

D. Steel, 'Out of Control—A Critical Examination of the Government of Scotland', Scottish Liberal Party, Edinburgh, 1968.

Appendices: **Party rules and constitutions**

A. Rules and Standing Orders of the National Union of Conservative and Unionist Associations

Rules

Rule I

The name of this organisation of Conservative and Unionist Associations shall be '*The National Union of Conservative and Unionist Associations*', hereinafter referred to as '*The National Union*'.

Rule II

The functions of the NATIONAL UNION shall be:
(1) To promote the formation and development of a Conservative and Unionist Association in every Constituency in England, Wales and Northern Ireland and to foster thought and effort in furtherance of the principles and aims of the Party.
(2) To form a centre of united action, and to act as a link between the Leader of the Party and all organisations of the Party in England, Wales and Northern Ireland.
(3) To maintain close relationship with the Conservative and Unionist Central Office.
(4) To work in close co-operation with the Scottish Conservative and Unionist Association and the Ulster Unionist Council.

For the attainment of the above functions the work of the National Union shall be dealt with through a Central Council, Conference, Executive Committee, General Purposes Committee, and Provincial Area Councils.

Rule III

The Association of the Party in each Constituency in England, Wales and Northern Ireland, and the Central Association for each Borough with two or more Constituency Associations, subscribing annually direct to the National Union not less than Two Guineas, shall, subject to the approval of the Executive Committee, be Members of the National Union.

The approval of the Executive Committee in respect of the membership of any such Association may be withdrawn at any time at the discretion of the Executive Committee whereupon such Association shall immediately cease to be a Member of the National Union.

Subscriptions, which shall not be returnable either in whole or in part in the case of cessation of membership, shall be due on the 1st January in each year and unless paid, together with arrears (if any), the privileges of membership shall be forfeited.

Rule IV

(a) The Central Council, at its Annual Meeting, shall elect a President, a Chairman and three Vice-Chairmen, who shall be known as Officers of the National Union.

(b) Past Chairmen of the National Union and the Past Chairmen of the National Union Executive Committee shall be invited to become Hon. Vice-Presidents of the National Union.

Provincial Area Councils

Rule V

The Council of each Provincial Area in England and Wales shall be constituted annually as follows:

(1) The Officers of the Provincial Area, and the Officers of each County Organisation (if any) within the Provincial Area.

(2) The Officers of each duly constituted and approved Provincial Area Advisory Committee.

(3) The members of the Provincial Area Executive Committee and members of the Executive Committee of the National union representing the Provincial Area.

(4) Representatives of each Constituency Association within the Provincial Area, as follows:

   (a) The members of the National Union Central Council, i.e.:

      (i) Two representatives (one of each sex) including, if possible, the Chairman of the Association and the Chairman of the Women's Divisional Advisory Committee.

     (ii) The Honorary Treasurer (or a deputy) of the Association.

    (iii) The Chairman (or a deputy) of the Young Conservative and Unionist Divisional Committee.

    (iv) The Chairman (or a deputy) of the Trade Unionists' Advisory Committee. The representative must be a bona fide member of a trade union.

  (b) Such numbers of representatives as the Provincial Area Council may decide, one-third to be men, one-third to be women, and one-third to be Young Conservatives.

  (c) The Certificated Agent.

  (d) The Certificated Organiser.

(5) Representatives of the Central Association for each Borough with two Constituency Associations, as follows:

  (a) The members of the National Union Central Council, i.e.:

     (i) Two representatives (one of each sex) including the Chairman (or a deputy) of the Association.

    (ii) The Honorary Treasurer (or a deputy) of the Association.

    (iii) The Chairman (or a deputy) of the Young Conservative and Unionist Committee.

  (b) Such numbers of representatives as the Provincial Area Council may decide, one-third to be men, one-third to be women, and one-third to be Young Conservatives.

  (c) The Certificated Agent.

  (d) The Certificated Organiser.

(6) Representatives of the Central Association for each Borough with three or more Constituency Associations as follows:

  (a) The members of the National Union Central Council, i.e.:

     (i) Four representatives (two of each sex) including the Chairman (or a deputy) of the Association.

    (ii) The Honorary Treasurer (or a deputy) of the Association.

    (iii) Two representatives of the Young Conservative and Unionist Committee, including the Chairman (or a deputy).

    (iv) The Chief Certificated Agent.

  (b) Such numbers of representatives as the Provincial Area Council may decide, one-third to be men, one-third to be women, and one-third to be Young Conservatives.

(c) The Chief Certificated Organiser.

(7) Not more than two representatives of each Subscribing Organisation and Club within the Provincial Area.

(8) Vice-Presidents and Honorary Members elected by the Provincial Area.

(9) Four representatives of each University and College Conservative and Unionist Association within the Provincial Area.

(10) The Conservative and Unionist Members of the House of Lords resident within the Provincial Area who are in receipt of the Party Whip.

(11) The Conservative and Unionist Members of the House of Commons representing Constituencies within the Provincial Area, who are in receipt of the Party Whip.

(12) The prospective Conservative and Unionist Candidates approved by the Standing Advisory Committee on Candidates and officially selected by Constituency Associations within the Provincial Area.

(13) The Chairman of the National Union, the Chairman of the Executive Committee, and the Honorary Secretary and the Secretary of the National Union.

(14) The Central Office Area Agents.

Rule VI

The Council of each Provincial Area in England and Wales shall, under Rules adopted by such Council, elect annually the following:

(1) The President, Chairman, Vice-Chairmen, Honorary Treasurer and Honorary Secretary.

(2) The representatives of the Provincial Area on the Central Council and Executive Committee of the National Union, as provided for under the terms of Rules IX (7) and XII (3).

Provincial Area Committees *with executive powers*

Rule VII

Each Provincial Area in England and Wales shall elect annually a committee having executive powers with such a constitution as in the opinion of the Area Council concerned shall be best suited to the needs of the particular Area.

In such constitution due regard shall be paid to the representation on that committee of men, women and Young Conservatives. Written nominations shall be received for the elected element (if any) of the committee.

The constitution of such committees shall be submitted to the Executive Committee of the National Union for approval.

Rule VIII

The powers and duties of the Executive Committee of each Provincial Area in England and Wales shall include the following:

(1) To promote, superintend, and carry through such work of organisation and political education within the Provincial Area as may be considered necessary.

(2) To receive reports from the Provincial Area Advisory Committees and to take such steps thereon as may be deemed proper.

(3) To advise the Executive Committee of the National Union.

(4) To keep the Chairman of the Party Organisation in touch with the needs of every Constituency within the Provincial Area.

(5) To obtain local views on public questions, and transmit them to Headquarters, or to Members of Parliament representing Constituencies within the Provincial Area.

(6) To be a channel of inter-communication between the particular Constituencies within the Provincial Area for the purpose of rendering mutual assistance, and of arranging concerted action.

(7) To administer the funds of the Provincial Area.

(8) To appoint such Sub-Committees and to delegate to them such powers as may from time to time be considered necessary.

(9) To summon the Provincial Area Council at such times as may be deemed necessary, and to draw up the Agenda for the Council Meetings.

(10) To submit a Report of the acts and proceedings of the Committee at every ordinary meeting of the Provincial Area Council.

(11) To frame By-laws for its own guidance, provided always that they are in accordance with the Rules of the National Union.

The Central Council

Rule IX

The Central Council shall be constituted annually as follows:
   (1) The members of the Executive Committee designated in Rule XII.
   (2) The Hon. Vice-Presidents of the National Union.
   (3) The Secretary of each National Advisory Committee.
   (4) Representatives of each Constituency Association as follows:
      (a) Two representatives (one of each sex) including, if possible, the Chairman of the Association and the Chairman of the Women's Divisional Advisory Committee.
      (b) The Honorary Treasurer (or a deputy) of the Association.
      (c) The Chairman (or a deputy) of the Young Conservative and Unionist Divisional Committee.
      (d) The Chairman (or a member) of the Trade Unionist Advisory Committee. The representative must be a bona fide member of a trade union.
   (5) Representatives of the Central Association for each Borough with two Constituency Associations, as follows:
      (a) Two representatives (one of each sex) including the Chairman (or a deputy) of the Association.
      (b) The Honorary Treasurer (or a deputy) of the Association.
      (c) The Chairman (or a deputy) of the Young Conservative and Unionist Committee.
   (6) Representatives of the Central Association for each Borough with three or more Constituency Associations as follows:
      (a) Four representatives (two of each sex) including the Chairman (or a deputy) of the Association.
      (b) The Honorary Treasurer (or a deputy) of the Association.
      (c) Two representatives of the Young Conservative and Unionist Committee, including the Chairman (or a deputy).
      (d) The Chief Certificated Agent.
   (7) Representatives of each Provincial Area of the National Union, as follows:
      (a) The President, Chairman, Honorary Treasurer and

one other representative of the Provincial Area Council.

(b) The Chairman (or a deputy) and one other representative of each duly constituted and approved Provincial Area Advisory Committee.

(8) Representatives appointed by other organisations as follows:

    (a) Two representatives appointed by each University and College Conservative and Unionist Association.

    (b) The Chairman, Secretary, and six other representatives appointed by the Governing Body of the Association of Conservative Clubs.

    (c) The Chairman and five other representatives of the Conservative Commonwealth and Overseas Council.

    (d) The Chairman and one other representative of the Conservative Overseas Bureau.

    (e) The Chancellor, Secretary, and four other representatives appointed by the Headquarters of the Primrose League.

    (f) The Chairman, one other representative, and the Honorary Secretary of the National Society of Conservative and Unionist Agents; and the Chairman and one other representative of each Provincial Area Branch in England and Wales.

    (g) Two representatives of the Society of Conservative Lawyers.

    (h) Forty representatives of the National Association of Conservative Graduates.

(9) The Conservative and Unionist Members of both Houses of Parliament in receipt of the Party Whip.

(10) The prospective Conservative and Unionist Candidates approved by the Standing Advisory Committee on Candidates and officially selected by Constituency Associations in England and Wales.

(11) The Central Office Agents for each Provincial Area.

(12) Representatives of the Scottish Conservative and Unionist Association as follows:

    (a) The President, two Vice-Presidents, the two Hon. Secretaries, the Hon. Treasurer, the Secretary, the Chairman of the Executive Committee, the Chairman and two Vice-Chairmen of the Women's Advisory Committee, and the Chairman of the Scottish Young Conservatives.

    (b) The Chairmen of Regional Councils.

    (c) Twelve members appointed by the Central Council of the Scottish Conservative and Unionist Association.

    (d) The prospective Conservative and Unionist Candidates approved by the Chairman of the Conservative and Unionist Party in Scotland and officially selected by Constituency Associations in Scotland.

(13) The Chairman, Deputy Chairman, Vice-Chairman, and National Treasurer of the Conservative and Unionist Party in Scotland.

(14) Representatives of the Ulster Unionist Council as follows:

    (a) Ten members of the Council.

    (b) The Secretary of the Council and the Secretary of the Women's Council.

    (c) The prospective Unionist Candidates approved by the Chairman of the Ulster Unionist Party at Westminster and officially selected by Constituency Associations in Northern Ireland.

(15) The co-opted members of the Women's and Young Conservative and Unionist National Advisory Committees.

Rule X

The Annual Meeting and an Ordinary Meeting of the Central Council shall be held each year at such time and place as the Executive Committee shall appoint, and the procedure for summoning such meetings shall be as follows:

(1) A preliminary notice shall be sent to every member of the Council not later than forty-nine clear days before the date appointed for such meeting.

(2) Notice of any special business for inclusion in the Agenda of an Ordinary Meeting shall be sent so as to reach the Secretary not later than thirty-five clear days before the date of the meeting. This may be submitted in the form of a Notice of Motion provided it has first received the endorsement of either a Provincial Area, a Constituency Association, or a Central Association for a Borough with two or more Constituency Associations, and authority has been given for it to be moved at the meeting by a representative nominated for that purpose.

(3) A Notice of Motion may also be submitted by any of the following Committees of the National Union: Executive Committee, General Purposes Committee, National Advisory Committees, the Commonwealth and Overseas

Council, the Association of Conservative Clubs, the Society of Conservative Lawyers, the National Association of Conservative Graduates, the Scottish Conservative and Unionist Association and the Ulster Unionist Council.

(4) The General Purposes Committee shall decide and arrange the order of the business to be brought before an Ordinary Meeting of the Council.

(5) Fourteen clear days before the date appointed for the meeting the Secretary shall send by post to every member of the Council an agenda paper stating the business to be transacted.

(6) The business of an Annual Meeting shall include the election of the Officers in accordance with Rule IV.

Rule XI

The Executive Committee may, and if required by not less than one hundred members of the Central Council shall, forthwith, summon a Special Meeting of the Council. Fourteen clear days' notice at least shall be given of any such special meeting, and the Agenda Paper shall accompany such notice. No business other than the business specified in the notice convening the meeting shall be transacted at such special meeting.

The Executive Committee

Rule XII

The Executive Committee shall be constituted annually as follows:

(1) (a) The Leader of the Party, and the Leader of the Party in the House of Lords.

(b) The Officers of the National Union.

(c) On cessation of Office, past Chairmen of the National Union shall continue their membership of the Executive Committee for three years and past Chairmen of the Executive Committee shall continue their membership of the Executive Committeee for three years, or for the term of office of their immediate successors, whichever is the greater.

(d) The Chairman, Deputy Chairman and Vice-Chairmen of the Party Organisation, and the Treasurers of the Party.

(e) The Chief Whip of the Party in each House of

Parliament (when the Chief Whip of the Party in either House is unable to attend his place may be taken by a junior Whip).

(f) The Chairman of the Party's Advisory Committee on Policy.

(g) The Chairman of the Conservative Party Board of Finance.

(h) The senior officers of the Organisation, Publicity and C.P.C. Departments of the Central Office and the senior officer of the Conservative Research Department.

(i) The Principal of the Swinton Conservative College.

(2) The Chairman of each National Advisory Committee, and the Vice-Chairmen of the Women's, Young Conservatives', Trade Unionists' and C.P.C. National Advisory Committees.

(3) (a) Seven representatives appointed by each Provincial Area—the Chairman, the Treasurer, the Chairman of the Women's Advisory Committee, one Young Conservative, one Trade Unionist, and two elected representatives. (The Trade Unionist representative shall be one of the two Area representatives elected to the Trade Unionists' National Advisory Committee.)

(b) Where a Provincial Area comprises more than thirty constituencies there shall be one additional representative for each additional ten constituencies (or a broken number of less than ten but more than five). The Northern Provincial Area shall be entitled to one additional representative so long as it comprises not less than thirty-four constituencies. In any Provincial Area in which are situated one or more cities which contain four or more constituencies, at least one elected representative shall be from a City Association. In addition to the above, Areas with fifty or more constituencies shall be entitled to appoint one extra Young Conservative representative to serve on the Executive Committee.

(c) In the event of Young Conservative representatives being unable to attend meetings, alternates may be appointed to represent them provided that such alternates are members of their respective Area Young Conservative Advisory Committees.

(4) (a) One representative of the Conservative and Unionist Peers.

(b) The Chairman, a Secretary and two members of the Executive Committee of the Conservative and Unionist Members' Committee (all four may be represented on occasion by alternates provided that those alternates are members of the Executive of that Committee).

(c) One additional representative each of the National Advisory Committees on Local Government and Education, and three additional representatives of the Federation of Conservative Students.

(d) Two representatives of the National Association of Conservative Graduates.

(e) The Chairman and two other representatives of the Association of Conservative Clubs.

(f) The Chairman and one other representative of the National Society of Conservative and Unionist Agents.

(g) The Chairman and one other representative of the Conservative Commonwealth and Overseas Council.

(h) The Chairman and one other representative of the Conservative Overseas Bureau.

(i) The Chairman of the Conservative and Unionist Agents' Superannuation Fund Management Committee.

(5) Five representatives of the Scottish Conservative and Unionist Association, viz: The President, two Vice-Presidents, the Chairman of the Executive Committee and the Chairman of the Women's Advisory Committee.

(6) The Chairman and Deputy Chairman of the Conservative and Unionist Party in Scotland.

(7) Three representatives of the Ulster Unionist Council—at least one of whom shall be a woman.

(8) Additional members not exceeding fifteen, of whom twelve shall, subject to the Standing Orders of the Executive Committee, be co-opted either wholly at the first meeting of the Committee after it has been annually constituted or from time to time throughout the year as the Committee may determine and three of whom shall be nominated for co-option by the Young Conservatives National Advisory Committee.

Rule XIII

The powers and duties of the Executive Committee shall be:

(1) To consider such aspects of the policy of the Party as may be selected from time to time.

(2) To recommend annually to the Central Council for election a President, Chairman and three Vice-Chairmen of the National Union.

(3) To elect annually its own Chairman, who shall be deemed to be an Officer of the National Union.

(4) To appoint an Honorary Secretary and a Secretary of the National Union.

(5) To fill any casual vacancies that may from time to time occur among the Officers of the National Union.

(6) To elect the representatives of the National Union on the Party's Advisory Committee on Policy and other bodies on which it is deemed necessary for the National Union to be represented.

(7) To exercise under Rule III powers of approval and withdrawal of approval in relation to membership of the National Union.

(8) To give decisions upon or take such steps as it shall think fit to bring about a settlement of any dispute or difference submitted by the Executive Council of a Constituency Association (being a Member of the National Union) after the officers of the appropriate Provincial Area shall have failed to bring about a settlement acceptable to all parties to the dispute or difference.

(9) To set up, under Rule XVI, such other National Advisory Committees as may be considered necessary.

(10) To receive reports from the General Purposes Committee and from sub-committees of the Executive Committee.

(11) To consider resolutions from Area Councils, Central and Constituency Associations, National Advisory Committees, and by the Commonwealth and Overseas Council, subject to such powers delegated to the Officers of the National Union from time to time in accordance with the Standing Orders of the Executive Committee.

(12) To consider any matter or motion submitted by any member of the Committee.

(13) To submit an Annual Report to the Conference, or to the Annual Meeting of the Central Council.

(14) To appoint such sub-committees as it may deem desirable for the discharge of its duties.
(15) To make Standing Orders for its own guidance.

General Purposes Committee

Rule XIV

There shall be a General Purposes Committee constituted annually as follows:
(1) (a) The Officers of the National Union (the Chairman of the Executive Committee to be Chairman of the Committee). The Immediate Past Chairman of the National Union shall continue to be a member of the General Purposes Committee for the remainder of the National Union Year after completion of his/her term of office.
   (b) The Chairman, Deputy Chairman and Vice-Chairman of the Party Organisation, and the Treasurers of the Party.
   (c) The Chief Whip of the Party in each House of Parliament (when the Chief Whip of the Party in either House is unable to attend, his place may be taken by a junior Whip).
   (d) The Chairman of the Party's Advisory Committee on Policy.
   (e) The senior Officers of the Organisation and Publicity Departments of the Central Office.
(2) The Chairman of each National Advisory Committee. (When a Chairman is unable to attend the place may be taken by another member of the Committee serving on the Executive Committee.)
(3) (a) The Chairman of each Area Council (when a Chairman is unable to attend his place may be taken by one of the Area representatives on the Executive Committee) and where a Provincial Area is comprised of ninety or more Constituencies, one elected representative from amongst the Area's representatives on the Executive Committee of the National Union.
   (b) Three Men, three Women, three Young Conservatives and three Trade Unionists elected annually by the Executive Committee from amongst its members by

209

postal ballots, nominations being invited from all members of that Committee.

(4) (a) The Chairman of the Conservative and Unionist Members' Committee. (When the Chairman is unable to attend his place may be taken by a member of the Executive of that Committee.)

    (b) The Chairman of the Association of Conservative Clubs. (When the Chairman is unable to attend his place may be taken by one of the two representatives on the Executive Committee.)

    (c) The Chairman of the National Society of Conservative and Unionist Agents. (When the Chairman is unable to attend, his place may be taken by the Society's other representative on the Executive Committee.)

(5) The President of the Scottish Conservative and Unionist Association and the Chairman of the Conservative and Unionist Party in Scotland.

(6) One representative of the Ulster Unionist Council (to be chosen from the three representatives on the Executive Committee).

(7) Co-opted members not exceeding five in number.

Rule XV

The powers and duties of the General Purposes Committee shall be:

(1) To perform all ordinary and emergency acts on behalf of the National Union, except those reserved by Rule XIII, to the Executive Committee.

(2) To consider reports of the National Advisory Committees, and to circulate them to members of the Executive Committee for information.

(3) To consider any matter or motion submitted by any member of the Committee, or referred to it by the Executive Committee.

(4) To prepare the Agenda for the Central Council and the Conference.

(5) To prepare an Annual Report for approval by the Executive Committee before submission, to the Conference, or Annual Meeting of the Central Council.

(6) To submit reports to meetings of the Executive Committee at appropriate intervals.

(7) To appoint such sub-committees as it may deem desirable for the discharge of its duties.

(8) To make Standing Orders for its own guidance.

National Advisory Committees

Rule XVI

(1) There shall be National Advisory Committees of the Executive Committee as follows:
Women's, Young Conservatives', Trade Unionists', Local Government, C.P.C., Education, Federation of Conservative Students.

(2) Each Advisory Committee shall have power to make Rules for its own composition and management, provided such Rules are approved by the Executive Committee.

(3) The Executive Committee shall have power to set up such other Advisory Committees, as may be considered necessary, and to give them similar recognition.

(4) The Chairman of the National Union and the Chairman of the National Union Executive Committee shall be ex-officio members of all National Advisory Committees.

The Conference

Rule XVII

The Conference shall be constituted annually as follows:

(1) The members of the Central Council provided for by Rule IX.

(2) Two additional representatives appointed by each Constituency Association. One of these representatives shall be a Young Conservative nominated by the Young Conservative Constituency Committee. Where only one Young Conservative Branch exists this Branch, for the purposes of this Rule, shall have the same powers as a Constituency Committee. Where no Young Conservative organisation exists one of the two additional representatives appointed by the Constituency Association shall be a member of the Association who is not more than 30 years of age.

(3) Each Constituency Association, and the Central Association for each Borough with two or more Constituency Associations, shall be entitled to nominate its Certificated Agent to attend.

(4) Each Constituency Association, and the Central Association for each Borough with two or more Constituency

211

Associations, employing a Certificated Organiser shall be entitled to nominate him or her to attend.

(5) Fourteen co-opted members of the National Advisory Committees, excluding the co-opted members of the Women's and the Young Conservative and Unionist National Advisory Committees already entitled to attend the Conference under Rule IX (17). If the number of co-opted members not entitled to attend the Conference in another capacity exceeds fourteen, attendance shall be determined by ballot.

Rule XVIII

There shall be an Annual Conference which shall be held at such time and place as the Executive Committee shall appoint, and the procedure for summoning such Conference shall be as follows:

(1) A preliminary notice shall be sent to every member of the Conference, not later than forty-nine clear days before the date appointed for such Conference.

(2) The date by which notice of any business for inclusion in the Agenda shall be sent to reach the Secretary shall be determined by the General Purposes Committee and circulated to Secretaries of Associations and Committees concerned not later than 31st May of the year concerned. Business submitted after the date determined for the receipt of ordinary business will be included in the Agenda only in exceptional circumstances and at the discretion of the General Purposes Committee.

(3) Business for inclusion in the Agenda may be submitted in the form of a Notice of Motion provided it has first received the endorsement of either a Provincial Area, a Constituency Association, or a Central Association for a Borough with two or more Constituency Associations, and authority has been given for it to be moved at the Conference by a representative nominated for the purpose. A Notice of Motion may also be submitted by any of the following Committees of the National Union: Executive Committee, General Purposes Committee, National Advisory Committees, the Commonwealth and Overseas Council, the Association of Conservative Clubs, the Society of Conservative Lawyers, the National Association of Conservative Graduates, the Scottish Conservative and Unionist Association and the Ulster Unionist Council. A Notice of Motion, submitted in accordance with this Rule,

which originates from a branch or committee of the Women, Young Conservatives, Trade Unionists, Local Government, C.P.C., Education and the Federation of Conservative Students in a Constituency Association or Provincial Area, must be identified in the Handbooks by the initial letters of such parts of the Party, *if so requested by the sponsoring body.*

(4) The General Purposes Committee shall decide and arrange the order of the business to be brought before the Conference.

(5) Fourteen clear days before the date appointed for the Conference the Secretary shall send by post to every member of the Conference:
  (a) An Annual Report prepared by the Executive Committee.
  (b) An Agenda Paper stating the business to be transacted.

(6) The power to cancel or postpone a meeting of the Council or Conference in exceptional circumstances shall be vested in the Officers of the National Union.

Rule XIX

The Executive Committee may, and if required by not less than fifty Associations or by five Provincial Areas shall forthwith, summon a Special Meeting of the Conference. Fourteen clear days' notice at least shall be given of any such Special Conference, and the Agenda Paper shall accompany such notice. No business other than the business specified in the notice convening the meeting shall be transacted at such special meeting.

Rule XX

Participation in Meetings of the Conference shall be strictly confined to those entitled to be present under the terms of Rule XVII.

General

Rule XXI

(a) The Young Conservative and Unionist representatives appointed under these Rules must not be over 30 years of age provided that in exceptional circumstances the Executive Committee may otherwise decide.

213

(b)   Where only one Y.C. Branch exists within a Constituency this Branch for the purposes of the appointment of Young Conservatives under these Rules, shall have the same powers as a Constituency Committee.

Rule XXII

The Central Council shall have power to make Standing Orders for the Central Council and Conference.

Rule XXIII

No new Rule of the National Union shall be adopted, nor shall any existing Rule be altered or repealed, except at a Meeting of the Central Council and with the support of not less than two-thirds of the votes of those present and voting.

Notice of the proposed adoption, alteration, or repeal shall be given with the notice convening the Meeting of the Central Council at which such proposed adoption, alteration, or repeal is to be considered.

Rule XXIV

The Executive Committee shall have power to interpret these Rules if there should be any ambiguity or difference of opinion concerning the purpose or intention of any Rule and shall have power to deal with any matter not provided for in these Rules.

Standing Orders *for the Central Council and Conference*

1.   The hours of sittings of the Council/Conference shall be issued with the Agenda.

2.   The Chairman of the Central Council, or in his absence one of the Vice-Chairmen present or if all are absent the Chairman of the Executive Committee, shall preside at meetings of the Council/Conference.
     If the Chairman, Vice-Chairman and Chairman of the Executive Committee are all absent then the members present shall elect one of themselves to preside.

3.   One hundred members present at a meeting of the Council shall form a quorum.
     Three hundred members present at a meeting of the Conference shall form a quorum.

4. The speech of a mover of a motion shall not exceed 8 minutes in length, and that of each subsequent speaker, including the mover of an amendment, 4 minutes, without the consent of the Council/Conference, such consent to be ascertained without debate. A seconder shall not be required for a motion submitted in accordance with Rule X (2) or (3) (Central Council), or Rule XVIII (3) (Conference). This Standing Order shall not apply to the 'winding-up' speech. (For definition see Standing Order No. 17.)

5. a. Any member of the Council/Conference may submit an amendment to a motion but such amendment must be submitted to the Secretary in writing with the names of the mover and seconder attached. An amendment may be submitted at any time but only those received at least 7 days before the opening of a meeting of the Council/Conference shall be printed in the Supplementary Agenda for distribution at the Council Meeting/Conference.

   b. The seconder of an amendment, as such, shall not have the right to speak to the amendment.

6. a. The Chairman shall have the absolute right to decide whether or not to call any one or more of the amendments submitted.

   b. Whenever an amendment upon an original motion has been moved and seconded no second or subsequent amendment shall be moved until the first amendment shall have been disposed of.

   c. If an amendment is carried, the motion as amended shall take the place of the original motion, and shall become the question upon which any further amendment may be moved.

   d. The Chairman may allow a debate upon the amendment and the original motion to take place concurrently.

   e. No member shall be at liberty to move or second more than one amendment upon any motion.

7. Neither a motion nor an amendment, which has been duly moved and seconded, may be withdrawn without the consent of the Council/Conference.

8. No member shall speak more than once on any motion or amendment. The mover of an original motion may, however, speak for three minutes in reply before the 'winding-up' speech. (For definition see Standing Order No. 17.) The right of reply shall not extend to the mover of an amendment which, having been carried, has become the substantive motion. After the 'winding-up' speech the question shall be put forthwith.

9. When a motion has been moved it shall be competent for any member to move without debate that the question be now put,

and if such motion shall be seconded it shall be put forthwith, unless the Chairman rules otherwise.

If, however, the Chairman has received notice of the desire of any member or members to oppose the motion under discussion, the question shall not be put until at least one of such members has been given the opportunity to speak.

Where an amendment is under discussion the motion that the question be now put shall apply only to that amendment. Subject to the above provisions the Chairman shall at all times have the right to decide the time of termination of a debate.

10. It shall be competent for any member, at the close of the speech of any other member, to move without debate that the Council/Conference do proceed to the next business, and if such motion be seconded it shall be put forthwith unless the Chairman rules otherwise.

When a motion 'that the Council/Conference do proceed to the next business' is carried, the question under discussion shall be considered as dropped.

When such a motion is defeated, a second motion 'that the Council/Conference do proceed to the next business' shall not be accepted during the following 30 minutes of the same debate.

11. Every motion shall be put to the vote by a show of hands. No division shall be taken unless the vote is challenged and in the Chairman's opinion is supported by one hundred members rising in their places, or the Chairman thinks a division desirable. In order to ascertain the vote on any division a ballot paper designated by the Chairman shall be used by each member present and entitled to vote. Scrutineers shall be appointed by the Chairman to cast up the votes and the Chairman shall announce the result as soon as practicable.

12. In the event of an equality of votes being cast for and against a motion or amendment, the Chairman may give a second or casting vote, and the result shall be determined accordingly.

Where a presiding Chairman declines to give a second or casting vote, the motion shall be deemed to have been not carried.

13. The motions selected for debate at a particular session but not reached when the time arrives to close that Session of the Council/Conference shall be adjourned sine die.

14. The Council/Conference may at any period of its meetings resolve itself, without debate, into Committee. When the Council/Conference resolves itself into Committee, all strangers shall withdraw immediately.

15. Matters which the Chairman considers urgent, and which have arisen too late to be specified in the Agenda, may be brought

before the Council/Conference by the Chairman with the consent of the majority of the members present.

16. The decision of the Chairman on any point shall be final.

17. The expression 'winding-up' speech shall mean the speech made at the end of a debate by a Minister or other person invited by the Chairman.

18. Any Standing Order may be suspended on a simple majority of the Central Council or Conference on the proposal of the Chairman; such proposition shall designate the limit of the suspension.

19. No new Standing Order for the Central Council or Conference shall be adopted, nor shall any existing Standing Order be altered or repealed, except at a Meeting of the Central Council and with the support of not less than two-thirds of the votes of those present and voting.

Notice of the proposed adoption, alteration or repeal shall be given with the notice convening the Meeting of the Central Council at which such proposed adoption, alteration, or repeal is to be considered.

Provincial areas

	Constituencies	Representatives on Executive Committee
1 Greater London	104**	15
2 Northern (Cumberland, Durham, Northumberland and Middlesbrough)	34	8
3 North Western (Lancashire, Cheshire, Westmorland)	79	13
4 Yorkshire (excluding Middlesbrough)	54	10
5 East Midlands (Derbyshire, Leicestershire, Lincolnshire, Nottinghamshire, Northamptonshire, Rutland)	42	8
6 West Midlands (Gloucestershire excluding Bristol, Herefordshire, Shropshire, Staffordshire, Warwickshire, Worcestershire)	60	11

** These figures include five constituencies which are partly in the Greater London Area and partly in other Areas. Pending possible boundary alterations these constituencies are also included in the figures of Eastern Area (3) and South-Eastern Area (2).

	Constituencies	Representatives on Executive Committee
7 Eastern	42	8
(Bedfordshire, Cambridgeshire, Essex*, Hertfordshire*, Huntingdonshire, Norfolk, Suffolk)		
8 South Eastern	36	8
(Kent*, Surrey*, and Sussex)		
9 Wessex	37	8
(Berkshire, Buckinghamshire, Dorsetshire, Hampshire, Isle of Wight, Oxfordshire, Wiltshire)		
10 Western	28	7
(Cornwall, Devonshire, Somersetshire, Bristol)		
11 Wales and Monmouthshire	36	8

* Excluding territory in the Greater London Area.

Notes

Date of Publication

The Rules and Standing Orders contained herewith include amendments made at meetings up to and including the Central Council Meeting held on 17 and 18 April 1970.

Effective Representation

In order to secure an effective representation, the several bodies entitled under these Rules to elect or appoint representatives are urged to obtain an assurance from all nominees or candidates for election or appointment that they will undertake regularly to attend the meetings to which, in a representative capacity, they may be summoned.

Appointment of Deputies

Where a Chairman elected under Rule IX (4), (5), (6) or (7) (b) is not able to attend a meeting of the Central Council or the Annual Conference a deputy may be appointed, provided such appointment is notified to the Secretary of the National Union.

[Marginal headings have been omitted—ed. note.]

B. The Constitution and Standing Orders of the Labour Party

as amended by the Annual Party Conference (Brighton, 1969)

Clause I.—Name

The Labour Party.

Clause II.—Membership

(For sections (1) and (2) see p. 18.)

(3) Political organisations not affiliated to or associated under a National Agreement with the Party on January 1, 1946, having their own Programme, Principles and Policy for distinctive and separate propaganda, or possessing Branches in the Constituencies or engaged in the promotion of Parliamentary or Local Government Candidatures, or owing allegiance to any political organisation situated abroad, shall be ineligible for affiliation to the Party.

(4) Individual Members shall be persons of not less than fifteen years of age who subscribe to the conditions of membership, provided they are not members of Political Parties or organisations ancillary or subsidiary thereto declared by the Annual Conference of the Labour Party (hereinafter referred to as 'the Party') or by the National Executive Committee in pursuance of Conference decisions to be ineligible for affiliation to the Party.

(5) British citizens temporarily resident abroad may become Individual Members, or retain such membership of the Party, by enrolment with the Head Office provided they accept the conditions of membership in Clause III.

Clause III.—Conditions of Membership

(See p. 17.)

Clause IV.—Party Objects

(See pp. 14–15.)

Clause V.—Party Programme

(1) The Party Conference shall decide from time to time what specific proposals of legislative, financial or administrative reform shall be included in the Party Programme.

219

No proposal shall be included in the Party Programme unless it has been adopted by the Party Conference by a majority of not less than two-thirds of the votes recorded on a card vote.

(2) The National Executive Committee and the Parliamentary Committee of the Parliamentary Labour Party shall decide which items from the Party Programme shall be included in the Manifesto which shall be issued by the National Executive Committee prior to every General Election. The Joint Meeting of the two Committees shall also define the attitude of the Party to the principal issues raised by the Election which are not covered by the Manifesto.

Clause VI.—The Party Conference

(1) The work of the Party shall be under the direction and control of the Party Conference, which shall itself be subject to the Constitution and Standing Orders of the Party. The Party Conference shall meet regularly once in every year and also at such other times as it may be convened by the National Executive Committee.

(2) The Party Conference shall be constituted as follows:

(*a*) Delegates duly appointed by each affiliated Trade Union or other organisations to the number of one delegate for each 5,000 members or part thereof on whom affiliation fees and by-election insurance premiums were paid for the year ending December 31 preceding the Conference.

(*b*) Delegates duly appointed by Constituency Labour Parties (or Trades Councils acting as such) to the number of one delegate for each 5,000 individual members or part thereof on whom affiliation fees and by-election insurance premiums were paid for the year ending December 31 preceding the Conference; where the individual and affiliated women's membership exceeds 1,500 an additional woman delegate may be appointed; where the membership of Young Socialist Branches within a constituency is 100 or more an additional Young Socialist delegate may be appointed.

(*c*) Delegates duly appointed by Central Labour Parties or Trades Councils acting as such in Divided Boroughs not exceeding one for each Central Labour Party provided the affiliation fees and by-election insurance premiums have been paid for the year ending December 31 preceding the Conference.

(*d*) Delegates duly appointed by Federations not exceeding one for each Federation provided the affiliation fees have been paid for the year ending December 31 preceding the Conference.

(*e*) *Ex-officio* Members of the Party Conference as follows:
(*i*) Members of the National Executive Committee.
(*ii*) Members of the Parliamentary Labour Party.

(*iii*) Parliamentary Labour Candidates whose candidatures have been duly endorsed by the National Executive Committee.

(*iv*) The Secretary of the Party.

Ex-officio Members shall have no voting power.

(*f*) Any special Party Conference shall be called on the same basis of representation as that upon which the last Annual Party Conference was convened.

(3) In the event of a duly appointed delegate being elected as Treasurer or as a member of the National Executive Committee, the Affiliated Organisation responsible for his or her appointment as a delegate may claim authority at subsequent Party Conferences during his or her period of Office, to appoint a delegate additional to the number applicable to it under paras. (*a*), (*b*) and (*c*) of Section 2 of this Clause, provided the delegate elected as Treasurer or as a member of the National Executive Committee:

(*i*) Remains qualified to be appointed as a delegate under Clause VII; and

(*ii*) Continues to be duly appointed as a delegate by the Affiliated Organisation claiming authority to appoint an additional delegate within the provisions of this Section.

Clause VII.–Appointment of Delegates to the Party Conference

(1) Every Delegate must be an individual member of the Labour Party as described in Clause II Section 4 except persons resident in Northern Ireland who are duly appointed delegates of affiliated trade unions and who individually accept and conform to the Constitution, Programme, Principles and Policy of the Party.

(2) Delegates must be *bona fide* members or paid permanent officials of the organisation appointing them, except in the case of Members of the Parliamentary Labour Party or duly-endorsed Parliamentary Labour Candidates appointed to represent Constituencies in accordance with Section 4 of this Clause.

(3) Delegates appointed by Federations or Central Labour Parties must be resident within the area of the organisation concerned or be registered therein as Parliamentary or Local Government electors.

(4) Members of the Parliamentary Labour Party and duly-endorsed Parliamentary Labour Candidates may be appointed as Delegates by Constituency Labour Parties responsible for their candidatures; otherwise, Delegates appointed by Constituency Labour Parties must be resident in the Constituency appointing them, or registered as Parliamentary or Local Government electors therein.

(5) No person shall act as a Delegate for more than one organisation.

(6) No person shall act as a Delegate who does not pay the political levy of his or her Trade Union.

(7) Members of Parliament not members of the Parliamentary Labour Party are ineligible to act as Delegates.

(8) The following are also ineligible to act as Delegates:

(*a*) Persons acting as candidates or supporting candidates in opposition to duly-endorsed Labour Candidates.

(*b*) Persons who are members of political parties or organisations ancillary or subsidiary thereto declared by the Annual Party Conference or by the National Executive Committee in pursuance of the Conference decisions to be ineligible for affiliation to the Labour Party.

Clause VIII.—The National Executive Committee

(1) There shall be a National Executive Committee of the Party consisting of 25 members and a Treasurer, elected by the Party Conference at its regular Annual Meeting in such proportion and under such conditions as may be set out in the Standing Orders for the time being in force. The Leader and Deputy Leader of the Parliamentary Labour Party shall be *ex-officio* members of the National Executive Committee. The National Executive Committee shall, subject to the control and directions of the Party Conference, be the Administrative Authority of the Party.

(2) The duties and powers of the National Executive Committee shall include the following:

(*a*) To ensure the establishment of, and to keep in active operation, a Constituency Labour Party in every Constituency, a Central Labour Party in every Divided Borough, and a Federation in every suitable area, in accordance with the Rules laid down by the Party Conference for the purpose.

(*b*) To enforce the Constitution, Standing Orders, and Rules of the Party and to take any action it deems necessary for such purpose, whether by way of disaffiliation of an organisation or expulsion of an individual, or otherwise. Any such action shall be reported to the next Annual Conference of the Party.

(*c*) To confer with the Parliamentary Labour Party at the opening of each Parliamentary Session, and at any other time when it or the Parliamentary Party may desire a conference on any matters relating to the work and progress of the Party.

(*d*) To see that all its Officers and members conform to the Constitution, Rules and Standing Orders of the Party.

(*e*) To present to the Annual Party Conference a Report covering the work and progress of the Party during its period of office, together with a Financial Statement and Accounts duly audited. The Report, Financial Statement and Accounts shall be sent to affiliated organisations at least two clear weeks before the opening of the Annual Party Conference.

(*f*) To propose to the Annual Party Conference such amendments to the Constitution, Rules and Standing Orders as may be deemed desirable and to submit to the Annual Party Conference or to any Special Party Conference, called in accordance with the Standing Orders, such resolutions and declarations affecting the Programme, Principles and Policy of the Party as in its view may be necessitated by political circumstances.

(*g*) To organise and maintain such fund or funds as may be thought necessary for any or all of the objects for which the Party exists, including a fund to finance Parliamentary by-elections and a fund established for the purpose of insuring against the forfeiture of Returning Officers' Deposits at every Parliamentary General Election.

(*h*) To secure advances from time to time or to raise loans, either on mortgage or otherwise and on such terms as it may deem expedient; to employ any part of the funds at its disposal in the purchase of any freehold or leasehold building or site and/or in the building, leasing holding or rental of any premises and in the fitting-up and maintenance thereof; and to invest any moneys not immediately required in such securities as it may deem proper and to realise or to vary such investments from time to time and to appoint Trustees and/or form a Society, Association, Company or Companies in accordance with the provisions of the Friendly Societies Acts or the Companies Acts for any or all of the above purposes and to define the powers of such Trustees, Society, Association, Company or Companies and the manner in which such powers shall be exercised.

(*i*) To sanction, where local circumstances render it necessary, modifications in the rules laid down by the Annual Party Conference for the various classes of Party Organisations in the Constituencies and Regions, provided that such modifications comply with the spirit and intention of the Annual Party Conference and do not alter the objects, basis or conditions of affiliated and individual membership, vary the procedure for the selection of Parliamentary Candidates (except as provided in the rules) or effect a change in the relationship of Central Labour Parties or Constituency Labour Parties with the Labour Party.

(3) The decision of the National Executive Committee, subject to any modification by the Party Conference, as to the meaning and effect of any Rule or any part of this Constitution and Standing Orders, shall be final.

223

(4) The National Executive Committee shall have power to adjudicate in disputes that may arise between affiliated and other Party organisations, and in disputes which occur within the Party's Regional, Federation, or Constituency machinery, and its decisions shall be binding on all organisations concerned.

Clause IX.—Parliamentary Candidatures

1. The National Executive Committee shall co-operate with the Constituency Labour Party for each Constituency in selecting a Labour Candidate for any Parliamentary Election.
2. The selection of Labour Candidates for Parliamentary Elections shall be made in accordance with the procedure laid down by the Annual Party Conference in the Rules which apply to Constituency and Central Labour Parties.
3. The selection of Labour Candidates for Parliamentary Elections shall not be regarded as completed until the name of the person selected has been placed before a meeting of the National Executive Committee, and his or her selection has been duly endorsed.
4. No Parliamentary Candidature shall be endorsed until the National Executive Committee has received an undertaking by one of its affiliated organisations (or is otherwise satisfied) that the election expenses of the Candidate are guaranteed.
5. Labour Candidates for Parliamentary Elections duly endorsed by the National Executive Committee shall appear before the electors under the designation of 'Labour Candidate' only. At any Parliamentary General Election they shall include in their Election Addresses and give prominence in their campaigns to the issues for that Election as defined by the National Executive Committee in its Manifesto.
6. At a Parliamentary By-Election a duly-endorsed Labour Candidate shall submit his or her Election Address to the National Executive Committee for approval. The National Executive Committee, whenever it considers it necessary, shall give advice and guidance on any special issue to be raised, or in the conduct of the Campaign during such By-Election.
7. No person may be selected as a Parliamentary Labour Candidate by a Constituency Labour Party, and no Candidate may be endorsed by the National Executive Committee, if the person concerned:
    (a) Is not an Individual Member of the Party and, if eligible, is not a member of a Trade Union affiliated to the Trades Union Congress or recognised by the General Council of the Trades Union Congress as a *bona fide* Trade Union: or
    (b) is a member of a Political Party or organisation ancillary or

subsidiary thereto declared by the Annual Party Conference or by the National Executive Committee in pursuance of Conference decisions to be ineligible for affiliation to the Labour Party: or (c) does not accept and conform to the Constitution, Programme, Principles, and Policy of the Party: or (d) does not undertake to accept and act in harmony with the Standing Orders of the Parliamentary Labour Party.

8. Any Candidate who, after election, fails to accept or act in harmony with the Standing Orders of the Parliamentary Labour Party shall be considered to have violated the terms of this Constitution.

Clause X.—Affiliation and membership fees

(1) Each affiliated organisation (other than Federations, Constituency and Central Labour Parties) shall pay an affiliation fee of 1s. 6d. per member per annum to the Party.

(2) Each Constituency Labour Party shall pay an affiliation fee of 1s. 6d. per annum on each individual member attached to the Party directly or indirectly through its local Labour Parties, Polling District Committees, Ward Committees, and Women's Sections, subject to a minimum payment of £75 per annum.

(3) Each Central Labour Party shall pay an affiliation fee at the rate of £5 per annum for each Constituency Labour Party within the Divided Borough.

(4) Each County Federation shall pay affiliation fees in accordance with the following scale:

			Per annum
Federations of 2, 3, or 4	Constituency or C.L.P.		£1 10s.
„	5 or 6 „	„	£2 5s.
„	„ 7, 8, or 9 „	„	£3
„	„ 10, 11, 12 or 13 „	„	£4 10s.
„	of over 13 „	„	£6 15s.

(5) Each Individual Member of the Party shall pay a minimum membership fee of one shilling monthly to the Party to which he or she is attached in the manner laid down in Constituency and Local Labour Party Rules except Old Age Pensioners who have retired from work and they shall be allowed Individual Membership of the Party on the minimum payment of 1s. per annum. These contributions shall be entered on membership cards supplied by the National Executive Committee to Constituency Parties at 1s. 6d. per card, which sum shall include the affiliation fee payable by such organisation to the Party in respect of such members.

Clause XI.—Party Conference Arrangements Committee

(1) There shall be appointed in accordance with the Standing Orders at each Annual Party Conference a Party Conference Arrangements Committee of Five Delegates for the Annual Party Conference in the year succeeding its appointment, or for any Party Conference called during the intervening period. A member of the Head Office staff shall act as Secretary to the Committee.

(2) The duties of the Party Conference Arrangements Committee shall be:

(*a*) To arrange the order of the Party Conference Agenda.

(*b*) To act as a Standing Orders Committee.

(*c*) To appoint Scrutineers and Tellers for the Annual Party Conference from amongst the Delegates whose names have been received at the Head Office of the Party two clear weeks prior to the opening of the Conference and submit them for approval to the Conference. In the case of a Special Party Conference called under Clause VI, the National Executive Committee may appoint a date prior to which such names must be received.

Clause XII.—Auditors

There shall be appointed in accordance with the Standing Orders at each Annual Party Conference two delegates to act as Auditors of the Party Accounts to be submitted at the Annual Party Conference next succeeding that at which they are appointed.

Clause XIII.—Alteration to Constitution and Rules

The existing Constitution and Rules, or any part thereof, may be amended, rescinded, altered, or additions made thereto, by Resolution, carried on a card vote at an Annual Party Conference (in manner provided in the Standing Orders appended hereto) held in every third year following the year 1956, unless the National Executive Committee advises that amendments shall be specially considered at any Annual Party Conference. Notice of Resolutions embodying any such proposals must be sent in writing to the Secretary at the Offices of the Party as provided in Standing Orders.

Clause XIV.—Standing Orders

The Standing Orders of the Party Conference shall be considered for all purposes as if they form part of this Constitution and shall have effect accordingly. New Standing Orders may be made when required, or the existing Standing Orders amended, rescinded, or altered by Resolution in the same manner as provided for alterations in the Constitution itself.

Standing Orders

Standing Order 1.—Annual Party Conference

(1) The National Executive Committee shall convene the Annual Party Conference during October in each year, in accordance with the conditions laid down in the Constitution and these Standing Orders. It may also convene Special Sessions of the Party Conference when it deems necessary.

(2) When a Party Conference is called at short notice, the Secretaries of affiliated organisations shall, on receiving the summons, instantly take steps to secure representation of their organisations, in accordance with the Constitution and these Standing Orders.

(3) Any Session of the Party Conference summoned with less than ten days' notice shall confine its business strictly to that relating to the emergency giving rise to the Special Session.

(4) A delegation fee of £2 per Delegate shall be payable by affiliated organisations sending Delegates to the Party Conference. *Ex-officio* members of the Party Conference in attendance shall pay a fee of £2. Such fees must be paid to the Secretary of the Party before credentials are issued.

(5) To secure the publication for circulation to affiliated organisations of an Official List of Delegates attending the Annual Party Conference, the names and addresses of Delegates appointed by affiliated organisations must be sent to the Secretary not later than three clear weeks before the opening of the Annual Party Conference. In the case of a Special Conference called under Clause VI, the National Executive Committee may appoint a date prior to which such names and addresses shall be sent to the Secretary.

(6) The National Executive Committee shall make arrangements each year for the pooling of railway fares in respect of delegations appointed by Federations, Central Labour Parties, and Constituency Labour Parties.

Standing Order 2.—Agenda

(1) Notice of Resolutions for the Annual Party Conference, not exceeding one resolution on one subject from any one affiliated organisation, shall be sent in writing to the Secretary at the offices of the Party not later than twelve clear weeks before the opening of the

Conference, for inclusion in the first Agenda, which shall be forthwith issued to the affiliated organisations. At any Annual Conference at which Amendments to the Constitution are to be considered each affiliated organisation may submit one Resolution in addition to a Resolution proposing to amend the Constitution. In the case of a Special Conference called under Clause VI, the National Executive Committee may appoint a date prior to which such notices shall be sent to the Secretary.

(2) Resolutions will be accepted only from those affiliated organisations which have paid affiliation fees in accordance with Clause VI, Section 2, paragraphs (a), (b), (c), (d), of the Constitution and Standing Orders and by-election insurance premiums for the preceding year, not later than twelve clear weeks before the opening of the Conference.

(3) Notice of amendments to the Resolutions in the First Agenda, not exceeding one amendment on one subject from any one affiliated organisation (consequential amendments to a main amendment shall not be counted), and nominations for the National Executive Committee, Treasurer, Auditors, and Party Conference Arrangements Committee, shall be forwarded in writing to the Secretary not later than six clear weeks before the opening of the Conference for inclusion in the Final Agenda of the Conference. In the case of a Special Conference called under Clause VI, the National Executive Committee may appoint a date prior to which such notices shall be forwarded to the Secretary.

(4) Amendments will be accepted only from those affiliated organisations which have paid affiliation fees in accordance with Clause VI, Section 2, paragraphs (a), (b), (c), (d), of the Constitution and Standing Orders and by-election insurance premiums for the preceding year, not later than six clear weeks before the opening of the Conference.

(5) No business which does not arise out of the Resolutions on the Agenda shall be considered by the Party Conference, unless recommended by the National Executive Committee or the Party Conference Arrangements Committee.

(6) When the Annual Party Conference has, by Resolution, made a declaration of a general Policy or Principle, no Resolution or Motion concerning such Policy or Principle shall appear on the Agenda for a period of three years from the time such declaration was made, except such Resolutions or Motions as are, in the opinion of the National Executive Committee, of immediate importance.

Standing Order 3.—Voting

Voting at the Annual Party Conference shall be by cards on the following bases:

(*a*) National and Constituency Organisations: One voting card for each 1,000 members or part thereof on whom affiliation fees were paid for the year ending December 31 preceding the Conference.

(*b*) Federations and Central Labour Parties: One voting card each.

Voting at any Special Party Conference shall be on the same bases as those upon which voting took place at the preceding Annual Party Conference.

Standing Order 4.—Election of the National Executive Committee

(1) For the purpose of nomination and election the National Executive Committee shall be divided into four Divisions:

Division I shall consist of twelve members, to be nominated by Trade Unions from among their duly appointed delegates, and elected by their delegations at the Annual Party Conference.

Division II shall consist of one member, to be nominated by Socialist, Co-operative, and Professional Organisations from among their duly appointed delegates, and elected by their delegations at the Annual Party Conference.

Division III shall consist of seven members, to be nominated by Federations, Constituency Labour Parties and Central Labour Parties, from among their duly appointed delegates, and elected by their delegations at the Annual Party Conference. A Constituency Labour Party may nominate its Member of Parliament, or duly endorsed Candidate attending the Conference as an *ex-officio* member.

Division IV shall consist of five women members, to be nominated by any affiliated organisation, and elected by the Annual Party Conference as a whole. A Constituency Labour Party may nominate its woman Member of Parliament or duly endorsed woman Candidate attending as an *ex-officio* member of Conference.

(2) The election for each Division shall be made by means of ballot vote on the card bases as provided in these Standing Orders.

(3) Nominations for the National Executive Committee shall be made in accordance with the following conditions:

(*a*) Except in the case of Members of Parliament and duly-endorsed Candidates representing Constituency Labour Parties, nominees must be *bona fide* paying members of the organisations submitting their nominations.

(*b*) Except where a Constituency Labour Party desires to nominate its Member of Parliament or its duly-endorsed Candidate, the nominees of Federations, Constituency Labour Parties, and Central Labour Parties must either reside in or be registered as Parliamentary or Local Government Electors in the area of the Federation or Party submitting the nomination.

(c) Only persons appointed to attend the Annual Party Conference as Delegates or, in the case of Division III and Division IV, Members of Parliament or duly-endorsed Candidates attending as *ex-officio* members of Conference shall be eligible for nomination for a seat on the National Executive Committee. Nominees who do not attend the Annual Party Conference shall be deemed to have withdrawn their nominations, unless they send to the Secretary, on or before the day on which the Conference opens, an explanation in writing of their absence, satisfactory to the Party Conference Arrangements Committee.

(d) Members of the General Council of the Trades Union Congress are not eligible for nomination to the National Executive Committee.

(e) Before sending in nominations affiliated organisations must secure the consent in writing of their nominees. Unless such consent is obtained and is attached to the nomination paper, nominations will be rendered null and void.

(f) Each affiliated organisation may make one nomination from among its duly appointed delegates, for its appropriate Division of the National Executive Committee. In the case of Division III a Constituency Labour Party may nominate its Member of Parliament or duly-endorsed Candidate attending as an *ex-officio* member of Conference. Where an affiliated organisation pays fees on 500,000 members or more it may make one additional nomination (either man or woman) for such Division.

(g) Each affiliated organisation may make one nomination for Division IV of the National Executive Committee.

(4) Any vacancy which occurs amongst members of the National Executive Committee between Annual Party Conferences shall be filled by that Committee by co-opting the highest unsuccessful nominee in the Division concerned, as shown in the results of the Election for the National Executive Committee at the Annual Party Conference immediately preceding the vacancy.

Standing Order 5.—Election of Officers

(1) The National Executive Committee shall elect its own Chairman and Vice-Chairman at its first meeting each year.

(2) The Treasurer shall be nominated and elected separately by the Annual Party Conference. Every affiliated organisation may nomi-

nate a person for Treasurer who is a duly-appointed Delegate to the Annual Party Conference, or a Member of Parliament or a duly-endorsed Candidate, attending Conference as an *ex-officio* member. (3) The Secretary shall be elected by the Annual Party Conference, on the recommendation of the National Executive Committee, and be *ex-officio* a member of the Conference. He shall devote his whole time to the work of the Party and shall not be eligible as a Candidate for or a Member of Parliament. He shall remain in office so long as his work gives satisfaction to the National Executive Committee and Party Conference. Should a vacancy in the office occur between two Annual Party Conferences the National Executive Committee shall have full power to fill the vacancy, subject to the approval of the Annual Party Conference next following.

(4) Every affiliated organisation may nominate one duly-appointed Delegate, or a Member of Parliament or duly-endorsed Candidate attending Conference as an *ex-officio* member, for a seat on the Party Conference Arrangements Committee, who, if elected, must be a Delegate to, or an *ex-officio* member of, any Party Conference held during his or her period of office. In the event of a member of the Party Conference Arrangements Committee being unable to fulfil his or her duties, the Delegate or *ex-officio* member who received the highest number of votes amongst those not elected shall be called upon, but should the voting list be exhausted the affiliated organisation to which the elected Delegate, or *ex-officio* member, belonged shall nominate a substitute.

(5) Every affiliated organisation may nominate one duly-appointed Delegate, or a Member of Parliament or duly-endorsed Candidate attending Conference as an *ex-officio* member, to act as Auditor. In the event of an Auditor being unable to perform the duties, the same procedure shall be followed as in the case of the Party Conference Arrangements Committee.

Standing Order 6.—Restriction of Nominations

No Delegate shall be eligible for nomination to more than one position to be filled by election at any Annual Party Conference. In the event of any Delegate being nominated for more than one such position, the Delegate shall be requested to select the position for which he or she desires to remain nominated. After the selection has been made the Delegate's name shall be omitted from the nominations for all other positions. Should no selection of position be made not later than six clear weeks before the opening of the Conference, all nominations made on behalf of the Delegate shall become null and void.

C. The Constitution of the Liberal Party
As adopted at Brighton 1969

Preamble:
The Aims and Objects of the Liberal Party (see pp. 15–16).

A. The Constitution

1. The Liberal Party of the United Kingdom of Great Britain and Northern Ireland shall be a Federal party with independent constituent parties in Northern Ireland, Scotland and Wales. This Constitution shall only govern the Scottish, Ulster and Welsh Liberal Parties in so far as its provisions are accepted by those parties. Although these three parties shall be recognised bodies in the sense of Clause A3, their independence shall not be prejudiced by anything in this Constitution.

2. The following shall be the constitutional organs of the Liberal Party:
   (a) Constituency Associations as defined in Section C;
   (b) Regional Parties as defined in Section D;
   (c) Regional Councils as defined in Section D7;
   (d) Regional Executive Committees as defined in Section D8;
   (e) The Assembly as defined in Section G;
   (f) The Council as defined in Section E;
   (g) The Standing Committee as defined in Section F;
   (h) The Council Agenda Committee as defined in Section F2;
   (i) The National Executive Committee as defined in Section I;
   (j) The Candidates Committee as defined in Section H;
   (k) The Finance and Administration Board as defined in Section J;

and any Committee set up by and responsible to any of the abovementioned bodies.

For section 3 see p. 19.

4. The following shall be the principal officers of the Liberal Party:
   (a) The Leader of the Party who shall be elected by the Liberal Members of the House of Commons. In order that the Parliamentary Party may be cognisant of opinion in the country the Chief Whip shall, prior to the election, convene a meeting of the National Executive Committee;
   (b) The Chief Whip in the House of Commons;
   (c) The Honorary Officer as defined in Section K;
   (d) The Chairman of the National Executive Committee who shall also be the Chairman of the Party;

(e) The Chairman of the Scottish, Ulster and Welsh Liberal Parties;

(f) The Chairman of the Regional Parties.

5. In the event of any dispute over the interpretation of this Constitution, the President shall give a ruling which shall be final unless reversed by a two-thirds majority of those present and voting at a meeting of the National Executive Committee.

6. This Constitution may only be amended by a two-thirds majority of delegates present and voting at the Assembly. Amendments may be proposed by the National Executive Committee, by any Regional Executive Committee, by any body recognised by this Constitution or by any five Constituency Associations. Notices of proposed amendments must be submitted in accordance with the Assembly Standing Orders.

B. Membership

1. Membership of the Liberal Party shall be open to all persons who subscribe to the Aims and Objects of the Party regardless of colour, race or creed.

2. Membership of the Party shall be by virtue of membership of a Constituency Association, or in the absence of a Constituency Association, through direct membership of a Regional Party. Members of the National League of Young Liberals and the Women's Federation shall automatically be members of their appropriate Constituency Association or in the absence of a Constituency Association, of their appropriate Regional Party.

3. Minimum subscription rates shall be laid down by the National Executive Committee subject to approval by the Assembly. The National Executive Committee may also lay down regulations governing the payment of such subscriptions and the calculation of membership for constitutional purposes, subject to approval by the Assembly.

4. The President may, with the prior approval of the Council, confer Honorary Membership of the Liberal Party on persons, not citizens of the United Kingdom, who have rendered distinguished services to Liberalism. Such Honorary Membership may be withdrawn by the President with the prior approval of the Council.

5. Membership of the Party may be refused or revoked by the enrolling body at any time on either of the following grounds:

(a) Membership of or active support for another political party;

(b) Disagreement with Liberal Party policy expressed in such a way and to such an extent as seriously to throw doubt on the person's support for the Aims and Objects of the Party.

6. Any member of the Party who stands at a Parliamentary Election

233

in opposition to an officially nominated Liberal Candidate automatically and immediately forfeits his membership of the Party without appeal. After the election in question, he may re-apply for membership and if his application is refused may appeal against the refusal according to Clause B8 below.

7. A Constituency Association may decide to incorporate a similar procedure for local elections as Clause B6 above to its Constitution; but otherwise the procedure shall not apply to municipal elections.

8. In the event of such refusal or revocation by a Constituency Association or Regional Party, the refusing or revoking body shall inform the President, the person concerned, and, if a Constituency Association, the Regional Executive Committee of its action, giving detailed reasons.

The person concerned may appeal from the decision of the Constituency Association to the Regional Executive Committee; and from the Regional Executive Committee to the President. In the event of the President refusing to endorse the action of the refusing or revoking body his decision shall be final. In the event of the President endorsing the body's action, the person concerned may appeal to the Assembly by means of a motion signed by one hundred registered delegates which shall be debated at the next meeting of the Assembly in accordance with Assembly Standing Orders. If such a motion is defeated it may not again be raised at the next two Annual Meetings of the Assembly.

C. Constituency Associations

1. Constituency Associations shall be formed in all Parliamentary Constituencies and shall have the following duties:
   (a) To maintain if possible an agent or organiser with an office;
   (b) To attend to the registration of Liberal Electors;
   (c) To be constantly engaged in recruiting new members of the Party;
   (d) To carry on continuous educational work drawing for this purpose upon the help provided by the Liberal Party at national and regional level;
   (e) To keep watch upon the legislative and administrative work of the Government especially as it affects the needs and interests of the district and to direct the attention of local authorities, the public and the press, to the importance of these subjects, and to the methods by which Liberals believe they should be handled;
   (f) To do everything in their power to secure that Liberals are elected to Local and Regional Authorities;

(g) To help all citizens, without respect to party, creed or race, to secure their rights, and to protect them against oppression;

(h) To provide wherever possible such social services as are not otherwise available;

(i) To raise funds for the work of the Liberal Party at National, Regional and Constituency levels;

(j) Finally, as the chief object of their efforts, to secure that the Constituency shall be represented in Parliament by a Liberal, and for this purpose to have always in the field a prospective Parliamentary Candidate who will be the focus of their activities.

2. Each Constituency Association shall be governed by a Constitution which shall include the following specific provisions:

(a) The primary aim of the Association shall be to contest and win Parliamentary Elections;

(b) The Association shall hold an Annual General Meeting at which audited financial accounts shall be presented and the Officers of the Association elected;

(c) All such contested elections shall be by secret ballot;

(d) Adequate notice of the Annual General Meeting and other General Meetings of the Association, including the date, time and place of the meeting and the business to be transacted shall be given to all members;

(e) No Chairman of the Association or person holding an equivalent post shall serve in the same office for more than three consecutive years. He shall be eligible for re-election to that office after a period of two years;

(f) Membership of the Association shall be defined and shall not conflict with Clauses B1 and B2 of this Constitution;

(g) Procedure for refusal or revocation of membership shall be in accordance with Section B of this Constitution;

(h) Procedure for the adoption of a prospective Parliamentary Candidate shall be in accordance with Section H of this Constitution;

(i) Agents and other Officials shall be appointed only by the Association's Executive Committee and paid only through Association funds;

(j) Local branches of the Women's Liberal Federation and the National League of Young Liberals shall be represented on the Association's Executive Committee;

(k) The Association's Constitution may only be amended at a properly convened General Meeting;

(l) The Association shall be subject to dissolution in accordance with Clause C11 of this Constitution.

When a Constituency Association first affiliates it shall supply a copy of its Constitution to the appropriate Regional Executive Committee which shall be responsible for checking the inclusion of the above provisions. The same procedure shall be followed when an Association amends its Constitution.

3. Liberal Clubs and Societies within the Union of Liberal Students may affiliate to Constituency Associations by mutual agreement. The National Executive Committee shall have power to determine minimum conditions of affiliation.

4. Constituency Associations shall affiliate to the Party by payment of fees, the basis and amount of which shall be decided by the National Executive Committee subject to approval by the Assembly. No Constituency Association shall be deemed affiliated unless it has at least fifty paid-up members. Constituency Associations shall only be entitled to representation within the Liberal Party if they are properly affiliated.

5. A Constituency Association shall be deemed affiliated until March 31st of the year following the year for which it has last affiliated. If it has not re-affiliated by then, it shall be ineligible for representation within the Liberal Party until such time as it re-affiliates.

6. Each Constituency Association shall supply to its Regional Party a copy of the audited financial accounts presented to its Annual General Meeting and any further information concerning the accounts that the Regional Treasurer deems necessary.

7. In the event of a Regional Party being unable to reach agreement with a Constituency Association on any matter arising out of Clauses 2, 4, 5 or 6 above, the dispute shall be referred to the Council.

The Council may by a simple majority deem unaffiliated any Constituency Association which contravenes these clauses.

8. The Council may by a two-thirds majority of those present and voting, refuse or revoke the affiliation of any Association which in its opinion does not support the Aims and Objects of the Party. Before exercising the power to dis-affiliate an Association, the Council shall draw the Association's attention to the grounds on which it is proposed to take this action, and shall give the Association at least two months in which to satisfy the Council that these grounds no longer exist.

9. Any Association aggrieved by any decision under Clause 8 above may appeal to the next meeting of the Assembly. The decision of the Council shall become null and void if it is not supported by two-thirds of the delegates present and voting at the Assembly.

10. In Parliamentary Boroughs divided into more than one Constituency, Constituency Associations may, with the consent of the Regional Party Executive Committee, be combined into Borough

Associations. Such Borough Associations shall be recognised as Constituency Associations for constitutional purposes with the following provisos:

(a) Their financial obligation to the Party under Clause C4 shall be the total obligations which would be owed if there were separate Constituency Associations;

(b) The maximum number of delegates to the Assembly under Clause G1(h) shall be twenty;

(c) General Meetings to adopt prospective Parliamentary Candidates in accordance with Clause H4 shall be held separately for each constituency and shall only be open to members of the Association resident in that constituency.

11. When constituency boundaries are altered, the Constituency Associations affected may agree the necessary adjustments in co-operation with the Regional Party concerned. If no such agreement is reached or if it is judged unsatisfactory by the Regional Executive Committee, the dissolution of the Constituency Associations affected may be decreed by the Regional Executive Committee which shall then be responsible for the reconstitution of Associations within the new constituency boundaries and for all the necessary consequent arrangements.

D. Regional Parties

1. Constituency Associations shall be combined in Regional Parties corresponding to the political regions of the country. Until such time as a democratic regional structure may be set up in the country, the boundaries of Regional Federations shall be decided by agreement between the Regional Parties concerned and the National Executive Committee.

2. Regional Parties shall be responsible for stimulating and co-ordinating Liberal activities within their areas. They shall act as the principal links and lines of communication between Constituency Associations and the Party's central organisation.

Regional Parties shall organise political activity on a regional level and shall be responsible for ensuring that there is an affiliated Association in every constituency. Regional Parties shall be responsible for ensuring that all Constituency Associations carry out the requirements of this Constitution.

Regional Parties shall give assistance and advice in the adoption of prospective Parliamentary and local government candidates, and shall assist and advise Constituency Associations in building up and maintaining organisations capable of securing the election of Liberal M.P.s.

Where appropriate, Regional Parties shall, in consultation with the Constituency Associations concerned, set up area groups for organising purposes within the Regional boundaries.

Where appropriate, Regional Parties shall, in consultation with the Constituency Associations concerned, set up County or Borough organisations for the purposes of local elections in divided Counties or Boroughs.

The National Executive Committee may delegate to Regional Parties such additional powers and duties as it sees fit.

3. Each Regional Party shall be governed by a Constitution approved by the National Executive Committee. Any amendments to such Constitution shall be made according to the methods laid down in the said Constitution, which shall include provision for reference to the Annual Meeting of the Regional Party and shall come into effect on approval by the National Executive Committee. Each Regional Party shall include specific provision for the implementation of the other requirements of this section of this Constitution.

4. Each Regional Party shall hold a General Meeting annually which the following shall be entitled to attend:

(a) Members of the Regional Council and Regional Executive Committee;
(b) The Vice-Presidents if any;
(c) A reasonable number of representatives from each Constituency Association;
(d) A reasonable number of representatives from the appropriate regional organisations of bodies recognised by this Constitution.

At this meeting audited financial accounts shall be presented together with reports from the Regional Council and the Regional Executive.

5. The Annual General Meeting shall elect the President, Chairman, Secretary, Treasurer and such other Honorary Officers as the Regional Constitution provides. The President shall be guardian of the Regional Constitution, and shall investigate complaints by individual members or Constituency Associations about the actions of the Regional Executive or Officers, in particular under Clause 9 below. The Chairman shall be Chairman of the Executive Committee.

The President and Chairman may serve for up to four consecutive years and then shall not be eligible for re-election for three years.

6. Each Regional Party shall appoint a council whose business shall be to formulate regional policy and to contribute to the shaping of national policy.

7. Each Regional Council shall consist of:

(a) Liberal Members of Parliament for constituencies within the region;

   (b) Candidates for constituencies within the Region;

   (c) All Liberal members of the appropriate elected regional authorities (including the Greater London Council);

   (d) One representative of the Liberal group on each Municipal Borough, Urban District or Rural District Council within the region, and representatives of the Liberal group of each London Borough, County Borough or County Council on the basis of one for a Liberal group of three or fewer members and two for a Liberal group of four or more members;

   (e) Representatives of each affiliated Constituency Association within the region in the proportion of one representative for each five hundred or part of five hundred members;

   (f) The members of the Regional Executive Committee;

   (g) Representatives from the appropriate regional organisations of bodies recognised by this Constitution;

   (h) Up to five co-opted members.

8. The remaining functions of each Regional Party shall be exercised by an Executive Committee responsible to the Annual General Meeting. The Executive Committee shall include the Honorary Officers other than any Vice-Presidents, and representatives of Constituency Associations and of the appropriate regional organisations of bodies recognised by this Constitution.

The representatives of Constituency Associations may be elected either by each individual Association, or by area and borough groups, or *en bloc* by the Annual Meeting, whichever method is most appropriate.

9. The Regional Executive Committee shall have the power to investigate the affairs of a Constituency Association where it seems likely that either the Association is not adhering to this or its own Constitution, or events have taken place or are about to take place which will be detrimental to the Liberal Party.

10. Federations of the National Union of Liberal Clubs may affiliate to Regional Parties and shall thereby be entitled to representation on the Executive Committee of the Regional Party. The National Executive Committee shall have power to determine minimum conditions of affiliation.

E. The Council

1. The Council shall consist of:

   (a) All members of the National Executive Committee, unless otherwise elected;

   (b) The Vice-Presidents of the Liberal Party;

   (c) Six members of the House of Lords who are members of the

Liberal Party to be chosen annually by the Liberal members of that House, one of whom shall be representative of Liberalism in Scotland. These members shall be in addition to those who may be otherwise appointed;

(d) Six members of the House of Commons who are members of the Liberal Party, one, the Chief Whip, or his nominee, whose duty it shall be to act as the official link between the members of the Party Organisation, and five to be chosen annually by the Liberal members of that House, provided that one of these shall be a member for a Scottish constituency;

(e) All members of the Standing Committee unless otherwise elected;

(f) Representatives of the affiliated Constituency Associations and the bodies recognised by this Constitution elected in the areas of the Regional Parties, the election of whom shall take place annually between the 1st January and 30th April. The number and allocation of representatives in this category shall be two from each Regional Party area with an additional representative for every ten or part of ten Constituency Associations affiliated. Should any Regional Party fail to elect its representatives the Council shall be entitled to fill the vacancies, but the persons elected must be drawn from the area in default. Casual vacancies shall be filled on the nomination of the Regional Executive Committees;

(g) Thirty representatives of the Party as a whole, to be elected by ballot of the Assembly. Nominations for these positions may be made by the Council, or by any Regional Party, or by any affiliated Constituency Association, or by any body recognised by this Constitution, not fewer than three weeks before the Annual Meeting of the Assembly;

(h) Not more than fifteen members appointed by the Women's Liberal Federation;

(i) Representatives of the Scottish, Ulster and Welsh Liberal Parties elected on the same basis as in Clause (f) above;

(j) Not more than fifteen representatives appointed by the Liberal Candidates Association;

(k) Not more than fifteen members appointed by the National League of Young Liberals;

(l) Not more than fifteen members appointed by the Union of Liberal Students;

(m) Not more than fifteen representatives appointed by the Association of Liberal Councillors;

(n) Two representatives to be appointed annually by the Liberal Agents Association;

(o) Two representatives to be appointed annually by the National Union of Liberal Clubs Ltd, in addition to those who may be otherwise appointed;

(p) Two representatives to be appointed annually by the Association of Liberal Trades Unionists;

(q) The Council shall have power to appoint not more than fifteen members, in recognition of distinguished service to the Party.

2. The duties of the Council shall be to do everything in its power to stimulate militant Liberalism in every part of the country and to express the views of Liberals on current political questions as they arise.

3. The Council shall meet at least four times a year.

F. The Standing Committee

1. The Standing Committee shall be responsible to the Council for the planning of the long-term evolution of Liberal Policy; for expressing between meetings of the Council the views of the Liberal Party on urgent political issues and for setting up and co-ordinating the work of policy committees and panels.

2. The Standing Committee shall also have general care of the presentation of Policy Motions to the Council. A Council Agenda Committee shall be set up for the detail work involved and shall consist of six members elected annually by the Council together with a Chairman appointed by the Standing Committee from among its own members.

3. The Standing Committee shall consist of:

(a) A Chairman appointed annually by the Parliamentary Party in the House of Commons from among their own members;

(b) Twelve persons elected annually by an electorate consisting of all members of the Council together with all M.P.s and candidates who are not members of the Council;

(c) One representative from each of the Scottish, Ulster and Welsh Liberal Parties;

(d) The holders of the following offices:
   The Leader of the Party
   The Chief Whip in the House of Commons
   The Leader of the Liberal Peers
   The Chairman of the National Executive Committee
   The Chairman of the Finance and Administration Board

(e) Up to three co-opted members.

4. The Leader of the Party shall be responsible for the compilation of the Party's General Election Manifesto in consultation with the Standing Committee and the Liberal Candidates Association.

G. The Assembly

1. The Assembly shall be composed of the following:
    (a) All members of either House of Parliament at Westminster and Stormont who are members of the Party;
    (b) All Parliamentary candidates;
    (c) Councillors and Aldermen who are members of the Association of Liberal Councillors;
    (d) The Honorary Officers of the Party;
    (e) All members of the Council;
    (f) All members of Regional Federation Councils;
    (g) All persons entitled to vote at the Annual Conferences of the Scottish, Ulster and Welsh Liberal Parties;
    (h) Representatives of Constituency Associations affiliated to the Liberal Party in England at the rate of one per fifty members or part thereof up to a maximum of twenty;
    (i) Representatives of each of the following bodies in the proportion of one for every twenty-five members or part thereof up to a maximum of two hundred representatives per body;
        The Association of Liberal Trades Unionists
        The National League of Young Liberals
        The National Union of Liberal Clubs
        The Union of Liberal Students
        The Women's Liberal Federation
        Any other body approved for this purpose by the National Executive Committee.
    (j) Agents and Organisers of Constituency Associations who are members of the Liberal Agents Association.
2. There shall be at least one meeting of the Assembly in each calendar year. Special Meetings shall, when necessary, be summoned by the Council or National Executive Committee. At a Special Meeting of the Assembly no business shall be taken except that specified in the notice convening the Assembly.
3. Regulations governing the procedures of the Assembly shall be drawn up by the Council; and the Council shall classify and arrange the business to be brought before the Assembly in such a way as to avoid repetition or overlapping and to ensure that adequate time is allowed for the discussion of important subjects.
4. The functions of the Assembly shall be:
    (i) To elect such Officers of the Party and members of the Council as are chosen in this way;
    (ii) To receive from the Council, and to consider, reviews of the progress and work of the Party; to receive and deal with an

annual statement of accounts; and to receive and consider the reports of the President and Treasurer;

(iii) To consider resolutions on public policy. Such resolutions may be proposed by the Standing Committee, the Council, the Scottish, Ulster or Welsh Liberal Parties, any body recognised by this Constitution or by any affiliated constituency, but no body recognised by this Constitution or Constituency Association may propose more than one resolution at any Meeting of the Assembly.

5. All members of the Assembly shall pay a registration fee in respect of each meeting of the Assembly, the amount of which shall be determined by the Council.

H. Candidates

1. All candidates, by virtue of consenting to their adoption as prospective Parliamentary Candidates, undertake a duty both to their Constituency Association and to the Party as a whole to promote Liberal policies.

2. A candidate within the terms of this Constitution shall be one of the following:

(a) A Member of the House of Commons in receipt of the Liberal Whip;

(b) A prospective Parliamentary Candidate selected and adopted by a Constituency Association in accordance with this Constitution;

(c) A member of the Party who has fought a Parliamentary Election as a Liberal candidate within the previous eighteen months.

3. A Candidates Committee consisting of the Chief Whip in the House of Commons as ex-officio Chairman, a Deputy Chairman appointed by him, two members elected annually by the National Executive Committee and three members elected annually by postal ballot of all candidates shall be responsible for the preparation of lists of approved potential candidates, for aiding Constituency Associations in the selection of candidates and for the training of candidates.

4. Constituency Associations shall use the following procedure when selecting candidates:

(a) The Constituency Association shall first inform the Secretary of the Candidates Committee of its intention to select a candidate;

(b) The Association Executive Committee or a Selection Committee set up by it shall consider all names submitted to it by the

243

Candidates Committee or by any member of the Association;

(c) This Committee shall submit three or more names of suitable candidates to a general meeting, but may submit fewer than three names if, in its opinion, there are not as many as three suitable candidates among the names submitted to it;

(d) The Association Executive Committee may, by a two-thirds majority, decide to propose to a general meeting the re-adoption of a previous candidate notwithstanding Clauses 4(b) and 4(c) above;

(e) At least two weeks' notice shall be given to all members of the Association and to the Secretary of the Candidates Committee of the place and date of the General Meeting and of the names to be submitted;

(f) The General Meeting, after hearing and questioning each of the proposed candidates, shall select one as their adopted prospective Parliamentary Candidate in secret ballot by the alternative vote.

5. The Candidates Committee may, in exceptional circumstances, authorise a Constituency Association to vary the procedure in Clause 4 above.

6. A representative of the Candidates Committee and of the Regional Party shall be entitled to attend and speak at any selection committee, executive or general meeting held under Clause 4 above.

7. If a Constituency Association adopts a person as prospective Parliamentary Candidate who is not approved by the Candidates Committee, that person shall not be accorded the status of a Liberal Candidate within the terms of this Constitution.

I. The National Executive Committee

1. The National Executive Committee shall consist of:
   (i) The President;
   (ii) The President Elect;
   (iii) The Immediate Past President;
   (iv) The Leader of the Party;
   (v) The Leader of the Liberal Peers;
   (vi) The Chief Whips in the House of Commons and House of Lords;
   (vii) The Treasurer;
   (viii) One representative to be nominated annually by each Regional Party having up to and including thirty-five affiliated Constituency Associations and an additional representative if the Regional Party has 100 per cent of its Constituency

244

Associations properly affiliated. Two representatives to be nominated annually by each Regional Party having over thirty-five and up to and including seventy affiliated Constituency Associations. Three representatives to be nominated annually by each Regional Party having more than seventy affiliated Constituency Associations;

(ix) Representatives of the Scottish, Ulster and Welsh Liberal Parties on the same scale as Sub-Clause (viii) above;

(x) One representative to be nominated annually by the Women's Liberal Federation;

(xi) One representative to be nominated annually by the Liberal Candidates Association;

(xii) One representative to be nominated annually by the Association of Liberal Councillors;

(xiii) One representative to be nominated annually by the Liberal Party Organisation Staff Association;

(xiv) One representative to be nominated annually by the National League of Young Liberals;

(xv) One representative to be nominated annually by the Union of Liberal Students;

(xvi) One representative to be nominated annually by the Association of Liberal Trades Unionists;

(xvii) One representative to be nominated annually by the National Union of Liberal Clubs;

(xviii) Eight members elected by ballot of the Council.

2. The National Executive Committee thus composed may co-opt up to five additional members.

3. The National Executive Committee shall elect annually a Chairman who, if not otherwise a member, shall become a full member of the Committee from the date of his election until twelve months after he has ceased to be Chairman. No person shall serve as Chairman for more than three consecutive years unless the Committee vote by a three-quarters majority to suspend this provision.

4. Within the limits of the Constitution the National Executive Committee shall direct the work of the Party.

5. In particular, it shall draw up regulations which shall govern elections to all bodies and offices set up by this Constitution.

J. The Finance and Administration Board

1. The Finance and Administration Board shall consist of the Treasurer and four persons to be elected annually by the National Executive Committee. The members of the Finance and Administration Board shall on election become members of the National

Executive Committee. They shall not however take part in the nomination or election of their successors.

2. The Party Treasurer will be elected by the delegates at the Annual Meeting of the Party Conference to hold office for a period of one year following 1st January and shall be eligible for re-election. Should he die or for any reason resign before the end of this year of office the National Executive Committee shall appoint a successor to fill the vacancy until the next 31st December. The Treasurer shall be the Party's Chief Executive Officer on all matters concerning finance. He shall have the right to attend the meetings and to see the Minutes, Bank Accounts and Auditors' Reports of any Constitutional Organ.

3. The Board shall appoint the Head of the Liberal Party Organisation who shall be salaried and shall become a full member of the Board.

4. The President and the Chief Whip in the House of Commons shall receive notice of and be entitled to attend and speak but not to vote at all meetings of the Board.

5. The Board shall not have power to co-opt but shall invite a representative of the staff to attend and may invite outside consultants to attend.

6. Within the limits of this Constitution, the Finance and Administration Board shall have authority to direct the administration of the Party. In particular they shall be responsible for the employment of staff and the running of Party Headquarters through the Head of the Liberal Party Organisation and for raising and administering the finances of the Party.

7. The Finance and Administration Board shall submit a written half-yearly report to the National Executive Committee on the finance and administration of the Party.

K. Honorary Officers

1. The Honorary Officers of the Party shall consist of a President and not more than fifteen Vice-Presidents. They shall not be Executive Officers.

2. The President shall be the guardian of the Party's Constitution. He shall be elected annually by the Assembly to take office from the end of the following Annual Meeting of the Assembly, and thereafter he shall be ineligible for re-election for a period of three years. He shall have the right to attend the meetings and to see the Minutes of any Constitutional Organ. He shall report to the Assembly at the end of his year of office.

3. When a President dies or resigns while in office, the National

Executive Committee may appoint a successor to complete the term of office.

4. There shall be not more than fifteen Vice-Presidents who shall be elected for life by a two-thirds majority of the National Executive Committee. They may be removed from this office by the President subject to ratification by the National Executive Committee.

The Schedule

1. No minimum subscription rates in accordance with Section B(3) may come into effect until 1st January, 1971.

2. Section C(2) shall apply immediately to all new formed Constituency Associations; existing Constituency Associations shall conform to this section and submit their constitution in accordance with it within six months after the next General Election.

3. The affiliation fees for the year 1970 shall, notwithstanding Clause C4, be decided by the L.P.O. Council.

4. The existing Area Federations within the existing boundaries and with their existing constitutions shall immediately become the Regional Parties provided for in Section D. Clauses D1, D2, D6, D7, D9 and D11 shall become effective immediately but the operation of the other Clauses of this Section shall be delayed until brought into effect in accordance with Clause 5 of this Schedule.

5. Existing Regional Parties shall adjust their constitutions according to Clauses D3, D4 and D5 as soon as may be convenient for them and in any case, not later than by six months after the next General Election. The National Executive Committee shall lay down procedure for this on the basis of the Constitutional Review Committee's proposals (Clauses 4 and 5 of the Schedule prepared by it) for any existing Regional Parties which have not done so prior to the next General Election. Clauses D3, D4, D5, D8 and D10 of this Constitution shall come into effect for each Regional Federation at a date to be decided by it provided that that date be not later than six months after the next General Election.

6. Each existing Regional Party shall convene a Regional Council to meet by 15th December, 1969.

7. There shall be no election of Vice-Presidents at the 1969 Assembly.

8. The Standing Committee shall be set up as from 1st November, 1969; the Finance and Administration Board and the Candidates Committee as from dates to be decided by the National Executive Committee.

9. Section H shall come into force as from a date to be decided by the newly set up Candidates Committee.

10. The existing L.P.O. Candidates Committee shall continue to

exist with its existing powers and functions, until the date fixed in accordance with Clause 8 above.

11. The elections for a President Elect and for not more than three Treasurers by the 1969 Assembly shall proceed as elections of the 1970–71 President and of the 1970 Treasurer under the new Constitution.

12. The President elected by the 1968 Assembly shall serve as President for 1969–70; the Treasurer elected by the 1968 Assembly shall continue to serve until 31st December, 1969.

13. The draft regulations for elections, prepared by the Constitutional Review Committee, shall come into force at the end of the first meeting of the National Executive Committee unless they be amended or suspended by that Committee.

14. Any dispute about this Schedule shall be subject to the same procedure for interpretation as the new Constitution.

15. Except as provided in this Schedule the existing Constitution of the Liberal Party shall be abrogated and replaced by this Constitution on 1st October, 1969.

D. The Constitution and Standing Orders of Plaid Cymru, 1970

Membership

1. A member of Plaid Cymru is he who is a member of a Branch, or where there is no branch, he who joins by accepting and by being willing to further the aims given below in Article 3, and by paying a minimum membership fee of *at least* 5/- (but 2s. 6d. for pensioners and for those from 18–21 not earning, and 1s. 6d. for non-wage earners under 18 who are not full members of Plaid Cymru) per annum to the Treasurer of a District Committee (Pwyllgor Rhanbarth) or to the Treasurer of the Pwyllgor Gwaith (Executive Committee) of Plaid Cymru.
2. A Branch (Cangen) is established as an official branch of the Blaid by the sanction of a District Committee, or, where there is no District Committee, by the sanction of the Executive Committee. (A Branch in this constitution henceforth means an official Branch.) Every branch must have 20 members, who have paid their annual membership fee. It must have contributed yearly a minimum of £20 to the Central Funds of the Party, but where it has fought a local election in the name of the Party during the year, its minimum (for that year) shall be £10. It must meet at least once a year.
3. No person may be a member of a Branch unless he accepts and is willing to further the principles enunciated below, and pays his annual subscription.

Principles

 (a) To secure self-government for Wales within the Commonwealth of Nations.
 (b) To safeguard the culture, language, traditions, and the economic life of Wales.
 (c) To secure for Wales the right to become a member of the United Nations Organization.

Branch

4. A member must subscribe a minimum of five shillings a year to the Branch Treasurer (but 2s. 6d. for pensioners and for those from 18–21 not earning, and 1s. 6d. for non-wage earners under 18 who are not full members of Plaid Cymru).
5. The officials of a Branch are: President, Secretary, Treasurer as well as any other necessary officials, elected annually, in November,

their term of office commencing in January, and their names and addresses are to be sent to the Central Office.

6. The Branch must pay every member's membership fee to the District Committee, and send the name and address to the Central Office.

7. The Branch is to pay over to the District Committee at least half its other receipts (profits on meetings, subscriptions over and above the 5s. membership fees).

8. The Branch is to arrange for its books to be audited annually and to forward the audited balance sheet to the treasurer of the District Committee.

9. The Branch shall have the following representation on the District Committee:

2 representatives if membership is from 20 to 39
3 representatives if membership is from 40 to 59
4 representatives if membership is from 60 to 99
5 representatives if membership is from 100 to 199
6 representatives if membership is over 200.

The representatives to be elected in November, their term of office commencing in January.

10. A Branch may elect one deputy representative when its representative or representatives cannot attend the District Committee.

11. A Branch with not more than 50 members has the right to elect two delegates to the Party Conference and a further delegate for each further 50 members or part of 50, to be elected at least one month before the Conference.

Section

12. A Section is formed officially by the permission of a Branch or Rhanbarth Committee or the Executive Committee. The Section may be for Youth, for Women, or for a village or ward, or a district, whether the members are members of a Branch or not.

13. A Section must have 6 or more members.

14. The Officials will be, President, Treasurer and Secretary; it will have one representative on the Rhanbarth Committee.

District Committee

15. A District Committee is established as an official Committee of the Blaid, by sanction of the Executive Committee, where there are at least three Branches.

16. A District Committee consists of representatives of the Branches and Sections to form a Rhanbarth Committee from representatives of Branches and Sections, who have the right to co-opt, for twelve

months from the date of their co-option, not more than twenty other members.

17. The District Committee officials are: President, Vice-President, Secretary, Treasurer, and any other necessary officials, to be elected annually in the January meeting and to be in office until the end of the Committee meeting of the following January.

18. The District Committee shall have two representatives on the National Council, with an additional member for every three Branches over and above the first six, to be elected every January; and one in the Conference to be elected at least one month before the Conference.

19. The District Committee is to meet at least six times a year.

20. A special meeting of the Committee may be called on the request of the Executive Committee, or on the request of one-third of the members, or on a resolution of a constitutional meeting of the Committee.

21. The quorum shall be one-third of the members.

22. All the Branches within the District shall be under the direction of this Committee.

23. The District Committee is responsible for all the arrangements of the Blaid in the District, including arrangements for local and parliamentary elections.

24. The right to present to the Executive Committee for its consideration the name of a candidate for a parliamentary constituency within the District rests with the District Committee.

25. The District Committee must have its books audited annually and must send its audited balance sheet to the Treasurer of the Executive Committee.

26(a). The District Committee must pay half the five shilling membership fee and the entire 2s. 6d. and 1s. 6d. membership fees to the Executive Committee's Treasurer, together with a proportion of all other receipts (namely contributions and the profits of meetings, etc.) —the proportion to be decided by the Executive Committee.

26(b). Every branch is to pay over to the Pwyllgor Rhambarth the 'representation levy' placed on it.

Executive Committee

27. The Executive Committee will be in charge of the whole organization of the Party and its committees, and will act on the resolutions of the Conference and the National Council, except only when the Conference or National Council is in session. But if 4 of the members representing the regions (28d) are against any resolution, the matter must be brought before the National Council to decide.

28. The members of the Executive Committee shall be:
   (a) The President and Vice-President elected by the Conference every two years, Chairman of the Party, who shall be Chairman of the Executive Committee and the Vice-Chairman of the Executive Committee.
   (b) The Treasurer elected by the Conference every year.
   (c) The President of the Youth Section and the President of the Women's Section elected by the appropriate Section every year.
   (d) Eight regional representatives elected by the District Committees of each region every year in a manner decided among the District Committees of each region. In the event of a region failing to elect a representative the National Council shall have the right of election. The regions shall be—Gwent, West Glamorgan (Swansea East, Swansea West, Neath, Aberfan, Gower); Mid Glamorgan (Merthyr Tydfil, Aberdare, Rhondda East, Rhondda West, Ogmore, Pontypridd); East Glamorgan (Cardiff North, Cardiff South East, Cardiff West, Barry, Caerffili); Dyfed; Canolbarth; Gwynedd; Clwyd.
   (e) The General Secretary, the Editor of *Y Ddraig Goch* and the Editor of *The Welsh Nation* appointed by the Executive Committee.
   (f) Not more than seven Directors, appointed by the elected members of the Executive Committee for a period of two years, these should include Directors of Finance, Organisation, Elections, Policy, Research and Publications.

29. The Executive Committee shall meet at least bi-monthly. The quorum will be a quarter of its members. Plaid Cymru Officials shall be the Committee's Officials.

30. A special meeting of the Executive Committee shall be called at the President's directive.

National Council

31. The National Council shall be in charge of the whole government of the Party and shall steer its activities in accordance with its aims and the resolutions of the Conference, except during a session of the Conference.

32. The members of the National Council are:
   (a) Two representatives from each District Committee, with an extra representative for every three branches over the first six.
   (b) The Officers of the Blaid, President, Vice-President, Treasurer, General Secretary, Chairman of the Party who shall be Chairman of the National Council and the Vice-Chairman of the Party who shall be Vice-Chairman of the National Council.

(c) Four members elected by the Conference—two elected each year for two years.

(ch) Past Presidents of the Blaid.

(d) The Editor of *Y Ddraig Goch*, the Editor of *The Welsh Nation*, the Editor of *Y Triban* and the Editor of Pamphlets and Books, who are appointed annually by the Executive Committee.

(dd) The Chairman and Secretary of the National Committee of the Women's Section and the Chairman and Secretary of the National Committee of the Youth Section.

(e) Members who are co-opted annually by the National Council, not more in number than a third of the members under (a).

(f) Any one who is a member of the Executive Committee not already a member of the National Council.

33. The appointment of the Secretary of the Blaid rests with the Executive Committee.

34. The Officers of the Blaid shall be the Officers of the National Council.

35. The National Council shall meet at least twice a year.

36. A special meeting of the National Council will be called on the written request of one quarter of its members, or at the request of the President.

37. The quorum shall be one quarter of the members.

Conference

38. The Conference is the highest authority of the Blaid.

39. The Constitution and Policy of the Blaid may not be changed except by the vote of at least two-thirds of the members present at a Conference, a notice of motion having been constitutionally given to the Conference through the General Secretary of the Party; but in all other matters, the vote of the majority will suffice to carry resolutions.

40. The Conference shall be constituted as follows:

(a) of delegates from all Blaid branches—two from every Branch of not more than 50 members with one additional delegate for every additional 50 members or part of 50;

(b) of one delegate from each District Committee in addition to members who are already members of the National Council;

(c) of the members of the National Council;

(ch) of any one who is a Blaid member of Parliament.

41. Members of the Blaid may attend the Conference and may speak even though they are not delegates, but may not vote.

42. The Blaid Officers shall be the Conference Officers.

43. The Conference shall be convened annually by the Executive

Committee, and all its arrangements shall be in the hands of the Steering Committee, whose function shall be:

  (a) To review all motions submitted to the Conference;
  (b) To formulate composite motions from motions submitted to the Conference when such motions are of the like subject matter, as considered necessary;
  (c) To arrange the sequence of motions to be debated by the Conference;
  (d) To allocate the debating time to each motion;
  (e) To present to the Conference a list of any motions excluded from debate because of shortage of time. From all such motions the Conference shall ballot for three motions which will be discussed in specially allocated time periods.

The members of the Conference Steering Committee shall be:

  (a) Chairman to be elected by the Pwyllgor Gwaith for one year;
  (b) Two members to be nominated by the Pwyllgor Gwaith for one year;
  (c) Two members to be elected by the National Council for one year who shall not be members of the Executive Committee;
  (d) Two members to be elected by the Annual Conference as set out in paragraph 47.

44. A special Conference may be called by the National Council.

45. The Vice-President shall be elected by the Conference every two years and the Treasurer every year.

46. The President, Chairman and Vice-Chairman of the Blaid shall be elected every two years by the Conference.

47. The Conference shall appoint four members as members of the National Council, who shall not be members of the Executive Committee, in addition to the Officers, two to be appointed each year for a period of two years, the candidate receiving the highest vote in each year shall be elected as the Conference's member of the Conference Steering Committee for two years.

48. (a) All motions for the Conference shall be in the hands of the General Secretary by June 30th, from whose hands they will pass to the Conference Steering Committee;

  (b) In the event of any dispute as to the right of any constitutionally endowed group to submit any motion, such a motion shall be printed with all others and therefore put before the Conference in session.

    The Conference will then decide by a simple majority and without debate whether or not to formally debate such motions.

  (c) No emergency motion may be presented to the Annual Conference unless it is concerned with an issue of political importance which has arisen within the two months before the opening of the Conference.

49. When the Conference or the National Council and the Executive Committee are not in session, the President of the Blaid is responsible for the government and organization of the Blaid.

Standing Orders of the Conference

1. Persons who are not members of Plaid Cymru may attend and hear the proceedings of the Conference, unless the Conference decides otherwise.
2. The order of business is to be as follows:
   i. Acceptance of the minutes of the previous Conference.
   ii. Announcement of the names of the Conference Officials.
   iii. Business required by the Constitution (elections, etc.).
   iv. Presentation of Annual Report and questions on it.
   v. Emergency motions from the National Council or the Executive Committee.
   vi. Other motions in the order and according to the time allotted by the Conference Steering Committee. Every motion will have been sent, one month previous to the Conference, to the Secretary and Delegates of every Branch and District Committee.

Motions

3. Every motion or amendment except a motion to adjourn the Conference or to adjourn the debate, or to put the matter to the vote or to leave the matter on the table, or that the Conference resolve into Committee must be submitted in writing to the Chairman or Secretary of the Conference.
4. If there is no member to propose a motion of which notice has been given, when its turn comes, it shall be passed over and cannot be moved afterwards without a notice of motion.
5. A motion, having been proposed and seconded, cannot be withdrawn without the consent of the Conference.

Debate

6. Neither a motion nor an amendment shall be open to discussion—not even by the proposer—until it is seconded; the seconder may postpone his remarks upon it until later in the debate.
7. Every speaker must direct his speech to the motion which is under

255

discussion, or to a motion or amendment which he is proposing or to a point of order.

8. A proposer may not speak for more than five minutes, a seconder not more than three minutes, and others not more than three minutes, except with the consent of the Conference.

9. No member may address the Conference more than once on any motion or amendment; but that immediately before the motion or amendment is put to the vote the proposer of the original motion may reply to previous speakers, but without introducing fresh matter into the debate or speaking for more than five minutes. Notwithstanding the above, a member may speak at any time on a point of order or a point of explanation.

10. A motion may be proposed to the effect that the Conference should go into Committee, and, if it is passed, members are not confined to one speech. After a matter has been discussed in Committee, it may be moved that the Committee shall report to the Conference, the report to be made by the Secretary or to be taken as read.

Amendments

11. An amendment must be relevant to the original motion and must:
    (a) omit certain words, or
    (b) omit certain words and insert or add others, or
    (c) add certain words.

12. When an amendment to the original motion has been moved, no other amendment can be proposed until the first amendment has been disposed of; but notice may be given of any number of amendments. If an amendment is rejected, another amendment to the original motion may be moved. But if an amendment is carried, it takes the place of the original motion, and an amendment to it may be moved.

Formal motions

13. At the end of any speech, a member may move that the question be now put to the vote, and if this is seconded and passed, the original question shall be put to the vote without further discussion.

14. When a member moves the adjournment of the Conference, he may speak for not more than five minutes, and if the motion is seconded, it shall be seconded without a speech, and put to the vote without discussion.

15. When moving that the matter be left on the table or that the debate be adjourned or that the Conference resolve into Committee, a member may not speak for more than five minutes, and if the motion is seconded it shall be seconded without a speech. The Chair-

man shall then call upon a member (preference being given to the proposer of the original motion) to speak on this motion, and it shall then be put to the vote forthwith.

16. A motion to adjourn the Conference may not be moved a second time within an hour, unless by the Chairman; and a motion to proceed to the next business, or that the debate be adjourned, or that the Conference resolve into Committee to discuss any matter, may not be moved a second time within half-an-hour, unless by the Chairman.

The Chairman

17. The Chairman and Vice-Chairman of the Blaid shall be the Chairman and Vice-Chairman of the Conference. In the absence of the Chairman or Vice-Chairman, the Conference shall elect an acting Chairman.

The Chairman's decision shall be final on any point arising from these Orders or on their interpretation, or on a point of order, and may not be debated.

18. The Chairman has power to adjourn the Conference.

19. When a member speaks, he must stand and address the chair; when the Chairman rises, all others must be seated.

20. When two or more members rise at the same time, the Chairman shall decide to whom priority shall be given.

21. The Chairman shall have an ordinary vote and a casting vote.

22. The Chairman may address the Conference in order to interpret or to administer these Orders, or to reply to any question on a point of fact; if he wishes to address the Conference on any motion which is under discussion, he may, with the consent of the Conference, vacate the Chair, which is then to be taken by the President or Vice-President.

Voting

23. Voting is to be by show of hands, unless the Conference decides otherwise; in electing Officers and members of the Executive Council, voting shall be by ballot, unless the Conference decides otherwise.

24. These Standing Orders may be suspended by a two-thirds majority of those present at the Conference; and this resolution shall remain in force until the matter under discussion is decided and the Conference proceeds to other business. (This is the Constitution and Standing Orders of Plaid Cymru as amended by the Party's Annual Conference, 1970.)

E. The Scottish National Party, Constitution and Rules

as passed by Annual Conference 1967

Part one

1. Name

The Scottish National Party.

2. Aims

A. Self-Government for Scotland—that is, the restoration of Scottish National Sovereignty by the establishment of a democratic Scottish Government within the Commonwealth, freely elected by the Scottish people, and whose authority will be limited only by such agreements as will be freely entered into with other nations or states for the purpose of furthering international co-operation and world peace.

B. The furtherance of all Scottish interests.

3. Policy and Direction

The Policy and Direction of the National Party shall be that laid down from time to time in accordance with the Constitution and Rules.

4. Eligibility for membership

Persons eligible for membership of the National Party shall be those who:
  (a) endorse the Aims of the National Party;
  (b) agree to abide by the Policy and Direction of the National Party;
  (c) accept the Constitution and Rules of the National Party;
  (d) are not members of any other Political Party;
  (e) and duly sign a declaration to the above effect.

5. Membership

A. Membership of the National Party shall consist of persons who, being eligible for membership, are elected members of a branch or group of the National Party, pay the contributions due and are duly

258

registered in the list of members. Persons not desirous of joining a Branch or Group may become members at Headquarters.

B. Members may be enrolled in any Group or Branch or attached to the Headquarters of the National Party, but, until the Secretary of the Branch or Group has sent the members' full names and addresses to the National Party Headquarters, membership shall not be effective.

C. Membership shall cease when a member is suspended or expelled from the National Party, intimates his resignation, fails to pay his subscription or other contributions timeously, or ceases to be eligible for membership.

D. No person who has been suspended or expelled or who has publicly intimated that he has resigned from membership of the National Party may become a member again without the prior consent of the National Council or Annual Conference.

E. No member may be transferred from one branch to another without the consent of the member's former branch, but any refusal to transfer membership may, on appeal, be overturned by the National Council.

F. Any person, otherwise eligible for membership of a Branch or Group, but who is resident outside Scotland may, on payment of the appropriate contributions, become an honorary member of a branch or at the Headquarters of the National Party. Such persons may form Branches or Groups outside Scotland. Such Branches or Groups will have the same privileges or responsibilities as Branches or Groups in Scotland with the exception that their delegates to National Conferences and National Council will have no voting rights.

6. Organisation

A. Branches and Groups
   (1) Branches shall consist of not less than twenty members.
   (2) New Branches shall not be deemed to be officially constituted until the names and addresses of all members have been lodged with the National Party Headquarters, and recognition has been granted by the National Council.
   (3) Groups of less than twenty members may be formed when considered necessary by Constituency Associations, Area Councils or the National Council, and such groups shall be entitled to representation at meetings of the Constituency Associations and Area Councils, but not at the Annual Conference, Special Conferences, and meetings of National Council.

B. Constituency Associations
   (1) Constituency Associations may be formed of two or more

Branches within a Parliamentary Constituency, subject to the approval of the National Council in consultation with the branches.

(2) Constituency Associations shall deal with the organisation of the National Party, the co-ordination and expansion of activity within a constituency, the setting-up of new Branches and Groups, the contesting of local authority and parliamentary elections and any other matters that may be remitted to them by the National Council or Annual Conference.

C. Area Councils

The National Council may authorise the setting-up of Area Councils to deal with the organisation of the National Party and the co-ordination and expansion of activity within defined areas covering two or more constituencies, but such Area Councils shall not have binding authority over branches or Constituency Associations. The constitutions of such Area Councils shall be subject to the approval of the National Executive.

D. National Conferences

(1) The Annual National Conference of the National Party shall be the supreme governing body of the National Party.

(2) The National Conference shall consist of:

(a) representatives from branches or Constituency Associations elected from among the members of branches or Constituency Associations respectively in accordance with the provisions laid down in Part Two of the Constitution and Rules;

(b) the chairman of the National Party, the National Secretary, the National Treasurer, together with the National Office-Bearers and ordinary members of the National Council elected in accordance with section 13 A, subsection 2, of Part two of the Constitution and Rules;

(c) The procedure including voting powers shall be as provided for in Part two of the Constitution and Rules;

(d) An Annual Conference shall be held once a year, and Special Conferences when necessary, in accordance with the provisions of Part two of the Constitution and Rules;

(e) The Annual Conference and Special Conferences may delegate such powers and directions as they may think fit to the National Council, or other committees or bodies of the National Party.

E. National Council

(1) Subject to the over-riding authority of the Annual Conference or Special Conferences, the National Council shall be the governing body of the Party between Conferences, and its

decisions binding upon the Party and all members unless and until rescinded or modified by the Annual Conference, or a Special Conference.

(2) The National Council shall be elected at the Annual Conference in accordance with the provisions of Part two of the Constitution and Rules.

(3) It shall be competent for the National Council to amend Part two of the Constitution and Rules in accordance with the procedure detailed under clause 9 of Part one hereof.

F. National Executive Committee

The National Executive Committee shall be constituted in accordance with the provisions of Part two of the Constitution and Rules. National Council may delegate to it such powers and duties as National Council considers necessary.

G. National Office-Bearers

The National Office-Bearers shall be:

(1) A President.

(2) Three Vice-Presidents.

(3) A Chairman of the National Party, who shall preside at all Annual Conferences, Special Conferences and meetings of the National Council and of the Executive Committee.

(4) Vice-Chairmen consisting of:

(a) a Senior Vice-Chairman, who shall act in the absence of the Chairman, and

(b) four Executive Vice-Chairmen.

(5) A National Secretary.

(6) A National Treasurer; and

(7) Such other office-bearers as may be decided upon by the Annual Conference.

All National Office-Bearers shall be elected at the Annual Conference in accordance with the provisions of Part two of the Constitution and Rules, provided always that if no nominations are received from Branches or no appointments are made by the Annual Conference for any particular office, or in the event of resignation or death of an Office-Bearer, the National Council shall have the power to fill the vacancy.

The powers and duties of the Executive Vice-Chairmen shall be those delegated from time to time by National Council.

7. Finance

A. All monies payable to the National Party shall be paid to the National Treasurer.

B. The National Council, except in such cases as the Annual

Conference may decide, shall have full control over all monies, funds, property, investments and securities of whatever kind and description belonging to the National Party.

C. (1) The National Council shall have power to invest the monies and funds of the National Party in Stocks and Shares of Public Companies, Bank Deposit Receipts, Savings or Deposit Accounts, Bonds and Debentures with or without security, heritable property or otherwise, in any manner of way, as they in their uncontrolled discretion shall think fit. In selecting suitable investments, the National Council will not be restricted to Trustee Securities.

(2) Without prejudice to the immediate foregoing sub-section, the National Council shall further have power to utilise the funds or monies of the National Party for the formation of, or obtaining an interest in, Companies whether public or private, for the purpose of furthering the interests of the National Party or the Cause of Scottish Self-Government. All investments of whatever nature shall, where practicable, be taken in the name of the Chairman of the National Party, the National Secretary and the National Treasurer, or their successors in office as Trustees for behoof of the National Party. No member of the Council shall be personally liable in respect of the depreciation of any investments made on behalf of the National Party.

D. The National Council shall have full power to purchase, acquire, accept (whether by gift, legacy or otherwise), hold, sell (whether by public roup or private bargain), excamb, feu, lease or otherwise intromit with heritable and movable property and real and personal estate, including power to borrow on the security thereof and to grant and consent to all usual and necessary deeds in connection therewith, including Dispositions and Bonds, and Dispositions in security leases and others as accord. The title to any inheritable property or real estate belonging to the Party shall be taken in name of the Chairman of the National Party, the National Secretary and the National Treasurer of the Party for the time being and their successors in office as Trustees for behoof of the Party. The Chairman, the Secretary and the Treasurer foresaid shall have power to grant in accordance with a resolution of the National Council and to execute all and any deeds as above-mentioned and any such deed purporting to be so granted and executed shall be valid, binding and effectual notwithstanding any alleged irregularity or proceedings or otherwise concerning the same.

E. For the purpose of the foregoing Sections C and D excerpts from the Minutes of the Meeting of the National Council certified by

262

the Chairman and the National Secretary shall be evidence of the proceedings of such meeting. A statement under the hand of the Secretary shall be sufficient evidence for all purposes as to the identity of the Chairman, Secretary and Treasurer foresaid for the time being.

8. *Amendment of Part one*

A. Amendments to the Constitution and Rules Part one may be proposed by a duly constituted Branch of the National Party or by the National Council.
B. Notice of Amendment by Branches shall be given in writing to the National Secretary at least three months prior to the date of the Annual Conference. Such notice must be dated and signed by the Chairman and Secretary of the Branch who shall certify that the proposed amendment has been carried at a duly constituted meeting of the Branch and that prior notice of the business has been given in writing to all members of the Branch.
C. The National Council shall regulate its own procedure for dealing with notice of amendment provided always that the provisions of Section D hereof are observed.
D. Amendments shall be circulated to all Branches not less than two months before the Annual Conference.
E. Amendments shall not be carried unless supported by at least a two-thirds majority of the votes cast at an Annual Conference by persons present and entitled to vote.

9. *Amendment of Part two*

A. Amendments to the Constitution and Rules Part two may be proposed by a duly constituted Branch or Constituency Association of the National Party or by the National Executive.
B. Notice of amendment by Branches, Constituency Associations or the National Executive shall be given in writing to the National Secretary at least three months prior to the date of the meeting of National Council to which the amendment is addressed. Such notice must be dated and signed by the Chairman and Secretary of the Branch or Constituency Association or by the Chairman of the Party and the National Secretary in the case of the National Executive who shall certify that the proposed amendment has been carried at a duly constituted meeting of the Branch, Constituency Association or National Executive respectively and that prior notice of the business has been given in writing to all members of the Branch, Constituency Association or National Executive as the case may be.

C. Amendments shall be circulated to all Branches, Constituency Associations, and members of National Council not less than two months before the said meeting of National Council.

D. Amendments shall not be carried unless supported by at least two-thirds of the votes cast at the said meeting of National Council by persons present and entitled to vote.

Part two

1. Branches

A. All applications for membership of a duly constituted Branch shall be submitted to a meeting of the Branch and, provided the applicants are found to be eligible for membership, they may, one month from the date of such submission, be elected to membership on payment of the appropriate fees.

B. In the case of Groups or new Branches, the National Council may waive the waiting period.

C. Each Branch shall appoint a Chairman, a Secretary and a Treasurer, and may appoint such other officials as they may deem necessary.

D. Branches shall appoint an Executive Committee and may appoint such other committees as they consider necessary.

E. All Office-Bearers shall be elected at the annual meeting of the branch of which meeting fourteen days' clear notice must have been given, except in the case of a new branch where the office-bearers may be appointed pro tem until the first annual meeting shall have been held.

F. Office-Bearers shall not be changed except through resignation, or by default, or at a meeting of the Branch of which fourteen days' clear notice of the intention to change office-bearers has been given, or by direction of the National Council or Conferences of the National Party.

G. It shall be the responsibility of the office-bearers and committees and members of the branches to ensure that:

    (1) adequate notice of all meetings is given, meetings are properly conducted, full records kept (including minutes of meetings, register of names and addresses of all members and receipts into and payments made from the funds of the Branch), and that all correspondence is dealt with promptly;

    (2) proper and adequate steps are taken to promote the cause of Scottish Nationalism and the interests of the National Party, within the area covered by the Branch, including the holding of meetings, canvassing, literature distribution and sales, and

264

that periodical reports of all activities are made to the Head-quarters of the Party;

(3) in particular every endeavour is made to carry out the Policy and Direction of the National Party as may be laid down from time to time by Conferences and the National Council, and that nothing is done to modify or prejudice the aims, policy, or general activities of the National Party;

(4) every endeavour is made in the mutual interests of Branches and the National Party as a whole to co-operate closely with the Headquarters of the National Party.

H. (1) Each Branch shall pay such affiliation fees per member and such other levies and in such instalments as the National Council may decide.

(2) All affiliation fees and levies in respect of the financial year to 31st December shall be paid by 28th February following and must be accompanied by the names and addresses of the members for whom fees and levies are being paid.

(3) Any Branch which has not paid the affiliation fees in full by 28th February shall not be entitled to representation at the Annual Conference, or, except as provided for in sub-section (5) hereof, and in clause 5, at Special Conferences.

(4) Should any Branch fail to pay the levies due in full by 28th February then representation at all Conferences shall be as provided for in clause 5.

(5) The National Council may, however, decide that if a Branch pays in full all affiliation fees and levies due at a date later than 28th February, such a Branch may be represented at any Special Conference held after the Annual Conference.

I. All books, records and documents pertaining to Branch business, or to the business of any subsidiary organisation shall vest in, and may at any time be inspected by the National Council.

J. The National Party shall not be liable for any debts contracted by Branches, Constituency Associations, Area Councils or Organisations or other bodies attached to the National Party.

K. No money shall be collected in the name of any Branch of the National Party, or the name of the National Party used for the collection of money and no payments shall be made from the funds of any Branch, except for such purposes as are covered by the Constitution and Rules of the National Party, unless, however, the approval of the National Council shall previously have been obtained.

L. In the event of any Branch for any reason whatsoever going out of existence, being disbanded by the National Council or National Conference, or seceding from the National Party, all funds or properties pertaining to the Branch shall, at the option of the National

Council, become the property of the Scottish National Party, as represented by the National Council and the National Office-Bearers.

M. All resolutions of Branches, or nominations sent to Headquarters of the National Party shall be certified in writing by the Chairman and Secretary as having been properly passed at a meeting of the branch of which due notice has been given to the members of the Branch.

N. Subject to the provisions of the Constitution and Rules, Branches shall have full authority to conduct their own affairs, and in particular to fix their own membership subscription, but any proposed Constitution and Rules of a Branch shall be submitted to, and confirmed by, the National Executive before adoption by the Branch.

2. Constituency Associations

A. Representation shall, unless otherwise agreed, be on the basis of one delegate from each Branch or Group in the constituency for up to twenty members and one additional delegate for every twenty members thereafter or part thereof.

B. A Chairman, a Vice-Chairman, a Secretary, a Treasurer and an organiser shall be appointed at each Annual Meeting of which one month's clear notice must be given, except that at the first meeting of the Association the officials may be appointed pro tem until the first annual meeting is held.

C. The expenses of the Association shall be met either by a levy on the Branches, or by such other means as may be decided upon by the Association.

D. The funds of Associations shall be used only for the purposes covered by the Constitution and Rules, and annual statements of accounts must be rendered to the Constituent Branches and Groups.

3. Area Councils

A. Representation shall, unless otherwise agreed, be on the basis of two representatives from each of the Constituency Associations in the area, two from each Branch and one from each Group within the area covered.

B. A Chairman, Vice-Chairman and Secretary shall be appointed at each annual meeting of which one month's clear notice shall be given, except that at the first meeting of the Area Council the officials shall be appointed pro tem until the first Annual Meeting shall be held.

C. An Area Organiser shall be appointed by the National Executive after consultation with the Branches and Constituency Associations and he shall be primarily responsible to the National Executive.

D. The Area Councils and organisers shall work in close co-operation with the National Organiser and under the direction of the National Executive.

4. Suspensions, &c., of Branches, &c.

A. It shall be within the power of the National Council to admonish, suspend or expel any Branch, Constituency Association, or Organisation subsidiary to the National Party, or any member or official of a Branch, Constituency Association, Area Council, etc., or of the National Party in consequence of any contravention of the Constitution and Rules or of any decision made thereunder, or of conduct inimical to the interests of the National Party. This power may be exercisable in the name of the National Council by the National Executive or by the Chairman or National Secretary but only in emergency and between meetings of National Council, and its exercise shall not become binding or final until a full report in writing shall have subsequently been submitted to and approved by the National Council.

B. Any such suspended Branch, Constituency Association, Area Council, official or member shall have the right of appeal to the first Annual Conference, whose decision shall be final and binding.

C. Suspension shall be for a specified period, at the end of which a motion may be made at the National Council or Annual Conference for re-instatement. Such motion shall require a simple majority only. Resolutions seeking to re-instate expelled members may not come up for consideration until a period of two years has elapsed from the date of expulsion.

5. Representation at Annual and Special Conferences

A. Provided affiliation fees and levies have been paid in full the representation shall be:

Two Delegates from each Branch whose membership does not exceed 50 and one Additional Delegate for every additional 50 members or part thereof.

No Branch shall be entitled to more than ten delegates.

Each Constituency Association shall be entitled to one delegate at both Annual and Special Conferences.

B. Affiliated Branches outside Scotland may send not more than two non-voting delegates who may take part in the proceedings.

C. Branches which have paid affiliation fees but have failed to pay levies in full shall be entitled to representation in proportion to the amounts of levies paid, representation to be decided as follows:

267

The total levies due by each Branch shall be divided by the number of delegates qualified for by membership, and a Branch shall be entitled to one delegate for each such proportion paid.

D. The National Treasurer shall be responsible for assessing Branch entitlement on the above basis and shall give adequate notice to Branches.

E. The Delegation from each Branch to a Special Conference shall remain at the same number as fixed at the previous Annual Conference, and the new Branches recognised since the previous Annual Conference shall be entitled to two delegates from each, provided affiliation fees and levies due are paid not later than 14 days before the Special Conference.

F. A list of the names and addresses of delegates duly certified by the Chairman and Secretary of each Branch shall be sent to the National Secretary prior to the holding of the Annual or Special Conference. The name and address of the Constituency Association delegate duly certified by the Chairman and Secretary of each Constituency Association shall be sent to the National Secretary prior to the holding of such Annual or Special Conferences.

6. Dates of Notice, motions, &c., for Annual National Conferences

The date, time and place of each Annual Conference shall be fixed by the National Council, and the following will apply:

(a) First Notice: The National Secretary shall give to all Branches, Constituency Associations, National Office-Bearers and members of the National Council, three calendar months clear notice of the date, time and place of the Conference.

(b) Branch Notices: All notices by Branches or Constituency Associations of resolutions or other matters to be placed on the Agenda, including all nominations of National Office-Bearers, shall be in the Head Office of the National Party addressed to the National Secretary at least two months prior to the date of the Annual Conference.

(c) Agenda: The Agenda shall be issued at least six weeks prior to the date of the Annual Conference.

(d) Notice of Amendments by Branches: Any amendments, except a motion of the direct negative, to be proposed by Branches or Constituency Associations, shall be in the hands of the National Secretary at least three weeks prior to the Annual Conference. Such date shall be intimated by the National Secretary in issuing the Agenda and shall be held to be final and binding on all Branches or Constituency Associations.

7. *Resolutions, Nominations, etc., by Branches, etc.*

All Resolutions and Nominations to Annual Conference, Special Conferences and the National Council by Branches, Constituency Associations, Area Councils and other bodies shall:

    (a) be written in ink or typewritten.

    (b) show clearly the Branch or other body by which the resolutions, etc., have been made.

    (c) bear a certificate by the Chairman and Secretary that the resolutions, nominations, etc., have been properly passed at a meeting of which adequate notice had been given to members.

    (d) in the case of nominations for positions such as National Office-Bearers, Members of the National Council, testify that the consent of the person nominated has beforehand been received in writing.

8. *Preparation of Agenda, etc., for Annual Conferences*

This section is printed on p. 30.

9. *Quorum at Conferences*

Delegates from at least one-third of affiliated Branches and Constituency Associations combined shall be present before a National Conference is held to be constituted.

10. *Procedure at Annual Conferences*

A. The Chairman of the National Party shall conduct the proceedings at the Annual Conference.

B. When the Chairman rises, all representatives standing shall instantly resume their seats, and refrain from making any observations.

C. Any representative, who after being invited by the Chairman to resume his seat, refuses persistently to do so, shall be named by the Chairman and without further discussion shall be suspended from the session in which the incident occurred, and shall then be requested to leave the hall of the Conference for the remainder of the session.

D. Any representative who is again suspended in another session of the Conference shall be prohibited from entering the hall of the Conference during the whole of the proceedings of the Annual Conference.

E. The Chairman at his discretion may permit a vote without discussion on verbal amendments to any resolution, provided always such amendments do not alter the sense of the resolution.

F. The Chairman shall be the sole judge of the order in which motions or amendments may be put to the Annual Conference.

G. Should representatives consider that any ruling by the Chairman is not in accordance with good procedure, then a motion may be put of 'no confidence in the Chair', but such motion may not be made or seconded by the aggrieved representative. On such a motion being seconded, the Chairman shall leave the Chair and be succeeded by the Senior Vice-Chairman, failing whom an Executive Vice-Chairman, failing whom the National Secretary. The motion shall then be put without discussion to the Annual Conference and voted upon.

H. Should two motions of 'no confidence in the Chair' be carried, the Chairman shall then leave the Chair and the Chair be taken by the Senior Vice-Chairman, failing whom an Executive Vice-Chairman, failing whom a representative elected by the Conference.

I. The National Council may decide upon and issue along with the Agenda to the Delegates, etc., attending an Annual Conference Rules of Procedure, always provided that such rules do not infringe the Constitution and Rules of the National Party. Such Rules shall be put to the Annual Conference at the beginning of the proceedings, and if passed shall apply to the whole of the proceedings of the Annual Conference in question and shall be final and binding upon all the representatives attending.

11. Voting at Annual Conferences

A. National Office-Bearers and members of the National Council shall be entitled to vote on all questions before the Annual Conference, except on the election of any Office-Bearer or any member of the National Council unless they are attending as Branch or Constituency Association Delegates.

B. Accredited Delegates of Branches or Constituency Associations shall be entitled to vote on any matter before the Annual Conference.

C. All persons entitled to vote at the Annual Conference shall be issued with a Card bearing their name and status. Cards shall be in different colours for (1) Office-Bearers and Members of National Council, and (2) accredited delegates from Branches or Constituency Associations.

D. The Annual Conference shall at each session select from amongst its members two or more tellers who shall count the votes for and against a motion and report to the Chairman who shall in turn announce the result to the Conference.

E. The Chairman may instruct a recount to be taken, or on a motion for a recount being passed, a recount shall be taken.

F. Should no recount be demanded, or when a final count has been taken, the Chairman shall declare that the motion has or has not been carried and no further discussion shall be permitted.

G. No voting by proxy shall be permitted.

12. Special National Conferences

A. A Special National Conference shall be held at the request of the National Council or of not less than one-third of the Branches.

B. Definite reasons for holding such a Conference shall be given in writing and the subject matter for discussion clearly stated.

C. Requests from Branches for a Conference must be passed at a meeting of each Branch of which due notice had been given to all members, and certified accordingly by the Chairman and Secretary of the Branch.

D. The National Secretary shall give all Branches, Constituency Associations and Members of the National Council at least three weeks notice, together with the Agenda.

E. No other business than that for which the notice had been given shall be dealt with at a Special National Conference.

F. The procedure at Special National Conferences shall be the same as at the Annual National Conference.

G. Representatives of Branches and Constituency Associations shall be as provided for in clause 5 of Part two hereof.

13. National Council

A. The National Council shall consist of:
   (1) National Office-Bearers as defined in Part one, 6 (G);
   (2) fifteen ordinary Council Members to be elected by the Annual National Conference from members of the Party other than the National Office-Bearers and Area Representatives;
   (3) one representative from each Constituency Association as nominated by the Constituency Association;
   (4) one representative from each Area Council as nominated by the Area Council, but only until such time as all constituencies in the Area covered by the Area Council are entitled to representation under the immediately preceding subsection; and
   (5) one representative from each Branch to be nominated by the Branch within twenty-one days from the date of the Annual Conference.

271

In the case of new Branches being recognised between Annual Conferences, such new Branches shall be entitled to nominate a representative within twenty-one days from the official recognition of a new Branch.

In the event of a Branch representative desiring to resign, intimation thereof in writing shall be made to the National Secretary who shall request the Branch involved to nominate a new Branch representative within twenty-one days of receipt of intimation.

B. Ordinary meetings of the National Council shall be held once a quarter, and special meetings as required by the Executive Committee.

C. A quorum of the National Council shall consist of one-third of the members, or thirty, whichever is less, who must be present throughout the meeting. If at any time the departure of members reduces the number below the required number, the meeting shall be adjourned.

D. The procedure regarding notice of meetings, matters concerning the Agenda, conduct of business, etc., shall be as adopted from time to time by the Council, except that the procedure adopted in regard to the Annual National Conferences as laid down in clause 10 of Part two hereof shall apply.

E. The National Council may appoint standing committees or other ad hoc committees with such powers as it may decide.

14. National Executive Committee

The National Executive Committee shall consist of:
(1) the National Office-Bearers as defined in Part one, 6 (G);
(2) fifteen other members to be elected by the Annual Conference;
(3) one representative from each parliamentary constituency in Scotland, to be elected by Constituency Associations in accordance with procedure and arrangements approved by National Council; and
(4) one representative from each organisation whose affiliation to The Scottish National Party is recognised by National Council.

15. Publications and announcements

A. No publications or official communications to the Press shall be issued in the name of the National Party without the official sanction of the National Council or the National Conference. The National Council may delegate this power to office-bearers.

B. Branches, Constituency Associations and Area Councils may, however, issue statements, pass resolutions and make announcements in their own name provided such are in accordance with the policy and direction of the National Party and do not deal with the internal affairs of the National Party.

16. Political parties

A Political Party for the purposes of clause 4 of Part one of the Constitution and Rules shall be defined as follows:
   (a) a Party or Organisation whose object is the furtherance of its own political, social and economic programme; or
   (b) a Party or Organisation whose policy is to put forward candidates in Parliamentary elections, or sponsor candidates of other parties on purely political grounds; or
   (c) a Party or Organisation which avows itself to be a political party.
The National Council shall decide what organisations come under the foregoing definition and such decisions shall be binding on all Branches and members of the National Party.

Provided always that the Parties and Organisations referred to under this clause are parties and organisations whose activities cover Scotland and that this power may be exercisable in name of National Council by the National Executive or the Chairman but only in an emergency and between meetings of National Council and its exercise shall not become binding or final until a full report in writing shall have subsequently been submitted to and approved by National Council.

17. Parliamentary elections procedure

A. No person who has not been a member of the National Party for at least the year immediately preceding may be nominated as a candidate.

B. All nominations of candidates shall be submitted for the approval of the National Council, which shall consult the Branches or Constituency Association concerned before reaching a decision.

C. Branches or Constituency Associations shall be entitled to nominate candidates only for the constituency in which they are situated, and must first obtain the written consent of the nominee.

D. In considering nominations, the National Council shall take into account:
   (1) the amount of preparatory work that has been done in the constituency;
   (2) whether the Branches or Constituency Associations have the

necessary organisation and support from members to conduct an election;

(3) whether the Branches or Constituency Associations can appoint a person as election agent who has the necessary experience to carry out the duties in a satisfactory manner; and

(4) whether the Branches or Constituency Associations can raise the necessary funds to pay the expenses of an election.

E. Before nominating a candidate, the Branches or Constituency Associations shall appoint an election committee which, after consultation with the Headquarters of the National Party, or the appropriate committee at Headquarters, shall make recommendations to the Branches on the selection of a candidate.

F. The decision of the National Council on contesting any election and the selection of a candidate shall be final and binding on Branches and members of the Party provided that no candidate can be nominated by the National Council for any constituency without first obtaining the consent of the Branches within the constituency or the Constituency Association.

18. Local Authorities elections

A. A member of the National Party may stand for election as an independent, if solely described as 'Independent', provided no member has been previously elected on the local authority as a National Party representative, and no duly authorised National Party candidate is standing for the same ward at the same local election. Branches may support such candidate provided the declared aims as an Independent do not compromise the National Party Policy.

B. In all cases where the Branch finances the campaign, the candidate shall stand as a National Party representative. Exception may only be made in the case of National Party members already established on the authority as Independent representatives as a result of previous Branch sponsorship.

C. Members standing as National Party candidates shall be nominated by a Branch covering the ward or district to be contested, and shall be approved of by the Constituency Association or by the Area Council or by the National Council.

19. Overseas and foreign members and organisations

A. The National Executive may appoint an Overseas and Foreign Secretary or Secretaries whose duties shall be to deal with Members or organisations outside Scotland.

B. Persons or organisations outside Scotland may become honorary members or organisations attached to the Headquarters of the National Party.

C. All Members or organisations outside Scotland shall adhere to the Aims, Policy and programme of the National Party.

D. Any Constitution and Rules of any organisation attached to the National Party shall, before adoption, be approved by the National Executive.

20. Finance

A. The financial year of the National Party shall be the year to 31st December.

B. All statements of accounts duly audited shall be submitted to the first Annual Conference held after 31st December.

C. The National Treasurer shall report the financial position of the Party quarterly to the National Council and as part of such report shall submit estimates of income and expenditure for the ensuing quarter.

F. Constitution and Rules of the Ulster Unionist Council

I—Title

The name of the Council shall be 'The Ulster Unionist Council'.

II—Objects

The objects of the Council shall be to maintain Northern Ireland as an integral part of the United Kingdom; to uphold and defend the Constitution and Parliament of Northern Ireland; to bring together all Unionist Associations in Northern Ireland, with a view to consistent and continuous political action; to act as a link between Ulster Unionists and their Parliamentary representatives; and to be the medium of expressing Ulster Unionist opinion, as current events may from time to time require, and generally to promote the interests of Unionism.

III—Membership of Council

(See pp. 18–19.)

IV—Party Leader

The Leader of the Party shall be appointed by the Standing Committee and shall remain Leader until his retirement or the determination of his appointment by the Standing Committee. He shall be responsible for guiding and directing the Party, organising and directing Propaganda and Publicity, and promulgating the Unionist Policy. He shall be an ex-officio member of all Committees and Sub-Committees.

V—Office-Bearers

1. At the Annual Meeting of the Council there shall be elected out of the membership the following Office-Bearers, viz.: President, four Vice-Presidents, four Hon. Secretaries, and one Hon. Treasurer. These Officers shall be ex-officio members of all Committees and Sub-Committees.
2. All elections shall be by secret ballot.
3. The President of the Ulster Unionist Council shall preside at all meetings of the Council or may nominate the Chairman of the Standing Committee to do so.

276

VI—*Meetings of the Council*

1. The Annual Meeting of the Council shall be held in February or March, the date, place, and time of meeting to be fixed by the Office-Bearers. At this meeting the Secretary, who shall keep a record of all business transacted at Council and Committee Meetings, shall submit his report for the year and the Hon. Treasurer shall present the Statement of Accounts.

2. Further meetings of the Council may be held as the Standing Committee consider necessary. Special Meetings shall be held upon a requisition to the Secretary signed by thirty members.

3. Ten days' notice of the Annual Meeting, and at least three days' notice of Special Meetings of the Council shall be given.

VII—*Election of delegates*

1. Notice shall be given in December by the Secretary to each Association affiliated to the Council, requesting the selection of delegates to the said Council in accordance with the number specified in the Schedule annexed.

2. To each County Grand Orange Lodge in Ulster similar notice shall be given one month prior to its November meeting for the election of officers.

3. A delegate unable to attend a meeting of the Council may nominate a member of the Association or County Grand Lodge which he represents to take his place; notice of the change to be given in writing to the Secretary prior to the meeting.

VIII—*Standing Committee*

1. The business of the Council shall be conducted by a Standing Committee composed of:

    (a) Two delegates nominated by each of the Divisional Associations; two delegates nominated by each Women's Association affiliated to the Ulster Women's Unionist Council; two delegates nominated by the Queen's University Unionist Voters' Association; two delegates nominated by each of the County Grand Orange Lodges; five delegates nominated by the Ulster Women's Unionist Council; five delegates nominated by the Ulster Unionist Labour Association; two delegates nominated by the Ulster Reform Club Political Council; two delegates nominated by the Unionist Society; two delegates nominated by the Association of Loyal Orange Women of Ireland, two delegates nominated by the Apprentice Boys of

277

Derry, and two delegates nominated by the Willowfield Unionist Club.

(b) The Northern Irish Peers, the Members of the Imperial House of Commons representing Constituencies in Northern Ireland, and the Members of the Senate and of the House of Commons of the Parliament of Northern Ireland, who are members of the Council.

(c) Twenty of the co-opted and ten of the ex-officio members of the Council referred to in Clause III (m) (n) (in addition to the said Peers, Senators and Members of Parliament), may be nominated by the President of the Council.

2. The Chairman of the Standing Committee shall be at liberty to invite prominent Unionist electors to confer with the Standing Committee at any time, but such electors shall not have the right to vote.

3. Standing Committee delegates must be selected from those elected to the Council. The names and addresses of the delegates should be sent to the Secretary, Unionist Headquarters, Glengall Street, Belfast, not later than the second Monday in January. A delegate unable to attend may appoint (in writing to the Secretary) a substitute from the Organisation or Lodge which he represents.

IX—Meetings of Standing Committee

1. The Standing Committee shall meet four times a year for the transaction of the business of the Council. Special Meetings may be called when necessary by the Hon. Secretaries. Ten days' notice of Ordinary and at least three days' notice, when possible, of Special Meetings shall be given.

2. Notices of Motion should be sent to the Secretary at least three weeks before a meeting, and will be placed on the Agenda for consideration at the next meeting of the Standing Committee.

X—Chairman and Vice-Chairman

The Standing Committee shall elect its own Chairman and Vice-Chairman, and they shall be ex-officio members of all Committees and Sub-Committees.

XI—By-laws and Sub-Committees

1. The Standing Committee shall have power to make by-laws for the internal management of the affairs of the Council relating *inter alia* to questions of finance, affiliation of Associations, and the procedure at meetings and elections.

2. The Committee shall also have power to appoint Sub-Committees to transact special business and to consider and deal with matters of importance to Northern Ireland.

XII—Changes in Constituencies

In the event of changes being made at any time in the Constituencies, the Standing Committee may take steps to deal promptly with the matter and to report to the next meeting of the Council.

XIII—Executive Committee

1. The Executive Committee shall be elected annually by the Standing Committee and shall consist of 36 (thirty-six) members. Two of these shall be chosen from the Ulster Unionist Labour Association, two from the Orange Institution, and two from the Young Unionist Associations.

2. A territorial basis of membership shall be maintained.

3. The Committee shall meet monthly and shall have authority to perform all ordinary and emergency acts on behalf of the Standing Committee during the intervals between meetings of the Standing Committee (other than the appointment of the Party Leader and the determination of his appointment) and report to the Standing Committee. Special meetings of the Executive Committee may be called on the instructions of the Chairman.

4. The Leader of the Party shall be entitled to nominate as a member of the Committee an Ulster member of the House of Commons at Westminster.

5. The Committees shall have power to appoint Sub-Committees, including, if necessary, a Consultative Committee, which may confer direct with the Leader of the Party.

6. All members of the Committee must be members of the Standing Committee and of Divisional Associations. The Committee shall elect its own Chairman, who shall be an ex-officio member of all Committees and Sub-Committees.

7. The Unionist Chief Whip shall be an ex-officio member of the Executive Committee and of any Sub-Committee appointed to advise the Leader of the Party.

8. The President and Hon. Treasurer of the Ulster Women's Unionist Council shall be ex-officio members of the Executive Committee.

XIV—Publicity

The Executive Committee shall appoint a Sub-Committee to advise and work in co-operation with the Leader of the Party on all matters appertaining to political Publicity and Propaganda.

XV—Finance Committee

A Finance Sub-Committee shall be appointed annually by the Executive Committee. It shall meet as often as necessary to attend to all financial matters and submit through the Hon. Treasurer, reports to the Executive Committee and an Annual Statement of Accounts duly audited.

XVI—Young Unionist Associations

Divisional Associations (both men and women) which have active Young Unionist Associations attached shall each be entitled to an additional delegate at the Ulster Unionist Council and Standing Committee, this delegate to be chosen from the Young Unionist Association.

XVII—New Associations

New Associations desiring to become affiliated to the Council must send in a written application to the Secretary of the Council. Such applications shall be considered by the Executive Committee and forwarded by it to the Standing Committee for final decision.

XVIII—Termination of the Affiliation of an Association

If the Affairs of any Affiliated Association or Associations are conducted in a manner which in the opinion of the Executive Committee is likely to prove detrimental to the best interests of Unionism or disadvantageous to the objects of the Council, the Executive Committee shall recommend to the Standing Committee such action as they may consider appropriate, including, where necessary, the termination of the affiliation to the Ulster Unionist Council of such Association or Associations and shall forward their recommendation to the Standing Committee for final decision. Before the Executive Committee arrive at a decision, the Association concerned shall be given the opportunity of appointing five delegates to appear before the Executive Committee to put forward their case.

The Standing Committee shall have power to take any action

which may appear to them to be appropriate, including the removal of the name of any Association or Associations from the List of Affiliated Associations to the Council and such Association or Associations shall thereupon cease to be an Affiliated Association and its representatives and members shall thereupon cease to have the rights or privileges of representatives or members of Affiliated Associations.

Where the Standing Committee decide to terminate the affiliation of an Association in accordance with the above provisions, the Executive Committee shall thereupon have power to take such steps as may appear to them in the circumstances to be desirable, including the formation of a new Affiliated Association in the place of that whose affiliation has been terminated, provided that the affiliation of any such Association so formed shall not be complete until its rules have been approved by the Standing Committee.

XIX—Unionist Conference

1. At least one Conference under the auspices of the Council shall be held in the year and Affiliated Associations shall be entitled to forward resolutions for consideration. These resolutions must be sent to the Secretary of the Council and submitted by him to the Executive Committee, who may approve, amend or reject any resolution.
2. The Executive Committee shall fix the date, place, and time of the Conference or Conferences, arrange the order of business, determine the membership, and draw up Rules and Regulations governing the Conference.

XX—Subscriptions

Each Divisional Association (excluding Women's Associations) shall subscribe annually to Headquarters such sum per head per Unionist Voter as the Executive Committee may from time to time fix. County Grand Orange Lodges and other Organisations as set out in the Schedule shall subscribe a sum of Five Guineas annually (except where the amount is altered on account of representation). The Ulster Women's Unionist Council shall pay an annual fee of Five Guineas for each of their affiliated Women's Associations. All other members, including ex-officio and co-opted, shall pay an annual subscription of Five Guineas. All Subscriptions are due on the first day of January and should be paid as soon as possible thereafter, but in any event not later than the 31st October in each year.

XXI—Constituency Organisers

A Divisional Association shall have power to appoint for its own Parliamentary Constituency an Organiser whose duties will include looking after organisation in the various polling districts, seeing that the name of every loyalist who is qualified is on the Register of Voters and generally furthering the Unionist cause. His remuneration shall be paid by the Divisional Association. If necessary, financial assistance may be given out of Party Funds on the Executive Committee being satisfied that the Organiser is carrying out his duties in a capable and energetic manner.

XXII—Travelling Organiser

There shall be a full-time travelling Organiser appointed by the Executive Committee and attached to Headquarters. His duties will include visiting the various Constituencies from time to time, to see that Unionist organisation is receiving proper attention, assisting the Office-Bearers of Local Associations in any way considered advisable, co-ordinating the activities of Constituency Organisers, giving advice and help in the formation and running of Young Unionist Associations and making reports in regard to organisation through the Chief Executive Officer to the Executive Committee.

XXIII—County Organisers

1. Where the majority of Divisional Associations within a County or County Borough, or within any area prescribed as a County area, are of the opinion that a County Organiser should be appointed to co-ordinate and work in conjunction with such organisers as may be appointed by Divisional Associations and to assist in the organisation of such Divisional Associations as may be without a Divisional Organiser, power shall be given to the County Committee to appoint such an Organiser.
2. The Executive Committee shall for this purpose have power (where it is considered necessary) to define a County area as one comprising the Divisional Associations with two adjoining Counties or alternatively within one or more Counties and a County Borough.
3. For the purpose of County organisation a County Committee, comprised of eight delegates from each Divisional Association within the prescribed County or County Borough area, may be formed for the purpose of promoting co-ordination and conference on all matters affecting organisation within the area. Such Committees shall meet at least twice in each year.

XXIV—Headquarters Staff

1. A Secretary and Staff of the Ulster Unionist Council shall be appointed by the Executive Committee.
2. The Secretary of the Ulster Unionist Council shall be the Chief Executive Officer at Headquarters.

XXV—Constitution

The Constitution and Rules of the Council shall not be altered or added to without the permission of the Council. Proposed alterations and additions must first be submitted to and passed by the Standing Committee.

XXVI—Quorums at meetings

The Quorum shall be: Standing Committee, 12 members; Executive Committee, 10 members, and Sub-Committees, 3 members.

The foregoing Constitution and Rules were adopted on 8th March, 1946. Rule XVIII was passed on 7th March, 1952. Amendments made: Rule V (I) (Office-Bearers), 2nd April, 1954, and Rule XX (Subscriptions), 8th March, 1957, and 14th April, 1961, and 6th March, 1970. Rule III (I) (a) and (b) amended 31st March, 1969, to make provision for delegates from the four new Associations of Laganvalley, Newtownabbey, Bangor and Larkfield.

(A committee has been set up by the Ulster Unionist Council to redraft the present Constitution and Rules.)

Index

Affiliation, 17–19: Labour Party, 17–18, 225; Liberal Party, 19, 236, 240; National Union, 19, 202–4; Ulster Unionist, 19, 280

Aims and objects, 14–16: Labour, 14–15; Liberal, 15–16; National Union, 14, 197; Plaid Cymru, 14, 249; S.N.P., 14, 258; Ulster Unionist, 14, 276

Amery, Julian, 99–104

Bagehot, W., 128
Barons Court, 158, 163–72
British National Party, 88

Candidates, 79–108: educational background, 85; incentive system, 166–8; local, 90–1; 'primaries', 80; Scottish Unionists, 42–4
— selection procedures: Conservative, 94–6, 107; Labour, 94–6, 224–5; Liberal, 92, 243–4; S.N.P., 91, 273–4; Ulster Unionist, 108
— sources, 83–4

Central offices: addresses, 31; Conservative, 54, 64, 66, 67, 81, 82, 148, 166–8, 170, 197, 203; Labour (Transport House), 54–5, 66, 81; Liberal, 13, 246; and local government, 149; nationalists, 13; Scottish Unionist, 36; Ulster Unionist, 283

Chichester-Clark, James, 106
Communist Party, 5, 88–91
Conferences, 29–30, 177–8, 181–2: Labour, 30, 55–62, 177–8, 181–8, 219, 220–2, 223, 224, 225, 227–9,

230, 231 — arrangements committee, 30, 226, 231; Liberal Assembly, 233, 236, 237, 240, 242–3; National Union, 197, 211–13, 214–17; Plaid Cymru, 29, 253–7; S.N.P., 259, 260, 261, 263, 265, 267, 268–71 — agenda, 30; Ulster Unionist, 281

Conservative Party: Board of Finance, 71; development of, 1–2; leadership, 82, 105; parliamentary, 6, 67 — rebellions, 130–5; regional officials, 64

Conservative Political Centre, 73, 134, 206, 211

Constitutions, 13–31, 197–283
— sources, 31

Co-operative Societies, 18, 66, 229
Crossman, Richard, 54, 55, 113, 124, 128

Dahl, Robert, 118
Davies, S. O., 81
Discipline, 21, 113–29, 138–9, 222, 233–4, 259
— local government, 149–52
Donnelly, Desmond, 81
Du Cann, Edward, 55

Elections, 156–72: available seats, 93; broadcasting time, 64; campaigns, 156–8, 163–72; deposits, 90; electoral pacts, 92; expenses, 63; local, 142, 158–9 — S.N.P., 274; party workers, 165 — incentives, 166–72; strategy, 90
— sources, 160–2

Electoral system and parties, 87–8

285